THE
GIPPER

Also by Jack Cavanaugh:

Damn the Disabilities: Full Speed Ahead!
Tunney: Boxing's Brainiest Champ and His Upset of the Great Jack Dempsey
Giants Among Men: How Robustelli, Huff, Gifford, and the Giants Made
New York a Football Town and Changed the NFL
Season of '42: Joe D, Teddy Ballgame, and Baseball's Fight to Survive a Turbulent
First Year of War

THE
GIPPER

George Gipp, Knute Rockne, and the Dramatic Rise of Notre Dame Football

JACK CAVANAUGH

Skyhorse Publishing

Skyhorse Publishing books may be purchased in bulk at special discounts for sales promotion, corporate gifts, fund-raising, or educational purposes. Special editions can also be created to specifications. For details, contact the Special Sales Department, Skyhorse Publishing, 307 West 36th Street, 11th Floor, New York, NY 10018 or info@skyhorsepublishing.com.

Skyhorse® and Skyhorse Publishing® are registered trademarks of Skyhorse Publishing, Inc.®, a Delaware corporation.

Visit our website at www.skyhorsepublishing.com.

10 9 8 7 6 5 4 3 2 1

Library of Congress Cataloging-in-Publication Data is available on file.

ISBN: 978-1-61608-601-5

Printed in the United States of America

To my favorite team:
Marge, John, Tara, Lance, and
our three wonderful grandsons,
Rogan Jack, Tanner Patrick, and
Rylan Donovan Alexander.

CONTENTS

"I felt the thrill that comes to every coach when he knows it is his fate and his responsibility to handle unusual great-ness—the perfect performer who comes rarely more than once in a generation."

—Knute Rockne referring to George Gipp, ten years after Gipp's death

INTRODUCTION

WIN ONE FOR *The Gipper.* Has there ever been a better-known and more widely uttered rallying cry in sports? Not likely. Indeed, the expression found its way into the American lexicon long ago, at first as an exhortation, and later usually in jest and totally unrelated to sports. No less a figure than Ronald Reagan was prone to use the phrase when he was president, four decades after he had spoken it during a memorable movie portrayal. Among other times, Reagan employed the phrase during a commencement address at Notre Dame in 1981 to the delight of the school's graduating class, most of whom no doubt were well aware of its origin.

Yet, unlike other well-known phrases associated with famous athletes, such as "Say it ain't so, Joe," the lament of a young boy to the great baseball player "Shoeless" Joe Jackson after he had been implicated in the infamous "Black Sox" baseball scandal in 1919, the origin of the *Win One for The Gipper* phrase is as shrouded in mystery as the mystical figure to whom it refers.

Just who was the "Gipper," this seemingly mythical athlete whose name has aroused, in turn, awe, wonderment, curiosity, and amusement since the early part of the twentieth century and whose death while still a student plunged the Notre Dame campus, the city of South Bend, Indiana, and indeed much of the country into collective grief? And how, in such a short period of time, during one of the most colorful eras in American history, could have George Gipp's exploits as a football player equaled or even overshadowed those of such football immortals as Jim Thorpe and Red Grange and elevated him into a pantheon of his own just before, during, and immediately after World War I, when most college players played all sixty minutes of every game?

Even more than eight decades after his death, Gipp is regarded by football historians as probably Notre Dame's best all-around football player—a dazzling runner who averaged 8 yards each time he carried the ball as a senior, a Notre Dame record that still stands today; the best college passer of his era, who completed more than 50 percent of his passes at a time when a football was blunt-shaped, more rounded, and more difficult to throw, than the sleek, much narrower ball that became popular in the 1950s; a punter who boomed most of his kicks more than fifty yards, and once drop-kicked a 62-yard field goal; and a defensive back who never, in four seasons, allowed a pass to be completed in his area. That he did so at a time when there was not yet a National Football League, and when college football was becoming one of the most popular sports in the country after baseball, boxing, and horse racing, made Gipp one of the most famous athletes in the country. His ascendance to fame came at a time when the so-called Golden Age of Sports was emerging with such legendary athletes as Jack Dempsey, Gene Tunney, Babe Ruth, Bill Tilden, Red Grange, Bobby Jones, and Ty Cobb, and while America was rejoicing in the aftermath of World War I in what became known as the "Jazz Age," an appropriate era for the fast-living lover of the nights, George Gipp.

The handsome and intelligent (albeit somewhat undisciplined) Gipp, Notre Dame's first first-team All-American, also established a reputation in South Bend, Chicago, and a number of other Midwestern cities as one of the best high-stakes billiards players and a skilled poker player at a time when prohibition already had taken hold in Indiana (in April of 1918, before it became the law of the land in 1920), not that it would have much, if any, effect on the ingenious Gipp. Though pursued by women who were attracted to him as much by his good looks as his celebrity as an athlete, Gipp seemed to disdain such attention until he met a stunning young woman who became the love of his life in what turned out to be a bittersweet romance.

Not surprisingly, Gipp's lifestyle, in particular his association with gamblers and fellow pool sharks along with his drinking and inattention to his studies, made him a cross to bear for both his coach, Knute Rockne, and administration officials at Notre Dame. Yet Gipp's name can hardly be mentioned without also mentioning the charismatic Rockne, with whom he became—and still is—inextricably linked, as much as a wayward son as he was a great player. Rockne, who like Gipp did not expect to play football at Notre Dame, also turned out to be an unlikely football hero thanks to his involvement in what became a touchstone victory for an unheralded Notre Dame team in 1913. That

Rockne became the nation's best-known football coach during the Roaring Twenties was a remarkable achievement, since his college counterparts included such coaching immortals as Pop Warner at Pittsburgh, Amos Alonzo Stagg at Chicago, Fielding Yost at Michigan, Bob Zuppke at Illinois, and Tad Jones at Yale. Yet Rockne, more than any other coach, put his school on the map, as bent on making Notre Dame famous as he was on winning football games.

The link between Gipp and Rockne had begun serendipitously when Rockne spotted Gipp, in street clothes, launching dropkicks of more than fifty yards on campus, and talked him into coming out for football. Or so, at least, claimed Rockne, who became renowned for stretching the truth and at times concocting stories, mostly to motivate his players before or during a game. Fortunately for Gipp, Rockne—alternately bemused, angered, and amazed at his supremely talented halfback—seemed willing to ignore his off-campus peccadilloes, his habitual tardiness, and his reluctance to practice as long as he performed well on Saturdays during the football season, which he unfailingly did. Gipp never let Rockne down on the field, and even demonstrated a leadership that he never manifested during the rare practice sessions he attended.

As it was, Gipp and Rockne, in tandem, were largely responsible for making the small Midwestern all-male school nationally known. Gipp became the most famous football player and Rockne the best-known, and most colorful, coach in the country by the beginning of the 1920s. But their names were to resonate well beyond that era as they attained immortal status, both because of their football achievements and their distinctive, albeit vastly different, personalities—Gipp, the enigmatic and undisciplined loner and Rockne, the charismatic, highly organized and disciplined coach, famous for his stirring orations to his players and his ability to bring out the best in the insouciant Gipp. It was the close and symbiotic relationship between the two disparate football legends that led to "Win one for The Gipper," an expression that Gipp—portrayed by Reagan in what he always said was his favorite role—may or may not have uttered to Rockne on his deathbed.

Well-known sportswriter George Trevor of the old *New York Sun* provided what turned out to be a prophetic observation following a spectacular performance by Gipp against Army at West Point in 1920: "He blazes fiercely like a meteor, not long destined to dazzle earthly eyes."

Nine decades later George Gipp remains an almost mythical sports figure, Notre Dame's most legendary football player, and an athlete for the ages.

—Jack Cavanaugh
July13, 2010

1

THE RELUCTANT DROPKICKER

—————————————————————————

THE YEAR WAS 1916, and much of Europe was already engulfed in The Great War. (Decades later, when another worldwide conflict broke out, it would be retroactively renamed World War I.) To hundreds of young American men, the closest thing to warfare at the time was the country's most popular team sport after major league baseball—college football. Typifying the growing popularity of the game, crowds of up to seventy thousand were common at the two-year-old Yale Bowl in New Haven, Connecticut, home of the perennial national powerhouse Yale Bulldogs, among the first schools to start playing football (or at least an early, much rougher, version of the game) in the 1870s. Professional football offered virtually no opposition at the time, with the formation of the National Football League six years away, and the pro game relegated for the most part to relatively small cities in Ohio and Indiana where teams of part-time players performed before paltry crowds for around twenty-five dollars a game. Thus, college football had a virtual monopoly on the sport on the national level in the fall. Although the nation's best teams were primarily in the Northeast, the sport was beginning to gain strength elsewhere, particularly in the Midwest and the South.

Baseball, though, remained the so-called "national pastime." Among the college athletes who preferred the game was George Gipp, who in September 1916 enrolled at a small school in northwestern Indiana, the University of Notre Dame, to play baseball and not football, which he had not played in high school and had scant interest. Yet on November 11, 1916, Gipp stood in a huddle wearing the uniform of the Notre Dame freshman football team on a snowy and cold day in Kalamazoo, Michigan, having been convinced by the varsity team's assistant coach, Knute Rockne, one month earlier to go out for a game he had never played on an organized level. Like the twenty-one-year-old Gipp, Rockne had been a late bloomer in the sport, having played very little football in high school—in his case because he was too small and too light—and had not enrolled at Notre Dame until he was twenty-two years old. But Rockne had gone on to become a star end and helped popularize the forward pass as a result of his play during a stunning upset of a powerful Army team at West Point in 1913, in the first game between the two schools.

By late in the 1916 season, amid a group of scholarship players who had been football stars in high school, the tall and slender Gipp had in a month's time established himself as the best player on the freshman team in scrimmages with the varsity. Though he'd come out for the team late and lacked experience, Gipp's leadership qualities soon manifested themselves and endeared him to his teammates, who elected him captain. He did not disappoint while establishing a reputation as a free spirit, unimpressed with his own talents and those of his opponents. A triple-threat halfback, he could run, pass, and kick as well as anyone on the Notre Dame varsity, with whom he was prohibited from playing because the rules of the day restricted freshmen to playing with other first-year student athletes.

With about two minutes remaining in the freshman team's second game against Western State Normal (now Western Michigan University) and the score tied 7–7, Notre Dame was positioned on its own 38-yard line facing a fourth down with about 15 yards to go for a first down. The situation obviously called for a punt.

"Punt it, George," quarterback Frank Thomas barked, relaying an order from the team's head coach, Freeman Fitzgerald, who stood like a sentry on the sidelines in front of the Notre Dame bench.

"Why settle for a tie, Frank?" Gipp asked a bemused Thomas in the huddle. "Let me try a dropkick. I'm sure I can make it."

Gipp's teammates smiled at their star halfback's suggestion, but Thomas did not.

"Just punt the ball, that's it," he said firmly, whereupon Notre Dame went into its punt formation.

Taking the subsequent high snap from center at his own 38-yard line, Gipp dropped the ball to the ground and then, with a powerful thrust of his right leg, sent a dropkick straight down the middle of the field to the astonishment of his teammates, their opponents, the coaches of both teams, the officials and the crowd of around 1,000 spectators. Onward the ball sailed, low and end over end until, finally, it cleared the crossbar 62 yards from the scrimmage line to make it the second longest field goal ever kicked in a college football game[1]. Since Gipp was positioned seven yards behind the scrimmage line, on the Notre Dame 31, the ball actually had traveled sixty-nine yards, which is how it would be recorded today when field goals are measured from the point at which they were kicked.

"I had caught a couple of 50-yard punts by Gipp during the game, so I was plenty far back," said Walter Olsen, a safety who ran back punts for Western State Normal. "But this time, to my surprise, the ball sailed over my head and then over the crossbar for three points. I couldn't believe it."

Olsen wasn't the only disbeliever. Sprinting down the field to cover what he believed would be a punt, Notre Dame end Dave Hayes thought Olsen was trying to fake him out when the Kalamazoo safety turned his head. Olsen was even more confused when he heard a sudden and collective crowd cheer.

"What happened?" Hayes asked.

"The son-of-a-gun kicked a field goal," replied an incredulous Olsen.

---

[1] Only one college player had ever kicked one farther, on November 30, 1882, when Jim Haxall of Princeton booted a 65-yard field goal, also a dropkick, against Yale, a record that still stood more than a century later. Haxall's kick, however, was a "free kick" from his own 35-yard line, which the rules permitted at the time. Thus Haxall's kick was unencumbered by any charging linemen. Gipp's kick, by contrast, was made hurriedly in the face of an oncoming herd and after he had to leap to catch a high snap from center Frank Coughlin. It also traveled a greater distance to reach the crossbar.

Upfield, Gipp was engulfed by his teammates for his improbable field goal, which would turn out to be decisive in a 10–7 Notre Dame victory, its second in a row.

Even though the field goal occurred in a freshman game, the Associated Press put an account of Gipp's kick on its wires throughout the country. Hearing about Gipp's dazzling kick—and how it was accomplished in defiance of his coach and quarterback—Knute Rockne, the chemistry assistant and assistant varsity football coach who had strongly suggested that a reluctant Gipp suit up for football, felt more than a sense of satisfaction when told about it by varsity coach Jesse Harper that night. Though he had barely gotten to know Gipp, Rockne, who at twenty-eight was only seven years older than his protégé, also felt that it very likely would not be the first act of disobedience on a football field, or elsewhere, by the unlikely halfback from Michigan's Upper Peninsula.

Relatively tall for the era at six feet and weighing around 175 pounds, about normal for a running back at the time, Gipp, as a runner, had already showed Rockne, in the freshman team's scrimmages against the varsity, that he was a marvel of speed, balance, and grace, who could slither through a defensive line with ease or streak around end. Rockne marveled at how the raw but talented running back utilized his blockers masterfully.

"Take 50 to the inside!" he would call out to a blocker in front of him. Or to another blocker he would bark out, "Get 62!" Then, once in the open field and on his own, he became almost impossible to get a hand on as he dodged, twisted, and cut. He was able to outrun almost every defensive back on the varsity, a team that would go undefeated in nine games in 1916. Rockne also marveled at Gipp's prudent tendency to run out of bounds when he knew he had no chance of making additional yardage, a rare technique at the time, feeling, correctly, that it was not worth risking injury.

Turning to Harper after one particularly dazzling run by Gipp, Rockne said, "Jesse, he's going to be something special."

A week after the dramatic victory over Western State Normal, the Notre Dame freshman team closed out its three-game season by losing to Kalamazoo College, 34–7, with Gipp accounting for the visitors' only touchdown on a 65-yard run.

⤜⤛⤜

Even by the standards of tramp athletes who often moved from school to school to play football before, during, and after World War I, George Gipp was in a class of his own as a freshman student at Notre Dame. For most of the football gypsies of the era, the sole reason for being at a university was to play football; they usually dropped out of school after the last game of the season, having attended few, if any, classes. Gipp, by contrast, was bright and capable of doing his course work at the small Catholic school eighty-five miles east of Chicago and actually did attend classes, albeit somewhat erratically. Like many college football players, Gipp was about three or four years older than most freshmen at Notre Dame, whose collegiate student body of about five hundred was predominantly made up of young Catholic men from families of modest means who were able to come up with the yearly tuition of $120. Notre Dame tried to help by offering jobs to needy students, but could offer little more, since the school had virtually no endowment. "We here at

Notre Dame have a living endowment," the school's president, John W. Cavanaugh, often said, meaning that the university relied heavily on donations from some of its alumni. In addition to the college students, Notre Dame, from the time of its founding, included male elementary students from grades one through eight, and a four-year preparatory school. If they didn't share the same classrooms, all of the students—from, roughly, the ages of six (the so-called "minims") into the twenties—did share the same sprawling campus, an egalitarian concept that George Gipp and many other collegians did not particularly appreciate any more than that Notre Dame was an exclusively male province.

❧

It was not uncommon in those days for outstanding football players to work for several years after leaving high school while playing amateur or semi-professional football until—bigger, stronger, and invariably better—they were lured to play on the college level, even though not many were cut out to be college students. Gipp's situation, though, was different, since he had not played football in high school and had played it only rarely with some Calumet area semi-pro teams. Possessing great speed, uncanny balance, natural athleticism, and the supreme confidence he seemed to have in any athletic endeavor he stood out as a running back, passer, and kicker nonetheless.

Many of the tramp athletes were lured to other universities by unscrupulous coaches and well-heeled boosters, in some cases even after they already had played four years of college football and then were paid to play football. The United States Military

Academy was one of the worse offenders in its recruiting, often bringing in outstanding players who already had played football for up to four years at other schools. In an era when there was no central watchdog organization like the National Collegiate Athletic Association, it was usually difficult to track the provenance of school-jumping football players, a few of whom, some coaches claimed, wound up at Notre Dame, although that was never determined. Many of the tramp athletes, along with more than a few legitimate college players who confined themselves to one school, also played with professional or semi-pro teams on Sundays, the day after college games, under assumed names (as Gipp would do on at least one occasion) and often with the knowledge of their coaches. Rockne had not only done so as a player but he had also coached several professional teams in the South Bend area. Though, like Gipp, he had never graduated from high school, Rockne still found the time—and had the inclination—to be an exemplary college student, graduating with an A average in 1914 after starring in Notre Dame's upset of Army the previous fall. By then, because of Notre Dame's propensity to schedule teams from as far off as Army, Penn State, and Syracuse in the East, South Dakota and Nebraska in the Northwest, and Texas and Rice in the Southwest, many sportswriters called the team the Ramblers, Hoosiers, Catholics, Westerners (when they ventured East), and even the Harps, Micks, Hibernians, and Papists—though not yet the Fighting Irish.

◈◈◈

Largely because of the age discrepancy and a maturity that belied his twenty-one years, Gipp, as a freshman, felt out of place and uncomfortable on the Notre Dame campus. From the time he arrived, he was bored and pretty much a loner who did not go out of his way to make friends at Brownson Hall, where freshmen were housed and which was one of the two wings on the administration building renowned for the golden dome atop it. During his first year, he took a full load of courses—English, biology, history, political science, and German—and earned his room and board waiting tables, a task that, according to students he served, he performed well and in a friendly fashion. But boredom soon set in, as Gipp recounted in a letter to a friend in his hometown of Laurium, Michigan. "I got here alright and got away with a pretty good start," he wrote, "but I'm in a mood tonight where I'd like to go straight up. I want to come and go as I please. Sometimes I wonder what I'm here for." The reference to go "straight up" apparently was an allusion to Michigan's Upper Peninsula. Gipp went on to say, "I'd like to give up and quit right now, chuck everything and go anywhere."

Gipp's letter reflected his difficulty in adjusting to a structured way of living, especially among much younger, and less mature, college students. Subsequent letters also manifested his discomfort, even though by then he had established himself as a burgeoning football star. This seemed to have given him little satisfaction. "Becoming in his freshman year a hero of campus talk is enough to inflate any youngster's head," Rockne was to write years later, "but this boy Gipp had the superb personal policy of being indifferent to everything." At twenty-one years of age, Gipp, of course, was hardly a "boy," but rather a street-smart and somewhat cynical young man who, having spent much of his last five years associating with men older than him playing cards and pocket billiards for money, was, not surprisingly, uncomfortable amid much younger freshmen both in his dormitory and during his classes. Making him all the more uncomfortable was the composition of the Notre Dame's unusual student body, which ranged from five-year-old first graders to twenty-five-year-old—and even older—college students, all of whom shared the same campus, if not the same classrooms and dormitories.

Gipp's first roommate, Elwin Moore, was hardly one to help Gipp assimilate to college life or convince him to savor his success as a football star. Nicknamed "Dope" because of his encyclopedic knowledge of sports statistics (and not because he was short on intelligence), Moore also enjoyed the nightlife in South Bend more than he did his studies. A polished three-cushion billiards player, he taught Gipp the finer points of the game. Because of his skill in straight pool, an easier game that he had mastered as a boy and young man in the Calumet area, Gipp soon became accomplished at three-cushion billiards, which does not require players to deposit balls in the six pockets of a conventional pool table. By late in the first semester in 1916, Gipp, already tired of campus life and with few friends, was spending much of his time around pool tables in downtown South Bend, then one of the major manufacturing centers in the Midwest, where bars, restaurants, cigar stores, and even pharmacies often served as hosts for high-stakes billiard and poker games and, in later years, speakeasies in the rear. Though South Bend, like much of Indiana, had gone dry well before the Prohibition amendment was ratified in 1919, Gipp, who enjoyed a drink and the convivial atmosphere of a pool hall or a poker table far more than that of a campus dormitory, soon realized it was his kind of town.

2

THE CHANCE MEETING OF A
LIFETIME

___

IN ADDITION TO his newfound downtown haunts, Gipp spent a considerable amount of time during his first semester at Notre Dame in the campus recreation room shooting pool. "He'd always be alone and would spend an hour or so playing by himself," said one of Gipp's few early friends on campus, Walter Miller, a fullback on the football team and one of five Miller brothers to play football at Notre Dame. "I remember watching him run off as many as eighty balls without missing a shot, and all the while not saying anything to anyone who might be watching him play alone. Students who'd watch him were amazed, since they'd never seen anyone play like he did. As for Gipp, he never said a word nor changed his expression."

Before long, aware that he had no competition in straight pool at the recreation center, especially for money, Gipp soon began to concentrate more on pool parlors in downtown South Bend, notably at Hullie and Mike's restaurant, speakeasy, and pool parlor on Michigan Street, where Rockne himself frequently ate both as a student and as an assistant coach. His success with cue and cards allowed Gipp to give up his waiter's job on campus without hurting his income. Along the way, Gipp paid less and less attention to his studies, although his grades were good, and he began to miss classes often. Never the picture of health to begin with, Gipp's lifestyle took a toll on him, which was reflected by a pallor and loss of weight that made him look older than his twenty-one years. By the spring of 1917, Gipp had become a familiar figure at the Hotel Oliver, an elegant six-story, 250-room South Bend landmark, distinguished on the outside by its Italian Renaissance architecture and on the inside by its ornate but tasteful lobby (which included sixteen life-size paintings representing, among other things, the four seasons and muses of dance, drama, and music). Regarded as one of the most opulent and stylish hotels in the Midwest, attracting a high-end clientele that included the cream of South Bend society, the Oliver also was distinguished by its basement, which hosted what were reputed to be the highest-stakes poker games in Indiana. While the clientele was neither as prosperous nor as elegant as that on the floors above, the billiard and poker tables drew some of the best players in the Chicago area, which by then included student-athlete George Gipp.

❦

If Rockne had nothing to do with Gipp coming to Notre Dame, he had everything to do with having Gipp come out for football through a fortuitous—and for Notre Dame propitious—

meeting. In the movie *Knute Rockne: All American,* Rockne (played very well, albeit much too saintly, by Pat O'Brien) is taken aback by an obviously long kick that had sailed onto the playing field during a Notre Dame practice in the early fall of 1916. Upon investigation, he discovers that the kicker is Gipp (played in the film by Ronald Reagan), whom he thereupon convinces to come out for the freshman football team. Closer to the truth, it seems, was Rockne's own version, wherein, while walking past a near deserted practice field on campus about midway through the 1916 season, he spotted a casually dressed student wearing street shoes booming punts and dropkicks to a freshman player in uniform, obviously bent on practicing fielding punts and kickoffs. For about ten minutes Rockne watched the pale-faced, somewhat emaciated-looking kicker sending long spiral punts through the air, along with gracefully dropping footballs to the ground and, in a fluid and smooth motion, kicking one ball after another fifty yards and longer straight down the middle of the field. Well aware that no Notre Dame player, freshman or varsity, could come close to drop-kicking a football that far, Rockne then approached the student and asked, "What's your name?"

"Gipp. George Gipp," he replied nonchalantly, not recognizing Rockne even though, by then, the assistant varsity football coach had become well-known on the Notre Dame campus. "I come from Laurium, Michigan."

"What led you to come to Notre Dame?" Rockne persisted.

"Friends of mine are here," Gipp responded, though in fact he was not aware of anyone on campus from the Calumet area.

"Played high school football?" Rockne asked.

"No," Gipp replied. "Don't particularly care for football. Baseball's my game."

Intrigued by Gipp's confident air, his matter-of-fact demeanor, and his athletic bearing, Rockne wasn't about to give up, and, after introducing himself, thereupon did what he usually did best: He made a command. "Put on a football suit tomorrow and come out with the freshman scrubs," Rockne said pointedly but with a smile. "I think you'll make a football player."

As Gipp nodded and walked away, the player who had been catching Gipp's punts and dropkicks said to Rockne, "He's been kicking those punts and drops with ordinary street shoes. What'll he do with football shoes on?" A smiling Rockne thought he knew the answer. The question, though, was whether the young man from Michigan could do anything else with a football.

That, of course, was Rockne's story of how Gipp came out for football at Notre Dame—a version that was told some time after Gipp had died. So far as is known, it was never corroborated. Many other stories Rockne told, some as part of his trademark pep talks, turned out to be apocryphal. But that was part of Rockne's charm.

Despite Rockne's persuasiveness and conviction that Gipp would "make a football player," Gipp had no intention of going out for the freshman team, which already had been practicing, often against the varsity, for more than a month, though it had yet to play a game. Afternoons, to Gipp, were for sleeping. By the following day, though, the highly competitive Gipp—motivated by Rockne's speculation that he might become a football player—would have had a change of heart and decided to show up for practice. Reporting to freshman coach Freeman Fitzgerald, who had been told about Gipp by Rockne, Gipp made an immediate impression when, at his suggestion, he lined up as a halfback and on his first carry burst through the line and raced forty yards for a touchdown. Looking on from an adjacent field where the varsity was practicing, Rockne felt a surge of satisfaction. *Not only can he kick like hell,* the young assistant coach thought, *but he can run like hell, too.*

Rockne saw even more of Gipp in the ensuing weeks during scrimmages between the freshman and varsity teams when, time and again, Gipp raced through and around the varsity defensive line for long gains or touchdowns. Inexplicably, this preternaturally cool and poised freshman with no football pedigree was turning out to be the best running back at Notre Dame.

Even though Gipp was restricted to playing with the Notre Dame freshman team, he was hardly missed by the varsity, at least through the first four games when the Ramblers, as they were called because of their increasingly national schedule, amassed 182 points while holding its opponents scoreless and extending its winning streak to nine games going back to the previous season. But a powerful Army team, led by All-American fullback Elmer Oliphant, a remarkably versatile athlete, loomed as the fifth opponent at West Point on November 4. Typical of the era, Oliphant was in his second go-around as a varsity athlete, having already graduated from Purdue in his native Indiana in 1914 after earning varsity letters in football, basketball, (in which he was an All-American in 1913 and 1914), baseball, and track while also competing with the varsity wrestling and swimming teams.

Only five feet seven inches tall and about 175 pounds, Oliphant won another eleven letters over a four-year period at

West Point in the same four sports he earned letters at Purdue, while also earning monograms in boxing, swimming, and hockey. The week before the Notre Dame game, Oliphant had scored six touchdowns and a total of 45 points in a 68–0 rout of Villanova. That was two more points than Oliphant had scored for Purdue four years earlier in 1912 when his 43 points set a Boilermaker record that still stands almost a century later.

Army's ability to recruit star football players from other schools where they had been sports letter-winners, frequently for four years, gave it what many schools felt was an unfair advantage and helped the Cadets win several national football championships during the first few decades of the twentieth century. It also kept a number of the nation's strongest college football teams from scheduling Army, forcing the Cadets to play lesser teams such as Lebanon Valley, Maine, and Springfield. Among the Army stars who played college football elsewhere for four years before coming to West Point was Chris Cagle, one of Army's greatest running backs, who after scoring a school-record 235 points while playing for (and graduating from) Southwestern Louisiana from 1922 through 1925, played four years of football at Army, where he earned All-American honors his last three seasons. While serving as Army's captain during his senior year in 1929, he was featured on the cover of *Time* magazine. Cagle, who sometimes played without a helmet and scored 169 points at West Point while averaging 6.4 yards a carry, later played five seasons in the National Football League, three with the New York Giants and two with the Brooklyn Dodgers. For two seasons, one of Cagle's backfield teammates was another Army legend and All-American, "Lighthorse Harry" Wilson, who also had an extended collegiate football career. After playing three seasons at Penn State, Wilson switched to West Point, where he was a halfback for four years and, as at Penn State, an All-American. He captained the Cadets in 1927. Given Army's propensity to recruit All-American players like Oliphant, Cagle, and Wilson— players who already had played as many as four seasons at other schools—it was no wonder that Army was one of the country's best teams in the 1920s and that many schools, which held themselves to a four-season eligibility standard, wanted no part of the Cadets. Indeed, to national powers like Yale, Harvard, and Princeton, Army's practice of importing All-Americans who had already played four years elsewhere made it a football pariah. Yet for an aspiring school like Notre Dame, a game against the Cadets guaranteed it national publicity, and, if the Ramblers won, increased self-esteem for the little university in Indiana.

❧❧❧

Impressed by Gipp's performances in scrimmages against the varsity, Rockne suggested to head coach Jesse Harper that Rockne explain Oliphant's style of running to Gipp so he could emulate the great Army running back in a scrimmage before the team left by train for West Point. The tactic, Rockne was sure, would be very beneficial to Notre Dame's defensive line when it lined up against Army, and Oliphant in particular, on Saturday. Notre Dame coaches in the past had had players imitate Oliphant before previous Army games, but to no avail.

"For three days I took him personally in hand, making him vary his pace, break his runs and cut back and dodge," Rockne later wrote in an article that appeared in *Collier's* magazine in

THE CHANCE MEETING OF A LIFETIME

November 1930. "The varsity knew Gipp was going to be sent in against them. They were primed to stop him. They didn't. Gipp gave a perfect imitation of Oliphant and ran wide around end, passing the secondary defense with ease, and scoring a touchdown."

Theoretically, that should have made Notre Dame ready to cope with Oliphant, who also was captain of the team as a senior. It wasn't. Despite Gipp's outstanding impression of Oliphant, Army's All-American fullback had an outstanding afternoon, running for more than 100 yards, catching a touchdown pass, completing a number of passes that led to two Army touchdowns, and kicking two field goals and two extra points as the Cadets scored 24 unanswered points in the second half to beat Notre Dame, 30–10. Asked about Oliphant's performance after the game by a South Bend sportswriter, Rockne smiled and, after relating Gipp's outstanding role as a doppelganger for Oliphant during scrimmages leading up to the Army game, said, "The only drawback was that Oliphant gave a perfect imitation of Gipp."

❧❧❧

As it developed, Army would be the only team to score against Notre Dame during the 1916 season. The Ramblers would go on to win their last four games, scoring 141 points while holding their opponents, including Nebraska, scoreless. With a solid nucleus of the 1916 team scheduled to return the following year, the outlook for another good season looked promising indeed. Not only that, Rockne mused, Gipp had three varsity years ahead of him. That was assuming that the enigmatic young man from

Michigan's Upper Peninsula, who seemed to take for granted his unmistakable talent in a sport he had hardly ever played, would even complete his freshman year—let alone return to Notre Dame the following fall since, in April 1917, the United States would declare war on Germany. As it was, Gipp made it through the academic year with decent grades, including three consecutive grades in the nineties—the equivalent of an A—in German during the four quarterly marking periods. In December, Gipp decided to go out for the freshman basketball team. Clearly one of the team's best prospects, Gipp lasted a few practice sessions before realizing that basketball was interfering with his lucrative pursuits of pocket billiards and poker, and to a lesser extent, his studies.

Gipp lasted a bit longer in baseball, playing in one game for the Notre Dame freshman baseball team. Instructed to bunt, Gipp was unable to resist a fastball right across the plate, swung away and belted a home run. Chastised by the coach for his disobedience, as he had been for refusing to punt and instead kicking a game-winning 62-yard field goal the previous fall, Gipp turned in his uniform the next day. A few weeks later, as a prelude to the traditional spring game between the varsity football team and an alumni squad, the alumni team (with Rockne at quarterback, no less) took on what had been the freshmen side the previous fall. It gave Rockne, who played both ways, a close-up look at Gipp. As it developed, the bigger alumni team beat the freshmen 14–7, with Gipp's passing leading to his team's only touchdown.

After the game, Rockne, never prone to applaud a team's players individually, praised Gipp for his play. Then, in a rare gesture for Rockne, he told Gipp he was glad he had come out for the freshman team, but not without applying what had become a Rockne trademark—a barb intended to deflate a player's ego. "I told you I thought you'd make a football player," Rockne said to a smiling Gipp as they walked off the field. "And if you keep up what you're doing, you will."

If not the beginning of a beautiful friendship, it marked another step toward the establishment of a close bond between one of the most charismatic and dynamic football coaches of all time and the baseball player Rockne had discovered—or so he claimed—booming out awe-inspiring dropkicks during a walk across the Notre Dame campus on a sunny, early autumn Sunday afternoon.

3

THE POOL SHARK FROM LAURIUM

BY ALL ACCOUNTS, George Gipp morphed from being a teenage truant during his high school days into a directionless young man whose main goals seemed to be winning as much money as possible playing poker and shooting pool in his hometown of Laurium, Michigan, and nearby Calumet, while also establishing himself as a potential big-league baseball player.

"George wasn't what you could call troublesome as a kid, but he was lazy and somewhat indifferent to his studies," Karl Gipp, a cousin, recalled. "He came from a strict family, but was very different from his father and his seven siblings. George pretty much did whatever he wanted to do, but he was never what you would call troublesome."

Another cousin, Harrison Gipp, remembered his first cousin well, especially his affinity for gambling on cards and billiards. "He was darn good at it," Harrison Gipp said, "but otherwise there didn't seem to be anything exceptional about George. He was a quiet, modest fellow, well-liked. He didn't seem to have any real close friends. I guess you'd call him a loner."

Where Gipp's seemingly diffident attitude came from is diffi-cult to ascribe. Gipp's father, Matthew, the son of German immi-grants, was a somewhat dour disciplinarian who was unable to inculcate his own values into the youngest of his three sons. In effect, Gipp became the family's black sheep during his teenage years and remained so until—to the astonishment of his family, friends, and even those who knew him remotely—he decided to go to Notre Dame at the age of twenty-one. From all accounts, the Gipp household was not a joyous one and was dominated by Matthew Gipp's wife, Isabella, who was of Scotch-Irish descent and had been born in Belfast in Northern Ireland.

That Gipp went to Notre Dame was surprising for two reasons. First, he had never expressed an interest in going to college, and, second, he had not graduated from high school—thanks to poor grades, even poorer attendance, and a number of infractions serious enough to get him suspended on several occasions, such as talking back to teachers or speaking up in class with what his classmates thought were witty remarks, but which infuriated his instructors. What was not surprising was that Gipp, on the recommendation of former Notre Dame catcher Wilbur "Dolly" Gray (who had played amateur ball with Gipp), had been offered a scholarship by Notre Dame to play baseball, which in the latter part of the nine-teenth century and up until around 1910 had been the dominant varsity sport at the small Catholic school. While playing with strong amateur teams in the Calumet area, Gipp had established a reputation as a power-hitting outfielder with speed and a strong arm, good enough to attract the attention of several major league scouts. One of Gipp's amateur clubs was in Elkhart, Indiana, not far from South Bend, where Gray, already aware of Gipp's talents as a baseball player, had watched him play.

When first approached by Gray about going to Notre Dame in the spring of 1916, Gipp told him, "I'm too old to go to college, and, besides, I don't have any money." That was hardly surprising since Gipp had worked sporadically—driving a truck for a construction company, climbing poles for a utility company, waiting tables at the Michigan House restaurant, and ferrying copper miners to bars and a house of prostitution in Calumet by taxi—while spending much of his time playing poker and shooting pool, almost always for money, usually winning more than he lost. In mid-May, Gipp received a scholarship offer to play baseball at Notre Dame from Jesse Harper, who in addition to coaching the football team, coached the baseball team and was the school's athletic director. That night, Gipp told his family about the letter, but said he was disinclined to accept it.

"What was the deal?" Alex Gipp, the oldest of the Gipp children, asked.

"A full ride for tuition, bed, and board," George replied. "For that I'd have to play baseball and wait on table[s]."

"What's wrong with that?" Alex responded.

"It's kid stuff, money," the younger Gipp replied.

"What do you want? Egg in your beer?" retorted an increasingly perturbed Alex Gipp.

"Look, if I'm a good enough ballplayer to have some college come after me, I figure I'm good enough to play in the minor leagues anyway," George said.

"It doesn't follow that because a college wants you, the pros will," Alex said. "And anyway, they can find you at Notre Dame just as soon as they can in the bush leagues."

"Like I say, Notre Dame won't pay money, and I wouldn't be able to hustle the students for the price of a haircut," George said in response.

"Aren't you pleased they asked you to play for Notre Dame?" Alex asked.

"Oh sure, that's jake," George replied, using a term popular at the time to denote good or even great.

"Well then, you're going to go," Alex said loudly, obviously determined to see that his younger brother would be the first of the eight Gipp children to go to college.

Alex Gipp thereupon went to a nearby butcher to borrow fifty dollars and launch a drive to finance his brother's trip to South Bend. Eager to help his former teammate, who he regarded as a big-league prospect, Dolly Gray, along with some of Gipp's closest friends, also pitched in, persuading a number of merchants in Laurium and Calumet to donate money to pay for Gipp's train fare and some necessary expenses once he got to South Bend. Finally agreeing to take advantage of the scholarship, Gipp boarded a train bound for South Bend in early September 1916 after being informed by a school official that he was being accepted as a conditional freshman, meaning he would have to make up necessary high school credits during summer school at Notre Dame (which Gipp never did). If Notre Dame thought it was getting a prototypical student, the school was mistaken. What it got was a twenty-one-year-old freshman known only to the school's baseball coach who would become an athlete for the ages—and not because of his prowess in baseball.

❧

How George Gipp developed into an athlete is hard to fathom. His five-foot eight-inch father was unathletic, as were his three brothers, none of whom appeared to have encouraged him to get involved in sports as a boy. Nor were his mother or his sisters of an athletic bent. If he inherited anything from his parents, it could have been their even dispositions, along with the brown hair and blue eyes of his mother. Taller than his father and his siblings, Gipp, from an early age, demonstrated talent in baseball, football, basketball, and as a sprinter, even winning the annual Laurium foot race while competing against grown men at the age of thirteen. But school was another matter. "George was a bright kid, witty and smart, but he hated being restricted as he had to be in school," said Fred "Ojay" Larson, a high school classmate of Gipp's who played with him at Notre Dame, shortly before he died in 1977. "And being absent so often he wasn't permitted to compete in sports beyond his freshman year. He made up for it, though, by playing with older guys on basketball teams at the Calumet YMCA and baseball teams in the Calumet area. The only football he played was on the amateur and sometimes a semi-pro level, but in all three sports he was outstanding, a natural athlete."

Neither Larson nor any other longtime friends from the Calumet area seemed to recall any particular reason why Gipp was so recalcitrant and rebellious as a teenager. "I don't think it had anything to do with his family," Larson said. "His parents had eight kids, and, as I recall, his father was strict, but then so were most of the fathers at the time. We were all competitive, but nowhere near as much as George, who hated to lose at anything, even marbles. But he never was nasty, and most of the other kids who played sports with him liked him. Even as a kid he was very cool and very confident in everything he did. And from the time he got into his teens, he tended to hang around with older guys, both while playing sports and gambling. I think he was attracted to the card-playing and pool-shooting because of his intense competitive nature. As I said, he hated to lose at anything."

Gipp's constant truancy in school, especially at Calumet High, prompted letters to his parents, who seemed to have believed they'd done all they could to get him to go to school on a regular basis. "I think they often assumed George had gone to school when he hadn't and spent most of the time playing poker with older guys," Larson said. At Calumet High, Gipp was a good enough basketball player to become a starter as a freshman, the only year he played, but he was ineligible to play football and baseball because of his absences and poor grades. "George was a very smart fellow, but just didn't care for school," Larson said. "If he'd been eligible to play, he probably would have been great on both the football and baseball teams, but he didn't seem to care about not being able to do so. But that was the way George was. He was a prankster as a kid, but never pulled anything that was serious or hurt anyone. And I certainly don't recall him ever being in trouble with the law."

Having dropped out following the fall semester in 1911, he spent the intervening years driving a construction company truck and a taxi in Calumet, playing semi-pro baseball for money and establishing himself as one of the best pocket billiards and baseball players in Calumet and, according to Larson, earning a considerable amount of money in the process. For unknown reasons, Gipp returned to Calumet High in the fall of 1914. Again ineligible for sports, he stayed until the end of the school year in June 1915, but still did not have enough credits to graduate. Fifteen months after leaving Calumet High for the last time, Gipp enrolled at Notre Dame, leading some friends to believe that, by returning to school for a year, he thought he could manage to pick up enough credits to get into Notre Dame or whatever big-time college would accept him, although, according to Larson, he never mentioned the possibility of going to college when he went back to Calumet High.

"Even though he never mentioned it, some of us thought that he came back to high school because he had begun to have thoughts of going to college, probably to attract the attention of baseball scouts since he was such a good baseball player," said Larson, who went on play five years with the Chicago Bears in the National Football League. "But certainly none of us ever thought he would go to college to play football. That wasn't his game, although we played together on some amateur and semi-pro teams around Calumet and George was very good, both as a runner and passer and as a defensive player."

Bob Erkkila, who taught in the Calumet school system for many years and has researched Gipp's career in the area, said Calumet's wayward son was a prankster and practical joker, albeit a harmless one. "But when it came to sports, he seemed to be good at everything he did," Erkkila said. "He just loved to compete. But he also definitely did not live by his family's code."

Erkkila's best source on Gipp was Wilfred "Jazzy" Giroux, whose older brother, Peter, was one of Gipp's best friends. "Jazzy was about six years younger than Gipp, and very small for his age. When he was about twelve and George and Peter were around eighteen, Jazzy would slide down a coal chute to get into the Elks club in Calumet when it was closed and then open the door to let in his brother and George so that they could play pool," Erkkila said. "Jazzy was in awe of Gipp, who often took him along in a World War I-era liberty truck that Gipp drove for the Houghton Traction Company in Calumet both before he went to Notre Dame and during summer vacations. Once, when Gipp had driven a shipment to Hurley, Wisconsin, which was a wide-open town, Gipp got into a dice game with some older local guys and began to win a lot of money. The local guys became furious at this outsider winning their money and eventually threw Gipp down a stairway. Gipp then got into the truck with Jazzy and drove it right into the front of the building where the dice game was going on, then said to Jazzy, 'Let's get out of here,' and drove off in a hurry. That was George. He wasn't afraid of anything or anyone."

Much of the money Gipp won at poker and at pool tables came from older men, many of whom worked in the Calumet area's mines, which contained some of the richest copper deposits in the world. Following the discovery of copper in the middle of the nineteenth century in northern Michigan's Keweenaw Peninsula, which projects into Lake Superior, thousands of potential miners from as far away as Europe (including Gipp's paternal grandfather) streamed into the area. This increased Calumet's population to almost 40,000, making it the second largest city in Michigan after Detroit.

Like many of their relatives, most male Calumet High School students in the early part of the twentieth century wound up working for the Calumet and Hecla Mining Company, a copper-mining behemoth that dominated the industrial landscape. Because of that predestined future for so many students, courses were offered in carpentry, blacksmithing, and other subjects that related to mining. Gipp was among the relative few who, having no intention of working for the C & H (as the mining company was called), took none of those courses. He did not fare well in any of those he did take, although he did display creativity, a sense of humor, and awareness of three famed writers in a poem that he wrote for a freshman English class.

After mentioning the early nineteenth century poets John Keats and Percy Bysshe Shelley in his first two stanzas, Gipp concluded:

> *Now Gibbons they say wrote a history true*
> *Of things that had happened after me and you*
> *Of battles and wars and of wayward sons*
> *Whose only ambition was great battles won*
> *Of great men I'd tell with their ways so quaint*
> *If I were a Keats and I'm sorry I ain't.*

This is the only sample of Gipp's high school work that lives on, so far as is known; it may have been his only effort, and an admirable one at that, at poetry.

Having played a varsity sport, in his case basketball, only during his freshman year, Gipp never achieved the Big Man on Campus status that usually accrues to high school sports stars. Several acquaintances, including Ojay Larson, claimed that Gipp was the high scorer on the Calumet High team during the one year he played, and once scored 52 points in a game. That seems to have been a mind-boggling feat, since Gipp played in an era when basketball teams rarely scored more than 40 points in a game. (A jump ball was mandated after each basket—a rule that lasted until 1936—which kept fast breaks to a minimum and slowed down the pace of games considerably.)

Given his diffident manner, it's unlikely that the lack of attention he drew while at Calumet High bothered him, nor did much of anything, it seemed, during most of the rest of his life. Yet he did feel ill at ease during his early days at Notre Dame. Fortunately, the relatively old freshman from little Laurium, Michigan, would soon get over his discomfort—mainly because of his superb athletic talents and his skill at the pool and poker tables.

4

THE MISSING ARMY INDUCTEE

WHEN GIPP RETURNED home to Laurium in mid-June 1917, he found that quite a few of his friends, including some former baseball teammates, had joined the Army in the two months since the United States—with an army of only 128,000 men—declared war on Germany. Members of other teams in the Trolley League, one of the best amateur baseball leagues in Michigan, had also entered the services, which was certain to diminish the quality of play in a circuit comparable to that of a modern low-level minor league.

Laurium still managed to field a reasonably good team, which often attracted as many as 2,000 fans to its home games. Gipp, whose exploits on the football field at Notre Dame had surprised sports fans in the Calumet area, was the main attraction, primarily because of his hitting prowess, but also thanks to his fielding, his speed, and his strong arm. As a baseball player, Gipp most closely resembled a later-era Joe DiMaggio, the Hall of Fame centerfielder for the New York Yankees, in that he hit for both power and high average, was an excellent base runner, and a graceful outfielder, who made even difficult fly balls look easy to catch.

"No one around Calumet thought of George as a football player until he went to Notre Dame," said Joe Savini, a former baseball teammate of Gipp from Calumet. "He was one of the best baseball players around Calumet, though. When we played an afternoon game at home on the weekend, we often had to go find George, but when we played out of town and stayed over after playing, there usually was no problem. Then, George would come around and wake us up to make sure we'd catch the bus home. The reason he'd be up so early was that he'd never got to bed in the first place because he'd found an all-night poker game somewhere or was shooting pool someplace, no doubt for money."

In early August 1917 a story appeared in the *Daily Mining Gazette,* the major newspaper in the Calumet area, that the Laurium draft board had released a list of forty-two young men who were to be inducted on September 21. Gipp's name was on the list, much to his chagrin, since unlike many young Americans he was not particularly interested in the prospect of firing a gun or being shot at. But when a train left the Calumet train station for an Army post in Battle Creek, Michigan, on the scheduled date, Gipp was not aboard—and no one seemed to be able to determine why. Gipp himself would not explain his absence, nor would the Laurium draft board, who raised eyebrows and also speculation that Gipp's sports stardom had earned him at least a temporary deferment, which was not unusual either during World War I or II. Since the board never did say Gipp had received a deferment—and there seemed no legitimate reason why he should have been given one—Gipp was technically a draft dodger and thus subject to arrest. But as a celebrity athlete in Laurium, where fans tended to worship sports stars—and Gipp was on the verge of becoming the biggest star in the local constellation, with his celebrity status now enhanced as a football player at Notre Dame—perhaps the Laurium draft board felt that Gipp would do best on the home front, helping people forget about the war "over there" (as George M. Cohan described the war in Europe in his rousing song about American troops who, as the lyrics forecast, "won't come back 'til it's over over there").

By the time the Laurium baseball team had played its last game and its first draftees had gone off to war, classes had started at Notre Dame, as had football practice. But Gipp, obviously in no hurry to return to South Bend, continued to drive a truck for the Roehm Construction Company, a choice, well-paying job that Gipp got more for his baseball ability than for his capacity to navigate a dump truck along Calumet area highways and side streets. Four days after the Laurium draftees had departed for Battle Creek, a story appeared in the sports section of the *South Bend Tribune* that reported that the Notre Dame football team was still awaiting Gipp's much-anticipated arrival. "Both Harper and Rockne presume at this time that Gipp must be in the Army," the story read in referring to head coach Jesse Harper and his chief assistant. That neither Harper nor Rockne tried to get in touch with Gipp is hard to comprehend today, but is relatively typical of the lack of communication between coaches of the era and their players during summer vacations, even potential star football players like Gipp. By contrast, well before the turn of the twenty-first century, most Division I football players stayed on campus most of the summer, attending required classes that they could not fit into their schedules during the normal academic year and, of course, practicing on their own, since coaches are forbidden to work with their players during the off season except for spring practice.

❧❦❧

Gipp finally returned to South Bend on Sunday, October 15, the day after Notre Dame's second game, a scoreless tie with Wisconsin in Madison and more than a month after classes had begun. Despite his late and unannounced return, Harper, Rockne, and most of the players were glad to see Gipp turn out for practice, particularly since Notre Dame had lost about a half dozen players to the military and because starting halfback Leonard "Pete" Bahan had been hurt in the Wisconsin game. What, if anything, Gipp told Harper and Rockne as to why he had returned so late was never disclosed, although certainly they must have asked. Likewise, it's not known whether Gipp told any of his teammates why he had shown up more than a month after preseason practice had begun and two games had been played. Most likely he did not, since Gipp always kept his own counsel and, with the exception of his new roommate, fullback Walter Miller, and center Frank Rydzewski, one of the best centers in the country, was not close to any of the returning lettermen or the current sophomores with whom he had played on the 1916 freshmen team.

Gipp's return came at a propitious time, since Notre Dame's next game was against powerful Nebraska in Lincoln. In practices leading up to the game, Gipp was obviously in good condition, mainly, no doubt, because of all the baseball he had played during the summer (and despite the all-nighters he had pulled playing poker or pocket billiards). Though both Harper and Rockne were cool toward Gipp in the days after his belated arrival, neither coach was about to be caustic toward him, knowing that, given his independent spirit, he might take umbrage at criticism and quit the team, as he had the freshman baseball team in the spring. They likely had no worries about how the team would react, since he had been popular with his freshman teammates and had even been elected as the team's captain.

During the week leading up to the Nebraska game, the *South Bend News-Times* mentioned Gipp for the first time since his arrival on campus. "Gipp is the long-distance dropkicker who starred as a freshman last year," the paper noted, while failing to mention that he also had been the freshmen team's best runner and passer. "If he can demonstrate any of his old-time acumen, dropkicking, he will be a very valuable man to have around for the Cornhuskers."

As it happened, Gipp never was called on to drop-kick in the Nebraska game. As much as his other skills were needed, he did not start, although he played more than half the game. His lack of practice and familiarity with the team's offensive plays showed, and for the most part, he was contained by a much bigger Nebraska defensive line and a strong secondary as the Cornhuskers prevailed, 7–0.

The defeat, which was hardly an upset, was followed by more bad news early the next week when starting quarterback and captain Jim Phelan (one of many early-day Notre Dame players who went on to coach in the National Football League) left for

Army service. Making up somewhat for the team's losses to the military were a number of outstanding freshmen who, under a temporary rule stemming from the war, were allowed to play with the varsity, as was the case at other schools that tried to play a schedule in 1917. They included lineman Maurice "Clipper" Smith, who became a well-known college coach; Joe Brandy, a 145-pound quarterback who would go on to become a college professor, an NFL head coach, the publisher of a newspaper and the founder of a radio station in his hometown of Ogdensburg, New York; and halfback Norm Barry, who would coach the Chicago Bears for two years after spending two seasons as a running back with the Bears. Barry would be the only player to spend his entire academic career at Notre Dame, from the first grade through his senior year.

(A year later, three more eventual National Football League coaches, Earl "Curley" Lambeau, Heartley "Hunk" Anderson, and Ojay Larson would join the Notre Dame varsity, as would Eddie Anderson, who would become both a physician and a Hall of Fame college coach, most notably at Holy Cross.)

Among those returning was the 220-pound Rydzewski, the biggest player on the squad and the anchor of one of the best defensive lines in Notre Dame history, who would go on to play with the Chicago Cardinals and the Chicago Bears in the National Football League.

Gipp, while still hardly a typical Notre Dame student, took up residence in the basement of Sorin Hall, named for the university's founder, which housed most of the team's thirty players, including his new roommate, Walter Miller, a junior fullback whose sense of humor, overall affability, and good study habits were expected—it was hoped by Harper and Rockne—to have a salutary effect on Gipp. They did to a degree, but before Gipp's first full week back was over, he had ventured downtown several times to visit Hullie and Mike's, the Hotel Oliver, and a few other favorite haunts. As the academic year went on, Miller found himself spending most nights alone in his basement room while his roommate worked at his off-campus job—shooting pool and playing poker for money (a lot of it, more often than not).

What Gipp saw on his first trip into town surprised him. South Bend, like many American industrial cities, had gone on a war footing, with the Studebaker Corp. plant and the Singer Sewing Machine Co. facility, among other factories, operating around the clock turning out products for the military. Gipp also saw more than a few servicemen home on leave and in uniform. Given his own close call with conscription, Gipp might have felt a twinge of guilt when he saw the military personnel, realizing that he had escaped the draft, which had already claimed about a half million young American men who, along with several hundred thousand who had enlisted, by early fall were already in harm's way in France. Just maybe, Knute Rockne thought, the realization that so many American men had gone to war might have a calming effect on Notre Dame's wayward football star and perhaps make him realize he was lucky to be going to college and playing football, a dangerous sport, to be sure, but nowhere as hazardous as wartime duty in France. Gipp might have thought that, but he was not about to admit it.

❧❦

Apparently trying to make up for his late arrival, Gipp was uncharacteristically punctual for practices from the time he

arrived back on campus. He also seemed intent on ingrati-
ating himself with his coaches, especially Harper, who was less
forgiving than Rockne about Gipp's tardy return. Harper and
Rockne could hardly have been more different. If Rockne was
fiery, passionate, and loud, the tall and slender Harper was taci-
turn, scholarly, and soft-spoken. They differed drastically in their
coaching demeanor as well, and even in how they dressed for
practice—Rockne in football pants, a sweatshirt, and football
cleats; Harper in a business suit and tie. Though he commanded
respect, Harper rarely raised his voice and was almost profes-
sorial in his coaching approach. Rockne, by contrast, was both
vocal and demonstrative, to the point of lining up at the scrimmage line without any protective gear and throwing a block or
making a tackle, to the amusement of the players.

A brilliant tactician, Harper had been a backup quarterback
to All-American Walter Eckersall at the University of Chicago
under the legendary and innovative Amos Alonzo Stagg, whose
coaching philosophy he tended to adopt, especially Stagg's
penchant for using the embryonic forward pass off play-action
fakes and having the passer throw to a moving, rather than a
stationary, target. At Notre Dame, the promethean Harper also
introduced a variation of the shift that Stagg is believed to have
devised, wherein all four backs shifted in unison before the
ball was snapped, thus distracting and confusing the opposing
defense. Stagg himself had learned from a master, Walter Camp,
while playing at Yale in the 1880s and was named to Camp's
first All-America team in 1889. Camp, a former player at Yale
who became known as the "father of American football," had
devised the line of scrimmage and the requirement of gaining at
least ten yards on three downs to retain possession of the football

(the possession rule ultimately was changed from three downs to four). As Rockne, aware of Harper's lineage, once said, "Notre Dame football goes back to Stagg and to Yale." And, he might have added, to Walter Camp.

An intellectual who majored in philosophy at the University of Chicago, where he had been an outstanding baseball player despite severe rheumatism, Harper had felt, from the time he was a player, that academics were more important than sports and that sportsmanship should trump winning—a heretical view among some big-time college coaches at a time when winning was everything, even if a coach relied heavily on tramp athletes. "It will take years to educate the public to the point where they will look down on the college that uses unfair methods to win," Harper wrote in 1911 in the college magazine while coaching at Wabash. "The American spirit is that we must win." A year later, after Harper announced he was leaving for Notre Dame, the magazine paid tribute to Harper: "Standing for fair play, square deal, and gentlemanly sport at all times and in every contest, he has helped establish among Wabash men a standard of sportsmanship that is becoming recognized in the college world."

⚘

In what would turn out to be Gipp's only home game of the 1917 season, Notre Dame crushed South Dakota, 40–0, the week before what had now become an annual meeting with Army, with whom the Ramblers had split their last four games. Playing about half the game, Gipp had a good but hardly spectacular day. That would usually be the case when Notre Dame played an overmatched opponent; Gipp would inevitably break off a few

THE MISSING ARMY INDUCTEE

long runs, as he did against South Dakota, but obviously would not go all-out. Saving his best for crucial situations in tough games would become a hallmark for the carefree running back.

Five days after the South Dakota game, a Notre Dame squad of twenty left South Bend for the fifth game in a series that began in 1913. What made that small number of players all the more remarkable is that it was the era of the two-way player—Gipp, for example, played cornerback on defense, punted, and drop-kicked extra points—and, on average, Notre Dame only used about four substitutes. Army, by contrast, dressed about thirty-five players. In Army, the "Hoosiers," as a *New York Times* headline referred to Notre Dame, would face a team that would outweigh it by an average of fifteen pounds a man. The Cadets also hadn't lost a game in two years.

Before a crowd of about 5,000 non-paying fans—there was no admission charge at Army games, which at the time were played in an open field with bleachers on both sides—the home team scored minutes after the opening kickoff when a punt by Gipp from the Notre Dame end zone was blocked, resulting in a safety that gave the "soldiers," as the unbylined *New York Times* writer called the Army team, a 2–0 lead. That lead stood until early in the fourth quarter. After Joe Brandy intercepted a pass by Army star Elmer Oliphant deep in Notre Dame territory late in the third quarter, Notre Dame, led by Gipp's running and passing, drove to the Army 7-yard line. Brandy, playing quarterback, then called Gipp's number on a power run on the right side. But Gipp, convinced that Army would expect him to carry the ball, persuaded Brandy to instead fake a handoff to Gipp who would then run right, drawing most of the Army line to that side, while

Brandy kept the ball and went up the middle. The play unfolded as Gipp suggested, and Brandy had no trouble running straight ahead through a huge hole and into the end zone unmolested for a touchdown, after which Gipp added the extra point.

Led by Oliphant, now in his seventh season as a varsity football player, Army then drove to the Notre Dame 19-yard line, where, on fourth down, the "soldiers" lined up for a field goal. Aware that a field goal made no sense at that juncture, since it would still leave Army trailing 7–5 with less than two minutes to play, Gipp called out from his right halfback post on defense, "Look out for the pass!" Sure enough, quarterback Hugh Murrill, on one knee in the holder's position, took the snap from center, bounded to his feet, faded back, and fired a pass into the end zone in Gipp's territory. Timing his leap perfectly, Gipp batted the pass down in what proved to be the key defensive play in a 7–2 Notre Dame victory. In hindsight, Army should hardly have expected a different outcome on the pass, since, as Rockne was to recount over the years, he could not recall a single pass ever having been completed in Gipp's part of Notre Dame's defensive secondary. That might have been a bit of Rockne hyperbole, but, in an era when most teams seldom threw more than a half dozen passes in a game, it might well have been true.

In his thousand-word story headlined "Light Notre Dame Team Downs Army," *The New York Times* reporter misspelled Gipp's name throughout, calling him "Gipe," indicating that word of Gipp's superb football abilities at that point apparently had been confined to the Midwest. In referring to Army, "They took too much for granted, and before the afternoon waned, the

Notre Dame youngsters had stopped the battering, line-smashing Oliphant in his tracks and administered a shocking defeat to a team which was being hailed as one of the greatest the Point had seen in years."

In truth, Oliphant had played very well, gaining more than 100 yards, mostly on power drives up the middle and also completing several passes, kicking off, and punting during what would be his final game against Notre Dame. But, as the *Times* reporter pointed out, Army was "a team of giants" whose "whole attack [was] built around Oliphant." (At five foot seven, Oliphant was hardly a "giant.") By contrast, he wrote, Notre Dame "has another of those quick shifty elevens," which, though outweighed considerably and at a disadvantage because of a muddy field, "was quick at starting and went through with a driving assault at great speed."

Though ecstatic with the team's performance, Harper and Rockne knew they had to worry about a letdown since Notre Dame's next opponent, Morningside College of Iowa, was hardly in Army's class and was regarded by many as a "breather" in an otherwise difficult schedule. As it turned out, it was a hard-fought contest, which Notre Dame won, 13–0. On the first play of the game, Gipp raced through a big hole on the right side, cut to the right and sprinted almost 40 yards before he was knocked out of bounds and into a metal fence post. Unable to get up on his own, he was helped to his feet by teammates and carried off the field with a broken right leg.

As Gipp lay on the ground, Horace Wulf, one of the players who had hit him, said, "I'm sorry. I hope it isn't bad."

"Forget it, pal," Gipp replied. "It's all part of the game."

Gipp, who had missed the first two games because of his late arrival, would now also miss the last two while spending almost two weeks in a Sioux City, Iowa, hospital. Fortunately for the Ramblers his absence was not costly, though he was missed. Notre Dame easily beat Michigan Agricultural College (now Michigan State), 23–0, but barely got by Washington and Jefferson, 3–0, on November 24 in the final game of the 1917 season. By then, although classes still had almost three weeks to go before the Christmas break, Gipp was gone from campus, having returned home to Laurium on crutches in time for Thanksgiving. Both Harper and Rockne knew that with the football season over, there was no guarantee that Gipp would return in January for the spring semester, given his injury, his mysterious draft status, and his personal state of mind. Perhaps Gipp would decide that he wasn't up to being a student-athlete (he had already demonstrated his distaste for the first half of that role) and could shoot as much pool and play as much poker, albeit not for as much money, in the Calumet area as he could in South Bend. One thing was certain, though; if Gipp did come back, he would have a new head coach.

5

THE BEGINNING OF A LEGEND

KNUTE ROCKNE, FOR one, was not about to let Gipp get away, not when he had at least two more years of eligibility at Notre Dame, assuming he attended classes once in a while. Aware that Notre Dame was bound to lose more than a few players to military service before the 1918 season began, Rockne wrote Gipp a letter in early December 1917.

"Dear George," the salutation read, "I hope you are recuperating from the broken leg that you received in the last game. Your teammates and I want you to know that we look forward to seeing you this coming year and need you for our football team. If there is anything that I can do for you, please do not hesitate to ask. Sincerely yours. Knute Rockne."

By then, Gipp had heard that Jesse Harper had resigned as head coach and athletic director, effective June 1, and that Rockne was a strong candidate to replace him. It would make no difference to Gipp, assuming he returned to Notre Dame, since he liked both men. Though he was a disciplinarian, Harper tolerated Gipp's idiosyncratic behavior and left it to Rockne to handle, or at least try to handle Gipp, mainly to see to it that he went to classes more often and showed up for more practices. Reflecting his respect for the far more emotive Rockne, Gipp, somewhat surprisingly, did respond to Rockne's letter. In a handwritten letter, Gipp wrote that his injured leg was getting better but still hurt. "I am hoping that I might return to school in time to start practicing for football," Gipp wrote.

Even though Gipp's letter did not guarantee that he would return—Gipp could still be pressed into military service—it most certainly lifted the coach's spirits. Rockne obviously had a vested interest in Gipp, who he was convinced had unlimited potential as a football player. At the same time, Rockne felt that Gipp "was dissipating his life," according to Chet Grant, a quarterback at Notre Dame in 1916, 1920, and 1921.

"Rockne knew that George had an innate intelligence and had great potential as a person besides as a football player," the erudite Grant said, "but he felt that George was drifting along without any particular goal in his life. That's the real reason, I think, that he wanted him to come back to Notre Dame."

Still limping when the spring semester began in early January, Gipp, as expected, did not return to Notre Dame, as much because of his draft status as his recuperation, and perhaps because of a blizzard, the worst ever in South Bend, which kept schools and many businesses closed for a week and virtually brought life in the city to a standstill. In late January, Gipp was ordered to report for a physical examination for the second time by the Laurium draft board. Limping noticeably when he arrived for his exam, Gipp was either given a six-month deferment or rejected for service—it never was made clear which—because of his leg injury. With the war still raging in France, the United States Army needed more men, but not men with only one good leg. While recovering that winter, Gipp sporadically drove a taxi in Calumet and spent much of his time shooting pool and playing poker, activities that did not require Gipp to be in great physical condition. By late spring, though, with his leg healed, Gipp signed on with the Laurium baseball team and had another very good season, hitting well over .400 and showing no ill effects from his broken leg, only to injure the other leg late in the season. Once again, a number of major league scouts drooled over Gipp's prowess as a baseball player and tried to get him to sign professional contracts, only to be rebuffed by Gipp, for reasons unknown, since his main objective was to play in the major leagues, preferably with the Chicago Cubs. If Gipp had any major disappointments during the spring and summer of 1918, it was that Indiana's prohibition act, prohibiting the sale and consumption of alcoholic beverages (enacted in February 1917), took effect on April 2, 1918, some two years before the Volstead Act became law. As in South Bend, Michigan's own prohibition laws had little impact on Calumet, where a large number of speakeasies soon sprung up, well-attended and pretty much ignored by the local police.

Successful as Gipp was at the pool and poker tables, his winnings weren't sufficient to help him survive, even though he lived with his family during some of his summer vacations. To make ends meet and supplement his gambling winnings, Gipp spent his weekdays driving a truck again for the Roehm Construction Company. Something of a dashing and handsome man about town, and now a Notre Dame football star to boot, Gipp had no trouble attracting women and dated a number of girls in Laurium and Calumet whenever such dates did not interfere with baseball, pool, or poker. From what some of his closest friends said, none of those relationships became serious, at least through the summer of 1918.

◈◈◈

Following the 1917 season, Jesse Harper informed Notre Dame's president, John W. Cavanaugh, that he was resigning because his father-in-law was seriously ill and Harper, who had grown up on a farm, had to take over the family ranch in Kansas. Harper was well aware that Notre Dame had a history of bringing in head football coaches from the outside, as had been the case with his own hiring. So before Father Cavanaugh even asked about a possible successor, Harper told him Rockne was perfect for the job. Cavanaugh paused for several moments, then said, "I have some doubts, Jesse. In the first place, I think he's too young."

Harper had expected that response. He also realized that Cavanaugh knew that Rockne, at the age of thirty, was not many years older than some of the players he might be coaching, especially those who eventually would be returning from military service. But then Cavanaugh also knew that Harper was even younger, twenty-nine, when he was hired away from Wabash in 1913 not only to coach the football team but also the baseball, basketball, and track teams, and to serve as athletic director. Probably more of a factor to Cavanaugh, Harper suspected, was his concern about Rockne's flamboyance and temper, which made him difficult for the Notre Dame administration to handle. Aware of what Cavanaugh's position on Rockne might be, Harper then pointed out that he—with Cavanaugh's permission—had hired Rockne as the school's track coach when he was a senior, and that the head of the chemistry department had given Rockne a job as an assistant and then hired him to teach chemistry classes in the preparatory school on the Notre Dame campus while he was still an undergraduate. Still, he sensed Cavanaugh was not convinced that Rockne was ready to coach the varsity football team. Then, using what he thought was his ace in the hole, Harper told the university president that Rockne had a chance to become head coach at Michigan Agricultural College for more money than he was now making as an assistant football coach, head track coach, and chemistry instructor combined, and might well take it since his wife, Bonnie, had given birth to their first child, a son, a year earlier.

Unwilling to make a decision right away, Cavanaugh stopped by Harper's office frequently in the week or so that followed to suggest coaches from other schools who he thought might do well at Notre Dame. Harper, who was highly respected by Cavanaugh, would shake his head and adamantly suggest his own choice—Rockne. Growing impatient with Cavanaugh's reluctance to name Rockne the head coach, Harper finally told the president that several years earlier he had promised Rockne the head coaching job when he stepped down. That did it.

"Well, Jesse, if you promised it to him, we certainly will have to offer it to him, won't we?" said Cavanaugh with a smile.

A week later, in March 1918, Rockne signed a contract to become the head football and track coach, as well as the athletic director, for $3,500 a year ($1,500 less than what Harper, reportedly, the highest paid employee at Notre Dame, had made). That, of course, wasn't saying much, since Notre Dame was still a small school striving for accreditation, better known for its football team than for its academics. Rockne's ascension would mark the beginning of the most colorful era in the history of Notre Dame sports.

∽❦❧∾

Much as Gipp liked the low-key and cerebral Harper, he was glad to know that Rockne had been named head coach. During their symbiotic relationship, Gipp had come to both like and respect the fiery assistant coach, aware that he had the knack to inspire players and get the most out of them, including Gipp. In large measure because of Rockne's hiring, Gipp, during the summer of 1918, convinced two longtime friends and outstanding all-around athletes, with whom he had attended Calumet High School—Heartley "Hunk" Anderson and Fred "Ojay" Larson—to attend Notre Dame and play football. Both had taken a year off after graduation to work while hoping to get scholarship offers to play football, and Gipp, aware that about a dozen members of the 1917 Notre Dame team had gone into military service, felt that Rockne would be more than glad to have Anderson and Larson on his depleted team. There were no guarantees, but Gipp, as smooth in conversation as he was on a football field, was certain he could convince Rockne to give scholarships to both his friends.

In late summer, Rockne, anxious to find out whether Gipp planned to return to Notre Dame, finally managed to reach him by phone to check on his draft status, his right leg, and, primarily, whether he would be returning to Notre Dame. "We need you, and I hope you're coming back," Rockne said. Expecting Gipp to waver and give a noncommittal answer, Rockne was amazed when Gipp said, "I'll be back, Rock. I look forward to playing with you." It was during this conversation that Gipp convinced Rockne to offer scholarships to Anderson and Larson without ever having seen them play—not uncommon at the time—or even having spoken with either man. That Gipp wanted them to play alongside him was good enough for Rockne to believe that they would be welcome additions to an undermanned Notre Dame team. Rockne knew that Gipp was smart and wouldn't recommend players who would be blocking for him just because they were boyhood friends.

Not only did Gipp agree to return, but he did so in time for the brief weeklong preseason practice sessions that were customary in the era. The coming academic year would turn out to be a much more comforting one for Gipp, since he would be playing alongside Anderson and Larson, and, at least for a while, living with Larson on campus in Sorin Hall. Gipp and Larson were on hand at the South Bend train station to meet Anderson when he arrived.

"George told me that Rockne was getting some cigars at Hullie and Mike's, which George had already told me about, and would be by to meet us soon," Anderson said. "When he did arrive, George introduced me to him and Rockne asked, 'What position do you play?'"

"I mainly play fullback," Anderson replied.

"That's fine, but what we really need are linemen," Rockne responded. "Can you play tackle or guard?"

"I can play anywhere on the line, " said Anderson, who had played both fullback and as a linebacker at Calumet High, although he only weighed about 170 pounds, which was about average for a lineman at Notre Dame, where Harper and Rockne put a premium on speed and quickness, not size.

"OK," Rockne said, seemingly impressed with Anderson. "See you at practice tomorrow afternoon."

⌘

If downtown South Bend had changed as its factories became defense plants, so, too, had the Notre Dame campus. Under a program begun that fall by the government, male students were able to enroll in the Student Army Training Corps, which permitted students to stay in school while undergoing military training in addition to attending classes. It was a win-win situation for the students, most of whom were of draft age, since the government also paid their tuition, albeit only 100 dollars a year plus room and board. As in the Army, students had to pass a physical to qualify for the SATC, which some students said, with tongue in cheek, stood for "safe at the college." Rockne, not surprisingly, suggested to most of his players, including Gipp, that they join the SATC and thus be able to play football. Both of Gipp's friends from Calumet, Hunk Anderson and Ojay Larson, were among those who joined and had to drill for two hours every morning before classes began. Gipp, however, was rejected, ostensibly because of the leg injury he had sustained playing baseball during the summer. That made it two draft board rejections, both based on injured legs, not to mention the mysterious circumstances of Gipp's first call to duty. Rockne, taking no chances, thereupon asked the head of the SATC on the Notre Dame campus to inform the draft board in Laurium that Gipp had flunked the physical, hoping, no doubt, that the draft board—which had already either rejected Gipp because of his first leg injury or given him a six-month deferment in January—would thus exempt Laurium's biggest sports star from military service. As it developed, Gipp never did hear back from the Laurium board after his physical examination in Laurium and was never summoned again for military service. Why the draft board never sought to charge Gipp with draft evasion for failing to report for induction on September 21, 1917, never was explained. Nor, it seems, did anyone in Laurium ever bother to ask. Perhaps members of the board were big Gipp fans who felt that the local sports hero was needed on the home front to entertain sporting crowds and thus help keep their minds off the war, both in the Calumet area and in South Bend and other college towns where the Ramblers/Hoosiers/Westerners played.

6

FOOTBALL'S ODD COUPLE

ON SUNDAY, NOVEMBER 2, 1913, high school dropout George Gipp, then eighteen, read about Notre Dame's stunning victory over Army in the *Daily Mining Gazette*. Living a carefree life as a taxi and truck driver, amateur baseball and basketball star, and skilled poker and pool player, Gipp had no particular interest in Notre Dame—still, like tens of thousands, if not millions, of newspaper readers he was surprised at the outcome. He also was delighted to read how the relatively new forward pass was the key to Notre Dame's victory, since he himself enjoyed throwing forward passes to friends, who marveled at how Gipp could fling the stubby football of the time up to 50 yards.

Because of his passing ability, his speed, and his all-around athleticism, Gipp was in demand by Calumet area semi-pro football teams, and occasionally played both halfback and as a lineman against much older players, some of whom had played on the college level. Gipp more than held his own in such games, as both Hunk Anderson and Ojay Larson were to recall, especially as a swift and elusive hard-to-bring-down runner. Quite often teammates suggested to Gipp that he pursue a football scholarship at Michigan, Notre Dame, or some other big-time football-playing college in the Midwest, where, they felt, he would be more than welcome. Gipp's automatic response was that, first, he hadn't graduated from high school, and, second, he had no interest in playing college football.

Like Rockne, his lack of organized football experience and years of work prior to entering Notre Dame was no deterrent to Gipp when he agreed, at Rockne's suggestion, to go out for football. By the 1918 season, Rockne's first as head coach, Gipp had established himself as the team's star player.

❧❧❧

Gipp's dual personality as a football star and a carefree, seemingly fatalistic, hedonist, coupled with his disdain of authority, both in sports and in academic life, begs the question of whether his behavior was a facade or an inexplicable character trait stemming from an early-life trauma. Yet despite his carefree and cavalier attitude at Notre Dame, Gipp never displayed any arrogance or hostility of the type often manifested by many latter-day sports stars, apart from an occasional outburst at a player who he felt had gone out of his way to rough him up. If anything, as a college football player, he was something of a charming rogue— liked and respected by his teammates and by his opponents on the field (as well as those at both the pool and card tables in South Bend and elsewhere), idolized by his fellow students and most of the faculty and staff at Notre Dame, and highly but grudgingly esteemed by Rockne despite his unconventional, even aggravating, off-the-field behavior, which often drove the coach to distraction.

From the beginning, when he was still an assistant, Rockne felt Gipp would be difficult to deal with as a player, and a challenge to him as a coach—which proved to be the case. Even in the quintessential tramp athlete era, many, if indeed not most, coaches would not have tolerated Gipp's off-campus gambling and his chronic absenteeism from classes, and often practices. Nor would many top administrative officials at most universities. But Rockne feigned ignorance of Gipp's off-campus activities and allowed him a huge amount of leeway, both because of his great talent as a player and because of the growing bond that had formed between them despite their disparate personalities. He was not about to try to transmogrify Gipp into a more conventional college student, realizing that it would be impossible. Also, Rockne obviously had a vested interest in Gipp, having recognized his greatness from the start, as he was to say some years later. "I felt the thrill that comes to every coach when he knows it is his fate and his responsibility to handle unusual greatness—the perfect performer who comes rarely more than once in a generation."

That may have been why Rockne put up with Gipp's absence at many practice sessions, the missed classes, the inordinate amount of time he spent shooting pool and playing poker in downtown South Bend, and during his last two years, his near full-time residence at the plush Hotel Oliver—all of which Rockne, with his downtown contacts, had to know about. Wayward and carefree as he was off the field, Gipp perceived Rockne's genius as a coach and motivator, even when, his voice dripping with sarcasm, he would direct a cutting remark at Gipp for his nonchalance during practice or even during a game. Gipp knew that the verbal attacks were justified and intended to show the rest of the Notre Dame squad that, even though most of the players sensed that Rockne tended to treat Gipp with kid gloves, the coach was not about to let his star halfback go too far over the line.

Rockne no doubt recalled that, as a player at Notre Dame, he himself had indulged in some questionable behavior. Like Gipp and many other Notre Dame players of the era, Rockne often played for money with semi-pro teams in South Bend and other Midwestern cities on Sundays, the day after college games (usually, but not always, under an assumed name), which he continued to do while an assistant and even as the head coach. Like Gipp, too, Rockne liked to gamble on games as a player and was known to frequent some of the same downtown South Bend establishments that Gipp later did.

To make extra money while he was an undergraduate, Rockne also boxed professionally throughout the Midwest as a welterweight (usually under the name of Frankie Brown, Jab Brown, or Kid Williams) for purses that generally ranged between five and ten dollars. Also like Gipp, Rockne, while a player and coach, would place bets on Notre Dame for gambling friends from downtown South Bend and himself, even though Rockne, so far as is known, did not come close to Gipp when it came to gambling and breaking university rules.

None of this was displayed in Pat O'Brien's somewhat saintly portrayal of Rockne in the movie *Knute Rockne: All American,* which also portrayed Gipp as a clean-cut All-American-boy sports hero without any shortcomings whatsoever. Even though many Midwestern sportswriters were aware of Gipp's gambling and late hours, Rockne ignored all the rumors and tried to convince nationally known writers like Ring Lardner and Grantland Rice that Gipp was close to being the very personification of the college football ideal, a star who had even fewer frailties than most athletes. That would seem to indicate that initially, Rockne also was unaware (perhaps willfully so) of Gipp's poor academic performance. Indeed, during two of Gipp's four and a half years at Notre Dame—the 1917–18 academic year and 1918–19, Rockne's first season as head coach—his transcript had no grades whatsoever. Certainly, someone must have brought Gipp's academic shortcomings to Rockne's attention, which he ultimately said he had become aware of.

As close as they became, Gipp and Rockne could hardly have been more different. At a shade over six feet and around 180 pounds by his senior year, Gipp was the personification of an athlete. On the football field—as on the baseball diamond and basketball court—he made everything he did look easy and effortless. Work hard at practice? No need to, Gipp felt. He knew what he could do and would do it on Saturday.

By comparison, Rockne, at five foot seven inches and, at most, around 160 pounds during his final season as a player, had to struggle and go all-out in practice to make the Notre Dame varsity, having played only intramural football for a while as a freshman. (He'd played football only sparingly in high school, as well, and had not played the game for five years before enrolling at Notre Dame.) It was while playing interhall football, which involved students from the six residence halls for Notre Dame's college students, that Rockne attracted the attention of the Brownson Hall team's coach, Joe Collins, an end for the Notre Dame varsity, who recommended the odd-looking, twenty-two-year-old freshman to varsity coach Shorty Longman.

Even after that, nothing in football came easy for the bandy-legged, prematurely bald, pot-bellied, undersized end with the pumpkin-shaped head, flattened nose, raspy voice, and the up-and-down staccato way of talking. Supremely organized, intense, and always looking ahead, Rockne was the antithesis of the carefree Gipp who rarely gave a thought to tomorrow (and not much to today, either) but yet somehow managed to compartmentalize his rampant gambling and his football-playing.

Academically, they were polar opposites. Rockne was a dogged, diligent student who graduated with a degree in pharmacy and a 90.52 scholastic average, played the flute in the school orchestra, appeared in a number of campus theatrical productions, was an editor of the campus magazine, *The Dome,* and was a student chemistry department assistant. Rockne's course load was a heavy one, including several chemistry courses, as well as biology, botany, human anatomy, geology, physiology, and philosophy. "He had a very good mind, and was an attentive student," Father Thomas Irving, Rockne's physics instructor during his junior year, said, "and you would never make the mistake of taking him for a dumbbell." Particularly impressive was that most of Rockne's grades during his freshman year—usually the most difficult year for a student—and his senior year, when he was captain of the football team and involved in a number of other extracurricular activities, were A's.

That academic determination enabled Rockne to overcome a stammering manner of talking that he'd brought to Notre Dame and was responsible for his shyness while an undergraduate. Later, as an assistant coach, he privately took elocution lessons, which rid him of his stammer and boosted his confidence when he spoke. Gipp, though demonstrably intelligent and well-spoken, never applied himself to his studies, cut classes repeatedly, and, apart from sports, had no interest in any extracurricular campus activities, or, if one would believe Rockne, in women.

Still, there were similarities that may have drawn Rockne and Gipp close together. Neither had graduated from high school, both came from families of limited means, both had worked for three years before coming to Notre Dame at an advanced age for freshmen, both were Protestants in a milieu that was heavily Catholic, and both arrived in South Bend unheralded and without scholarships, and felt, once they got there, that they might have made a mistake in coming.

"I think that Rock may have envied George in a way, mainly because of his carefree devil-may-care manner," Hunk Anderson was to say five decades after he played under Rockne. "Rock was too organized and too disciplined to ever have been that way, and yet I think he probably understood George better than anyone."

Ojay Larson agreed with Anderson. "I think Rock also secretly got a kick out of how George could spend most of a week staying up much of the night shooting pool and playing poker—and for a lot of money, at that—but still went all-out and would play so brilliantly during a game on Saturday," Larson recalled. "He also could relate to George's playing professionally on a number of occasions while at Notre Dame, since he had done the same and had run the risk of getting kicked off the team as Gipp did."

Though he made his high school team in Chicago as a scrawny, seldom-used 125-pound end and halfback, Rockne's first love in sports was track. He excelled in the half-mile run and as a pole-vaulter. Rockne later held the Notre Dame record for fifteen years—remarkable given his relatively short stature. After spending a year at a variety of odd jobs after leaving high school, Rockne worked as a clerk and then a dispatcher for the United States Post Office in Chicago for two and a half years. During that time, he became one of the best distance runners in the Chicago area while totally forsaking football, even though he had filled out to 145 pounds. Only at the insistence of his sister did Rockne begin to think of enrolling at a college, preferably the University of Illinois. However, two fellow members of the Illinois Athletic Club who were going to Notre Dame to join the track team talked Rockne into come along, convincing him that he, too, could make the team. So it was that at the age of twenty-two Rockne enrolled at a school he claimed never to have heard of, although that seems to have been a stretch of the truth. (Chicago newspapers regularly carried stories about Notre Dame sports teams, especially its rapidly improving football team, which in 1909, after losing to Michigan all eight times they had played, upset the highly rated Wolverines, 11–3.)

"I went to South Bend with a suitcase and a thousand dollars, feeling the strangeness of being a lone Norse Protestant invading a Catholic stronghold," Rockne was to say. Prematurely bald with a nose that had accidentally been flattened by a baseball bat while he was a teenager in Chicago, Rockne appeared about ten years, if not more, older than his twenty-two years and hardly like a typical freshman. But he was hardly the lone Protestant at the school, since, by 1910, of its approximately five hundred college students, about one hundred were not Catholic. Indeed, anyone who could come up with the $120 yearly tuition fee at the time was welcome at Notre Dame, even if, like Gipp and Rockne, they hadn't graduated from high school. It was—and was indeed perceived as by larger and far better known colleges and universities such as Michigan—a school for boys from families with limited means.

Gus Dorais, who became Rockne's roommate and football teammate, said Rockne (like Gipp) was ill at ease during his early days at Notre Dame, when he slept in a single room in Sorin Hall that was not much bigger than most closets. "Don't forget, he was about four years older than the rest of us at school," said Dorais, the first in a long line of outstanding quarterbacks at Notre Dame. "He also had kind of a rough edge and certainly was not a genteel character."

Regarding Rockne's odd staccato speaking style, Dorais, who was from the small town of Chippewa Falls, Wisconsin, said years after their Notre Dame days, "His thoughts tumbled out in such bursts that he was inclined to stammer. This was the reason for his machine gun type of oratory later on. But he had trouble becoming a speaker. For a long time, he was always threatening to quit school, for one reason or another, but, of course, he never got around to it." Rockne came closest to leaving Notre Dame when, during his sophomore year, his father died, but he was encouraged to stay by his mother and his sister.

Not only did Rockne overcome his shyness and come to love Notre Dame, but by the 1920s he had become a much sought-after speaker, and a very good one, at that. Indeed, his staccato speaking style became a trademark and enhanced his appeal as a speaker. By the 1920s, too, Rockne, in the eyes of many, had become an archetype of a college football coach, with a style that was the envy of other coaches, many of whom would try to emulate the dynamic and creative Norwegian Protestant who would become the face of Notre Dame football.

7

DEADLY FLU PANDEMIC CUTS
SHORT ROCKNE'S FIRST SEASON

KNUTE ROCKNE COULD hardly have become Notre Dame's head football coach at a worse time. When preseason practice began, not only was World War I still being fought in France, but the deadliest flu pandemic in history had spread throughout the globe, infecting about a third of the world's population, including millions in the United States. Among the least significant developments stemming from the pandemic was a drastic curtailing, and in some cases even a canceling, of the 1918 college football season.

Believed to have originated in the Far East, the flu spread rapidly, and was first detected in the United States at about the same time (March 1918) at Fort Riley, an Army base in Kansas, and in the borough of Queens in New York City. A more virulent strain of the influenza manifested itself in late August by which time millions of people had died on virtually every continent, including more than 20,000 in New York City, then a city of six million, and about 13,000 in Philadelphia. Particularly puzzling was that most of the victims were healthy young adults, rather than infants and the elderly who were usually most vulnerable to outbreaks of influenza. That made it of special concern to high schools and universities, including Notre Dame, which, like many colleges, canceled most of the 1918 football season because of the outbreak of the pandemic. (The deadly disease had been named the Spanish Flu because most of the reports about the flu had come from Spain, a neutral country, during World War I and whose press thus was not hindered by the censorship on the epidemic imposed in most of the countries involved in the war.)

As the epidemic spread into Indiana, the state board of health on October 10 prohibited all public gatherings in the state. By then about eighty cases of Spanish Flu had been reported in South Bend, and downtown movie theaters had closed. Then, during a single day, forty-two people in South Bend died of the disease, including two students and a nun at Notre Dame. By October 25, the flu had claimed eighty-seven lives in South Bend. After abating for a while, the epidemic resurged in early November when more than 750 additional cases of the Spanish Flu were reported in South Bend. By the end of the month, 152 South Bend residents had lost their lives.

Making conditions worse and contributing to the spread of the deadly virus was the closeness of soldiers during the massive troop movements in the United States, in Europe, aboard cramped transport ships, and in their close living quarters. Described by medical experts as the worst medical holocaust in modern history, the pandemic—which began to wane in late 1918—killed more than fifty million people, including more than a half million in the United States while infecting another half million.

As a result of the pandemic, Notre Dame played only five of nine scheduled games during the 1918 football season and just one at home, a contest against a team from the Great Lakes Naval Training Station, which was arranged after the season began. For Rockne, the shortness of the season was welcomed since most of the 1917 starting team was gone, either graduated or inducted into the armed forces, including virtually all of the defense, which had allowed only one touchdown the season prior. Fortunately for Rockne, freshmen had been made eligible to play varsity football in 1918, mainly because the military draft had depleted rosters, and the incoming group of freshmen was one of the best Notre Dame had ever had. Seven freshmen would become starters in 1918, including Anderson and Larson; ends Eddie Anderson and Bernie Kirk; tackle Charlie Crowley; quarterback Bill Mohn; and fullback Earl "Curly" Lambeau, who would drop out of Notre Dame before his sophomore year because of a severe case of tonsillitis and in 1919 become a co-founder, player, and coach of the Green Bay Packers.

At Gipp's suggestion, Larson roomed with him at Sorin Hall—at least occasionally, as Larson was to recall years later. "When we roomed together, George would often come in during the middle of the night, or later, usually after playing cards or shooting pool downtown," Larson said while working in the Cook County Assessor's Office in Chicago while he was in his eighties. "Of course I knew he did a lot of gambling, and

I'd played cards with him myself. He was an uncanny poker player, the kind who never gave you the slightest hint of what he had. George wasn't the type who would volunteer personal information, but I once asked him how he was doing at poker and pool, and he told me he had made at least $5,000 the previous year (the equivalent of $50,000 in 2010), and from the looks of things, would top that amount that year we roomed together."

"He was a helluva card player, one who could deal them off the top, the middle, or the bottom," Anderson recalled. "He'd win four or five hundred a night playing cards, but sometimes, instead of settling for that, he'd try to double it in craps. Unfortunately, he was a lousy crap shooter—probably the only thing he couldn't do well. He would make eight or nine passes, but then blow it all on one throw of the dice. But then George always said he preferred poker or pool because you had control over what you were doing. With dice, as he said, it's all luck. But one thing's for sure: George made everything he made on his own" In saying that, Anderson no doubt was alluding to his knowledge of some star football players accepting payments from well-to-do alumni. Whether it happened at Notre Dame was never proven. The practice was still prevalent in the twenty-first century.

Gipp's old schoolmate also remembered Gipp's talent with a pool cue. "He was the best shooter around Calumet before he even came to Notre Dame, where, even as a kid, he was winning lots of money," Anderson said. "And he became the best around South Bend, too. He was the classic hustler—although he didn't look like one—who would play a stranger for a dollar or two at straight pool and do real bad, but then raise the stakes and clean up at twenty-five or fifty dollars a game. Once in a while, some hotshot players from Chicago would come to South Bend looking for some fresh action, knowing it was a good gambling town. As I was to find out, George would take them on at a hundred dollars a game at places like Hullie and Mike's. They were crackerjack players who made their living shooting pool, but George would take them almost every time. He'd also go to Elkhart, which is about fifteen miles from South Bend, to play cards on some Friday nights. Elkhart was a railroad town, and Friday was payday, and a lot of the railroad workers liked to play poker, and George knew it. George would go over to Elkhart and make the railroad workers' paydays his paydays at the poker table," Anderson said with a laugh.

As for Gipp's usually pale and sallow complexion, "It was the smoking and the hours he kept," Anderson said. "If you stayed out all night, night after night, chain-smoking, playing cards, and shooting pool, usually for a lot of money, and hardly getting any sleep, you'd be pale, too. Let's face it—George didn't take very good care of himself."

The evidence also seems to indicate that Gipp liked to drink, sometimes a lot, while playing poker or shooting pool, although none of his teammates interviewed said they ever saw him drunk, contrary to some reports. "From what I saw, George carried his liquor very well," said Chet Grant, who took the odd path of going from a sportswriter for the *South Bend Tribune* to a five-foot seven-inch 135-pound backup quarterback for Notre Dame in 1916, 1920, and 1921 (he was a lieutenant in the Army from 1917 until 1919), when he was twenty-nine years old. "He was a gentleman in every way and that included his drinking."

❧❦❧

When Rockne held his first practice on September 18, he didn't know what to expect, given that he now had so many new players who he knew little about. Missing were practically the entire defensive unit that had allowed only one touchdown in 1917, most of whom had graduated. Also gone were seven lettermen who had been called to Army duty—quarterbacks Joe Brandy, Tex Allison, and Grant; linemen Slip Madigan and Dave Hayes; halfback Grover Malone; and fullback Walter Miller, Gipp's roommate during Gipp's sophomore year. As it was, the outlook for the 1918 season looked bleak indeed, and grew even bleaker when only twenty prospects turned out for the first practice on September 17 on a field made muddy by a steady rain. At his oratorical best, Rockne reminded the players that they faced an uncertain season because of the flu pandemic and that some games might be scheduled at the last minute, which turned out to be true. At that twenty players comprised a decent turnout. As few as a dozen showed up for the initial practice sessions at some well-known football schools, such as Minnesota, and, because of the dearth of players, many schools canceled the 1918 season. Rockne, his voice softer than usual, also pointed out that since they were all of draft age, the Notre Dame players were lucky to be playing football at a time when young men their age were dying on battlefields in France and tens of thousands of others had died of the Spanish Flu.

Writing about the initial practice, a sportswriter for the *South Bend Tribune* reported in the next day's editions, "Green is the word to describe the material for the gold and blue"—the team's colors—"Not that the youngsters do not know any football at all, or that they are an awkward squad. Some of them look promising, but they have a long way to go to measure up to traditional varsity standards."

It was also a very light team, even by the standards of Notre Dame, where Harper, like Rockne, put a far greater stress on speed than weight. Only one starter, tackle Rollo Stine, weighed more than 185 pounds, while four weighed less than 170 pounds, including guards Hunk Anderson and Maurice "Clipper" Smith, and end Eddie Anderson, another future coach, who weighed 149 pounds. The only other player on the eventual twenty-nine-man squad who weighed more than 200 pounds was reserve tackle Romanus "Peaches" Nadolney. And this, mind you, was on a team whose starters played both offense and defense, as was the case with every collegiate team at the time when rules forbade unlimited substitutions and mandated that a player leaving the game could not return until the following quarter. Indeed, the two-platoon system, wherein one set of players play on offense and one on defense, was still three decades away.

In the coming days, Gipp, fellow halfbacks Pete Bahan, the team captain, and Norm Barry, along with the other three returning letterman, found that Rockne was essentially staying with Jesse Harper's playbook, both on offense and defense. Considering that while playing for one season under Harper and serving as an assistant with him for four seasons Notre Dame had won thirty-four games and lost only five, Rockne was not about to interfere with a winning style of play. Moreover, he admired Harper, both as a person and as one of football's most innovative and cerebral coaches. Rockne also appreciated the fact that Harper, soft-spoken and not given to inspirational pregame or halftime talks, had often delegated that task to his far more outgoing and glib chief assistant. As it was, the only noticeable change Rockne made was slightly altering the shift Harper had instituted by having both ends shift along with the four backs, who under the Notre Dame formation had the quarterback line up to the left or right of the center and the other three backs in a line about six feet from the center. Under Harper, only the backs had moved in unison before the ball was snapped in what had become known as the "Notre Dame shift," even though the Notre Dame version was patterned after the shift originated by Walter Camp at Yale and modified by Amos Alonzo Stagg at Chicago, where Harper had learned it as a player. In an unusually candid moment, Rockne, asked where, if anywhere, his version of the shift had come from, said, "From Yale, where everything in football comes from." Given the fertile football brain of the great Yale coach Walter Camp, that, of course, was very close to being the truth.

Despite its lack of heft, Notre Dame had no trouble in its opening game against Case Tech (now Case Western Reserve) in Cleveland on September 28. After the home team had taken a 6–0 first-quarter lead, Notre Dame responded with 26 unanswered points, the first a touchdown by Curly Lambeau in the second quarter and two touchdowns by Gipp in the third period. Pointing out that it was the lightest team Notre Dame had fielded since he came to Notre Dame in 1910, Rockne said, "This team, despite its light weight, has all the spirit and fight that any of the older and heavier teams had." Overall, though, Rockne was not satisfied with the team's play, which he described as "ragged" while also criticizing it for poor tackling and blocking. Above all, Rockne never tolerated poor blocking. A player could miss a tackle or drop a pass, but, to the onetime 165-pound end, missing a block was inexcusable. It was one of the reasons Rockne often went out on the practice field to physically demonstrate the proper way to block.

Because the Spanish Flu intensified in the Midwest, as it did across most of the United States that fall, the team did not play again until November 2, canceling all four scheduled games in October. Practices were also sharply curtailed, giving Gipp more time to sleep off his many all-night gambling sessions in downtown South Bend. The November 2 game was hastily arranged after Nebraska canceled out against Notre Dame just before the Ramblers were to board a train for Lincoln after the city's city council banned all sporting events because of the flu pandemic. Somehow, Rockne managed that night to arrange a game with Wabash in Crawfordsville, Indiana, for the following afternoon, which required Notre Dame to board a train before daybreak for the 185-mile trip to Crawfordsville. Even lighter and with a smaller squad than that which had been crushed by Notre Dame, 60–0, two years before, Wabash lost by the same margin again, 67–7, even though Gipp spent most of the second half on the bench because of the one-sided score. Rockne was not about to risk injury to his best player when he wasn't needed.

While Gipp was playing, though, Wabash had difficulty containing him. "I may have laid a hand on him once or twice, but that was all I could do," said John Ott, a Wabash end. "He didn't seem extra fast, but that was good enough, combined with his elusiveness and strength." In its remaining three road games in the abbreviated season, Notre Dame lost to Michigan Agricultural in a game in which Gipp sustained a broken blood vessel in his face and missed most of the second half; beat in-state rival Purdue as Gipp accounted for almost 200 yards running and passing; and, in a make-up game, played a 0–0 tie against Nebraska. As against the future Michigan State, the Ramblers were without Gipp for most of the Nebraska game after he was forced to leave in the first half with a severe sore throat that hampered his breathing.

The team's best effort came in its only home game, on November 9, against a strong Great Lakes Naval Training Station team comprised mainly of former college stars, including former All-American Paddy Driscoll and the later legendary George Halas, both of whom eventually played for and coached the Chicago Bears. Though outweighed by an average of ten pounds per man, Notre Dame scored first on a touchdown by Gipp in the first quarter, which was quickly matched by a touchdown run by Driscoll. Thereafter, Notre Dame played Great Lakes on even terms in a game that ended in a 7–7 tie. After the game, both Driscoll and Halas paid tribute to their much-younger and lighter opponents, especially Gipp and his fellow halfback, the 155-pound Pete Bahan.

Two days after the Great Lakes game, South Bend, like cities and towns across the United States, erupted with joy on the morning of November 11 when news of the war's end—the armistice—was announced on radios throughout the country.

As many as 15,000 people assembled in downtown South Bend, where a spontaneous parade began through the city's streets and a huge bonfire was set in the courthouse square. Even George Gipp, never prone to showing emotion, exulted when Larson awakened him to tell him that the war was over. Gipp's concerns about being drafted, after so many close calls, were now assuaged for good. On hearing the news, Rockne, never one to hide his inner feelings, was ecstatic, hugging his wife, Bonnie, before leaving for his office that morning. Rockne had another reason to be happy; the armistice meant that as many as a half dozen players with remaining eligibility would probably return from military service to resume playing football at Notre Dame in 1919.

That night, Larson and Anderson, anxious to celebrate the war's end but unable to leave campus, found themselves stymied by Indiana's premature prohibition law, which had taken effect earlier that year. "Then I realized that George might be able to help us," Larson said. "So I got in touch with him downtown, and before we knew it he was back on campus with a bottle, which didn't surprise us at all considering his connections downtown. But I also remember that he didn't take a drink."

Maybe Gipp was just hung over from the night before.

❧❧❧

Because of the impact of the Spanish Flu on college football teams, the 1918 season did not count against a player's eligibility, which meant that Gipp, among others, would have an extra season of eligibility, assuming, of course, that he would take advantage of it. Rockne was well aware that there was no guarantee Gipp would. Between the last game on November 28 and the Christmas break, Gipp again spent more time gambling in South Bend than he did on campus. "George made a lot of money during that period," said Hunk Anderson, who, like Larson, tended to speak of Gipp in reverential terms. "I mean a lot—hundreds of dollars." Because of the extra time the players had, Gipp and Pete Bahan, one of his closest friends on the team, bought a quantity of blue and gold pennants, buttons, pins, and campus calendars, which they sold on campus for a considerable profit.

Gipp invested much of his share of that profit, along with his gambling earnings, in a sizable quantity of bootleg liquor to take back to Calumet. Gipp's intention was hardly altruistic nor was he smitten by the Christmas season. Shortly before Christmas, Gipp boarded a train for Calumet with Anderson and Larson, along with two suitcases of whiskey stashed below their seats. As Anderson recalled, somewhere along the way, the train was stopped for an inspection, not uncommon at the time, since it was illegal to carry liquor aboard trains in the Midwest.

"Spotting the suitcases, one of the inspectors asked us what was in the bags, which George had put under our seats," Anderson recollected. "We were worried, to say the least, and we had to think fast. I finally said, 'Our clothes are in the bags.' The inspector looked at the bags again and thankfully he walked away. When we got back to Calumet, George sold the booze for about $500. It was a risk—arrest and confiscation of the liquor—he was willing to take. And, as usual, George came out ahead."

8

THE FIGHTING HIBERNIANS

GIVEN THAT NOTRE Dame was founded by seven French-speaking priests, it is somewhat ironic that the university's sports teams became known as the "Fighting Irish." At that, credit for the nickname is hard to pin down, although it appears that it was first used by the *Notre Dame Scholastic*, a weekly campus newspaper, as early as 1917, George Gipp's second season in South Bend. Regardless, the nickname stuck, supplanting Hoosiers, Ramblers, Westerners, Micks, Catholics, Hibernians, Harps, and Papists, even though the football team was rarely dominated by players of Irish descent. That was the case on Gipp's teams, when, on average, about a third of the thirty or so players could have lived up to the name "Fighting Irish."

Ever since 1909, when Notre Dame upset Michigan and beat Michigan Agricultural, Pittsburgh, and Miami of Ohio, while yielding only three points (to Michigan) in that span, Notre Dame had made its mark in football in the Midwest. But it wasn't until 1913 that the school became nationally known, at least in the sports world.

Even though Dorais and Rockne had been involved in only one losing game since their freshman year, a span of twenty-four games, the Ramblers were a heavy underdog to a heavier and also undefeated Army team when they met on The Plain at West Point. Harper knew that his team could not beat Army with its ground game, even though in fullback Ray Eichenlaub it had an outstanding runner; the only path to victory lay with its passing attack against a team that rarely threw the ball and had never played against one that passed very often.

Remembering the success Amos Alonzo Stagg had enjoyed with the pass when Harper was a backup quarterback at Chicago, the new coach had used the pass often and effectively as Notre Dame scored 169 points during its first three games while yielding only one touchdown. Fortunately for Harper, Dorais and Rockne—while working at a resort hotel in Cedar Point, Ohio, on the bank of Lake Erie during the previous summer—had spent hours of their spare time throwing and catching passes on the beach and on a grass field near the resort's main building.

They did so after Harper had told Rockne, the incoming captain, before the summer break that Notre Dame would be playing Army during the 1913 season. Harper welcomed their plan and gladly loaned Rockne and Dorais two footballs they had requested to take to Cedar Point. As he did, Harper suggested to Rockne, by no means an outstanding receiver, that he start catching the ball with his hands, rather than with his arms and chest, which was the conventional way to catch a forward pass at the time. "Jesse stressed catching the ball with what he called soft hands, and I worked on that at Cedar Point," Rockne said. Even more important, Harper told Rockne and Dorais to work on pass patterns wherein Rockne caught passes on the run, rather than as a stationary target, as was the norm during the early days of the forward pass.

That summer, Rockne also worked on developing a relationship with a young waitress at the resort named Bonnie Gwendoline Skiles. The following July, a month after Rockne's graduation, they were married at a nearby Catholic church in Sandusky, Ohio, shortly after Bonnie had converted to Catholicism (Rockne was still a Protestant). Dorais was the best man. Shortly after the wedding, Rockne and Dorais wound up as the two finalists for the head football coaching job at St. Joseph's College in Dubuque, Iowa. Rather then both apply, the two friends decided to settle the issue with a coin toss, which Dorais won. He then got the job. Rockne, who had always harbored thoughts of becoming a doctor, enrolled in medical school at St. Louis University while taking a job coaching football at a high school in order to cover some of his expenses. However, when medical school administrators got wind of Rockne's off-campus job, they told him it wouldn't be feasible for him to attend classes and coach football, prompting Rockne to drop out of school and return to South Bend, where Harper hired him as an assistant and he was made a chemistry instructor in the prep school.

⚭⚭

Although he was an early exponent of the forward pass, Harper had used it sparingly while coaching at Alma College in

Michigan and at Wabash College in Indiana after it was legalized in 1906. The legalization of the pass—which had been used occasionally, albeit illegally—came about after President Theodore Roosevelt had summoned representatives from Yale, Harvard, and Princeton to the White House in October 1905 because of his concern over an increase in football-related deaths. It was an era when football was, in effect, a no-holds-barred, anything-goes sport in which linemen faced each other only inches apart, holding and even punching were condoned, and many players played without helmets. Glenn "Pop" Warner, the legendary coach for whom Pop Warner youth football is named, was coaching at Cornell at the time and had invented shoulder and thigh pads that year, but while they were credited with reducing injuries at Cornell, they seemed to have had little bearing at some other schools, which also began to use the new safeguarding equipment.

A physical fitness buff himself, who liked to box and wrestle, President Roosevelt had been alarmed over how football, in trying to eliminate its rugby elements, had become more vicious and even brutal. In meeting with the representatives of the three Ivy League schools, which usually produced the nation's best football teams, Roosevelt had let it be known that unless steps were taken to curb the violent play, he might call for the abolition of the game. By the end of 1905, as Roosevelt was well aware, eighteen football players had been killed and 159 seriously injured that year, according to the *Chicago Tribune.* Over a twenty-five-year period, from the virtual onset of college football in 1880 through 1905, 325 deaths had occurred along with more than 1,000 serious injuries. Roosevelt was hardly the only one concerned. Because of the growing violence in the sport and the increasing death toll, a number of schools abandoned their football programs by the end of 1905, among them Columbia, Stanford, the University of California, and Northwestern, although all of them eventually would reinstate the sport.

In early December, two months after Roosevelt's summit meeting on college football, the chancellor of New York University, which had what would develop into a big-time football program, assembled representatives from thirteen other football-playing schools to discuss ways to end the violence in the game. Two weeks later, representatives from sixty-two schools assembled in a follow-up meeting and formed the Intercollegiate Athletic Association of the United States, the first organization to oversee collegiate sports in the country. Then, in January 1906, the organization, the forerunner of the National Collegiate Athletic Association, established a rules committee. Among the new rules promulgated was the legalization of the forward pass, albeit it with rules that hardly encouraged its use. For one, before throwing a pass, a player had to run at least five yards to the left or right of center after taking a snap and could not throw the ball more than twenty yards. If throwing the stubby, oblong ball was difficult, catching it was not easy either, since a defender could hit and knock down a potential receiver before he could get his hands on the ball. One of the few advantages of throwing a pass was that, on last down, a pass thrown out of bounds gave the ball to the opposing team at that point, making a long sideline pass as effective as an out-of-bounds punt. Most college teams were slow to incorporate the pass into their offensive repertoire because of some of the aforementioned rules and because the ball—about three inches bigger in circumference than the ball in use today—was difficult to throw. Some players placed the ball on the palm of their passing hands and hurled it, often end-over-end, in a sort of shot-put fashion. Gipp, though, had long fingers that enabled him to get a better grip on the ball and throw a spiral, which was much easier to catch than an end-over-end pass.

Another change, in 1912, which would last far longer than some of the new rules on passing—gave teams four downs to make ten yards for a first down, replacing the old rule wherein teams had three downs to gain five yards in order to retain the ball. Furthermore, the size of the field was reduced from 110 yards to 100 yards and the time of games was shortened from seventy minutes to sixty, broken into two halves of thirty minutes each.

Forever innovative, Amos Alonzo Stagg, the head coach at Chicago, was among the first coaches to take advantage of the new rules by throwing the ball more often. In Stagg's case, he had his quarterback or a halfback take the pass from center, then turn and fake a handoff to another back, and throw a pass to an end or another back who had been split wide, a maneuver that became known as a play-action pass. Eddie Cochems, the coach at St. Louis University, used the pass even more than Stagg, and it paid off handsomely. Throwing the ball as often as ten times a game, the Billikens went unbeaten in eleven games in 1906, the first year that a team could legally throw the football, albeit for no more than ten yards.

Even Yale coach Walter Camp began to use the pass in 1906, often having a player in punt formation throw the ball. As it was, Yale's ground game was so good that the Bulldogs rarely had to pass as they went unbeaten in ten games while giving up only six points and scoring 144.

Some coaches remained reluctant to throw the ball, mainly on the grounds that only three things can happen when you pass and two of them are negative—the pass can be incomplete and, worse, it can be intercepted. Most of those coaches eventually came around, though, realizing that in long-yardage situations, the pass usually could be more effective than a running play. At any rate, 1906 clearly proved that the forward pass not only was here to stay, but would probably revolutionize college football. But it would take several more years for that to happen, given the reluctance of Eastern powers such as Yale, Harvard, Princeton, Rutgers, and Army to throw the ball, which their coaches thought was an unnecessary, and dangerous, affectation that they could succeed without. One of the main reasons for that reluctance was that the ball was not designed to throw, but to kick. It was far more rounded than the modern-day ball, and at least an inch-and-a-half thicker.

The pass would continue to evolve as a weapon thanks to further rules changes. In 1910 the rules were changed so that a back no longer had to run at least five yards sideways behind the line of scrimmage before throwing a pass, though he still had to be at least five yards behind that scrimmage line. Even more dramatic changes occurred in 1912, when backs were permitted to throw anywhere behind the line of scrimmage without any distance limitations. Under other rules changes that year, an end zone of ten yards was established beyond the goal line, and a pass caught in the end zone was a touchdown and not a touchback. In addition, the value of a touchdown rose from five to six points, the field was shortened from 110 yards to 100 yards, and teams now had four downs to gain ten yards and a first down rather than three downs. All of those new rules remain in effect today, almost 100 years later.

That same year, Pop Warner, then the head coach at Carlisle, unveiled the single-wing formation, which made the halfback receiving the snap from center a triple-threat who could run, pass, or punt. That fitted his star back, Jim Thorpe, perfectly, since he could do all three very well. Warner's single-wing was used for the first time in 1912 against Army and flummoxed a Cadet team that was beaten, 27–6. By the start of the following season, in 1913, almost every major football power in the country was using a variation of Warner's single-wing, which remained the primary offensive formation until the introduction of the T-formation and its ensuing popularity starting in the late 1930s.

More than the T-formation, the 1913 game at West Point between Army and little-known Notre Dame became not only significant and momentous but changed football forever—in large measure because of the stage on which the Army–Notre Dame game was played—because of the mighty-mite passing tandem of Gus Dorais and Knute Rockne and their novel system of executing a successful pass play.

9

DORAIS TO ROCKNE AND AN
UPSET FOR THE AGES

IN THE LONG and mostly glorious annals of Notre Dame football, no game has ever come close to rivaling the significance of the one played against Army at West Point on November 1, 1913. And no player's performance has ever been as important as the one put on by an undersized quarterback named Charles "Gus" Dorais in that game. For all of their brilliance, even the best games ever played at Notre Dame by Joe Montana, Paul Hornung, Angelo Bertelli, Johnny Lujack, Joe Theismann, Terry Hanratty, John Huarte, Jimmy Clausen, or any other outstanding quarterback pale in comparison to the significance of the performance by Dorais on that raw afternoon on the banks of the Hudson River in New York.

The game had come about a year earlier, in December 1912, when Jesse Harper, the newly named football coach and athletic director, wrote a letter to the Army manager of athletics expressing an interest in playing at West Point during the 1913 season, which would be Harper's first as the Notre Dame head coach. With the approval, if indeed not the urging of the university's president, the Reverend John W. Cavanaugh, Harper wanted to book well-known football schools such as Army in order to enhance Notre Dame's name recognition and its prestige as a university. As it was, Notre Dame was still being ignored by most of the members of the Western Conference (later to become the Big Ten), mainly, Notre Dame officials thought, because of a perception that the Catholic school was recruiting academically ill-equipped players and because of an anti-Catholic bias by some of the Western Conference schools or its coaches. In fact, Notre Dame was no more guilty of recruiting players of dubious scholastic gifts than were Michigan and other members of the Western Conference, which consistently had rebuffed Notre Dame's efforts to join. A number of other schools with strong football programs used a similar rationale in refusing to play Notre Dame. Army, meanwhile, was having difficulty scheduling games for another reason—its policy of using star players who already had played as many as four varsity seasons elsewhere, and thus, in the opinion of some prospective opponents, had an unfair advantage. At least in part because of that scheduling problem, Army, to Harper's surprise, wrote back saying the Cadets would be willing to play Notre Dame on November 1 of the following year. Unlike many Eastern schools, Army knew about Notre Dame, mainly its baseball team, which, while barnstorming in the East, had played the Cadets twice and would play them again during the spring of 1913. Army's football coaches also knew that Notre Dame was developing into a football power in the Midwest and would be a formidable opponent, albeit unlikely to beat the Cadets, one of the best teams in the East where college football was predominant.

In subsequent discussions, Army offered Notre Dame a $400 guarantee, barely enough to cover the team's travel expenses, but, at Harper's request, raised the ante to $1,000—still a piddling amount for a team traveling slightly more than 700 miles to play a football game.

As one of the top-ranked college teams in the country, Army was a heavy favorite to beat the "Westerners," as West Point press releases and stories in New York City newspapers referred to Notre Dame. In addition to playing a stronger schedule than Notre Dame, the Cadets were bigger, heavier, and had the advantage of playing all of their games in an open field at West Point (except for the Navy game, which, in alternate years, was played in Annapolis). Leading up to the Army game, Notre Dame had outscored its first three opponents 169–7, but those opponents were Ohio Northern, South Dakota, and Alma College, hardly college football powers and well below the caliber of opposition Army usually faced. The new Army coach, Charley Daly, who like so many other Cadets had played football at two schools (in his case Harvard and Army, where he had been an All-American at both), had dispatched an assistant and former teammate, Tom Hammond, to scout Notre Dame. By then an Army captain, Hammond watched Notre Dame rout Alma, 62–0, the week before the Army game. In that contest, Harper had Gus Dorais pass infrequently, since outstanding fullback Ray Eichenlaub, halfback Joe Pliska, and Dorais, a swift and elusive runner, had little difficulty penetrating Alma's porous defense. Thus the scouting mission accomplished little, apart from determining that in Eichenlaub Notre Dame had one of the best fullbacks in the country and that the diminutive Dorais was almost equally as dangerous as a runner. Notre Dame was able to conceal its plan to primarily attack Army with the forward pass, something its opponents rarely used. Had the Army scout viewed any of the long and grueling practices Harper conducted on the following Monday, Tuesday, and Wednesday, he would have seen a number of plays that Harper had designed specifically for the Army game, most of them focusing on passing—to moving targets—which Harper was convinced his team would have to rely on if it were to beat the Cadets in Notre Dame's biggest football encounter of the year.

Apart from the 210-pound Eichenlaub, Notre Dame's key players on offense were also its smallest, the five-foot seven-inch Dorais and Rockne, who was an inch taller and, at 165 pounds, twenty pounds heavier than the little quarterback. Though Rockne had been a starter the previous three seasons, he had blossomed into a far better receiver under Harper. "I told Rockne that he'd never be a really good receiver until he learned to catch passes with his hands," Harper was to say years later.

After receiving a raucous send-off from several hundred Notre Dame students, a traveling squad of nineteen players (but only fourteen pair of cleats), carrying their own football gear, along with sandwiches from the campus cafeteria, boarded a train at the South Bend station on the morning of Thursday, October 30. "Everyone in the dorms got up early and marched downtown accompanying the team to the train depot," Rockne was to recall.

The team's supplies were minimal, mainly a few trunks, several rolls of tape and bandages, and bottles of iodine and liniment. To allow for more space in their suitcases, some of the players wore their game jerseys under their coats on the twenty-two-hour trip. At Buffalo, the players boarded a sleeper, which arrived in West Point at eight o'clock on the morning of Friday, October 31. Also on board were a half dozen Notre Dame fans, including George Hull and Mike Calnon, the proprietors of Hullie and Mike's restaurant in downtown South Bend, a favorite gathering place for Notre Dame students, including Rockne. One of Hull and Calnon's missions on the trip was to place bets for some of those students and other fans in South Bend.

After checking in at Cullum Hall, a dormitory adjacent to Cullum Field where the game was to be played, the players had lunch in the West Point mess hall, and then practiced for about an hour. A story in *The New York Times* on game day claimed "the visitors seem particularly heavy and look to outweigh the Army by at least ten pounds to the man." That was far from correct, since Notre Dame's seven-man line—almost all teams employed seven men up front in those days—averaged only 180 pounds, about ten pounds lighter than that of the Cadets' line, which included two All-Americans. Of the Notre Dame starters, only Eichenlaub, at 210 pounds, weighed over 200, compared with about a half dozen on the Army side. Then, too, the *Times'* pregame story also described Dorais as "stocky," which, at 145 pounds, he was anything but.

Though he was twenty pounds heavier, Rockne was not much bigger. That Rockne was the team captain in 1913 and a starting end for the third straight year was a surprise in itself. Always quick to deprecate his athletic ability, Rockne reveled in saying that he was an abject failure when he first went out for the varsity. "I was a dub, a washout, not even good enough for the scrubs," he would write years later. In fact, Coach Shorty Longman was impressed by the raw and tough undersized freshman's determination and latent football talent. Longman first tried Rockne at fullback, then switched him to end, where, as a backup, he saw considerable action. Rockne then was a starter his last three seasons, first under Jack Marks as a sophomore and junior, and then under Harper in 1913. "Having Knute was like having a coach out on the field," Harper once said.

❧

A crowd of about 5,000, about normal for an Army home game, turned out on a raw, cold, and cloudy afternoon, to sit on rickety wooden bleachers set on an open field on the famed West Point Plain. There was no admission charge to Army games at the time, and seats were on a first-come, first-served basis. As usual, the crowd was made up almost entirely of cadets and Army fans. The days of Notre Dame's "subway alumni" were still years away. Since almost all of Army's opponents were from the East, the crowd was curious to see how the "Westerners" would fare against the home side. Notre Dame was so little known in the East that a writer for one New York paper referred to the "Ramblers" as being from South Bend, *Illinois*. What the spectators saw would be both memorable and, in a way, historic in the annals of college football.

At the start, it appeared that Army's heavier line would overwhelm its Notre Dame counterpart. "They really pushed us around at the start," Rockne was to say later, "but we held our own." Indeed, Notre Dame did. The lightly regarded visitors struck first, scoring midway through the first quarter on a 42-yard touchdown pass from Dorais to Rockne. Dorais then kicked the extra point to make it 7–0, Notre Dame.

Rockne said later that a faked injury enabled him to get wide open for his touchdown catch. "I came out of one scrimmage limping and continued to limp for the next few plays, which convinced the defensive back on my side that I wasn't worth watching," Rockne said. "So when I started limping down the field on the touchdown play, he ignored me and I put on a burst of speed that left him flat-footed."

In the second quarter Army scored twice after long drives to take a 13–7 lead. With Harper having instructed Dorais to "open it up," meaning to throw more often, Dorais did just that, completing three consecutive passes to put the ball on the Army two-yard line, from where halfback Joe Pliska bolted into the end zone. Dorais's point after then gave Notre Dame a 14–13 halftime lead. By then, to the astonishment of the hushed crowd, Dorais had completed 12 of 14 passes. Among those stunned by Notre Dame's wide-open style of play was a reserve Army linebacker and halfback named Dwight Eisenhower, who was sidelined by an injury and did not play in the game.

Concerned that Army, with its greater depth and size, might overcome Notre Dame in the second half, Harper decided to have Dorais throw even more. "We figured it was the best chance we had," Harper said later. "Gus could throw the ball as well as any man who lived, and I think he proved it in the game."

As it developed, for reasons Harper never did explain, Dorais threw only one pass (it was incomplete) in the third quarter, which was scoreless but marked by a stalwart goal-line stand by Notre Dame. With first down at the Notre Dame two-yard line late in the period, Army was repulsed on two rushing attempts, after which Vernon Prichard threw a pass into the end zone that was intercepted by Dorais.

At Harper's direction, Dorais went to the air again, with great success, in the fourth quarter, as Notre Dame stunned the Cadets by scoring three unanswered touchdowns, all of them set up by Dorais's passes. Two of the touchdowns were scored by Eichenlaub, who gained more than 100 yards rushing, while the third was on a pass from Dorais to Pliska as the visitors prevailed, 35–13. By midway through the final period, even many of the Cadets were cheering Dorais's heroics. Certainly no one watching the game had ever seen such a demonstration of pin-point long passing.

"Army had its usual great team, but the passes completely demoralized them," Harper said. "By the time the game ended, we could do anything we pleased, running or passing. They didn't know what to expect or what to do about it." Harper also noted that Army appeared confused by Notre Dame's style of passing, which had receivers catching passes on the run in an era when passes were almost always thrown to stationary receivers. "Our style opened up the game considerably," Harper said, "and many schools copied it."

In what for the time was a masterful performance, Dorais completed 14 of 17 passes for an astounding 243 yards. "A frail youth of 145 pounds, as agile as a cat and as restless as a jumping jack, Dorais shot forward passes with accuracy . . . often as far as 30 yards away," exulted the *New York Times* reporter, who was obviously not the same one who had described Dorais as "stocky" in a pregame story. He went on to say, "The Army players were hopelessly confused and chagrined before Notre Dame's great playing, and their style of old-fashioned close-line smashing play was no match for the spectacular and highly perfected attack of the Indiana collegians."

Remarkably Notre Dame never called for a time-out during the game and used only one substitute, against twelve by Army. At that, the substitute, Art Larkin, was inserted into the game after halfback Sam Finegan broke a shoelace. With no extra football shoes, Harper had no choice but to replace Finegan with Larkin in the final minutes of the game. Harper never did say why he never let any of the other Notre Dame substitutes play in the momentous victory. As for Notre Dame's tendency to play its starters all sixty minutes, John Voelkers, a reserve halfback on the 1913 team, said years later, "Harper was a stickler on condition. We had two or three scrimmages during the week, and they were rough. And they ended with wind sprints and then runs to the locker room. Those scrimmages were harder than the games we played."

The victory made sports pages across the country. It also boosted the spirits of an untold number of Catholic sports fans and non fans, too, in an era when Catholics still encountered discrimination in employment and other segments of American society. Above all, the spectacular use of the forward pass by Notre Dame against Army was credited with helping change the game. Years later, highly respected *New York Times* sportswriter

Allison Danzig was to write that Notre Dame's upset triumph over Army was "the greatest impetus of all to the use of the forward pass." Danzig went on to say that the game "brought Notre Dame from obscurity to national fame and did more to make coaches pass-conscious than anything that had happened since the pass was put into the game in 1906."

The stunning victory by the visitors from the small Midwestern school also helped launch one of sport's greatest rivalries, with games that would attract as many as 60,000 spectators to Yankee Stadium and, some years, decide national championships. Notre Dame would end the season unbeaten for the third straight year, meaning that the three teams on which Rockne had been a starter had never lost a game. It was a harbinger of things to come when Rockne became Notre Dame's most famous head coach.

10

SHARPHOOTER WITH A BASKET-BALL AND A CUE STICK

WITH THE ABBREVIATED 1918 football season over, George Gipp surprised his football teammates by going out for the varsity basketball team in January of the new year. Considering how Gus Dorais, Knute Rockne's best friend and former teammate, was the new varsity basketball coach, some observers of the Notre Dame sports scene thought that Rockne had perhaps encouraged Dorais to ask Gipp to come out for the team to ensure that he would stay in shape and spend more time on campus and less time gambling in downtown South Bend.

Rockne always insisted that he never knew about Gipp's gambling proclivities, but that was hard to believe in light of Rockne's downtown connections and his friendship with George Hull and Mike Calnon, the owners of Hullie and Mike's. Furthermore, by early 1919, Gipp's accomplishments as a pool player were even being reported in the city's two dailies, and Rockne, an avid newspaper reader, read both the *South Bend Tribune* and the *South Bend News-Times.*

Dorais welcomed Gipp with open arms when he showed up for team tryouts. Before coming to Notre Dame, Gipp had played far more basketball than he had football, including his one season at Calumet High, where he starred as a freshman on a very good team. An excellent shooter and solid all-around player, Gipp had a strong background in the sport.

Typical of the era, the Notre Dame basketball team was made up mainly of football players, including four of the five start-ers—Gipp, Joe Brandy, Pete Bahan, and Raleigh Stine. Most of its home games were played in the afternoon, which freed Gipp's nights for poker and billiard games, and, occasionally, even studying. But basketball still apparently interfered with his lifestyle, since he played in only four games before, for reasons unknown, leaving the team. Notre Dame lost three of those games—the team wound up winning only one of eight games—which could have accounted for the departure of Gipp who had become accustomed to winning. In an era of low-scoring games, largely because rules called for a jump ball after each basket or free throw (which did not change until 1936), Gipp scored 12 points all told for an average of three points a game. Because of the jump-ball rule, Gipp, as the starting center, was forced to jump after every field goal or free-throw. At six feet, Gipp was tall for the era and was an excellent rebounder. Yet, a story about Notre Dame's first game of the season in the *Notre Dame Scholastic* said, "Gipp handles the circle job nicely"—meaning the area in front of and just beyond the foul line—"except that he needs to jump a little higher."

Just maybe Gipp jumped only as high as he wanted to. At any rate, because he played in only half of Notre Dame's eight games, Gipp did not earn a monogram, the school's version of a varsity letter. Given that he seemed to care little about publicity or recognition of his athletic achievements, it is unlikely that that caused Gipp any concern. Still, the four games were more than he would ever play for the varsity baseball team, for which he seemed to make cameo appearances every year or so, to the chagrin of, first, Jesse Harper, and then Dorais, who were the baseball coaches during Gipp's time at Notre Dame and knew that he was the best baseball player they had, albeit very briefly. Gipp also went out for track that winter, and, considering that he had been timed at ten seconds in the 100-yard dash in full football gear, was welcomed. But after several practice sessions as a sprinter, Gipp never returned and never did compete for the varsity track team.

"I remember George being in the gym in street clothes when some track guys challenged him to a race," Hunk Anderson recalled. "George reluctantly agreed and he ran away from the two sprinters in a 100 yard race—with shoes on, no less."

It is more than just possible that other sports interfered with his poker-playing and pool-shooting. By the 1918–19 academic year, Gipp had become one of the best pocket and three-cushion billiard players in South Bend and, indeed, probably in the entire Midwest. His earnings, especially from playing pool, had soared, and, as Hunk Anderson was to tell this author years later, it was not uncommon for Gipp to return to campus after a night at the billiards tables with hundreds of dollars in winnings. "George would ask me to put the money in a trunk I had in my room for safekeeping, which I did," Anderson said.

Gipp was so good with a pool cue that big-time pool shooters from Chicago and some other Midwestern cities were lured to South Bend to play him in either pocket billiards or the three-cushion game, always for high stakes, usually at Hullie and Mike's. In such games, Gipp had nothing to lose and a lot to gain, since, apart from often betting on himself, Hull and Calnon and other Gipp fans bet on him to win, which he usually did, and gave him a share of their winnings. The games attracted hundreds of spectators, most of whom bet on Gipp, who had helped enrich many of them with his football exploits and now was doing it on pool tables. Chain-smoking as he played and also occasionally sipping on scotch or bourbon, Gipp was both nerveless and seemingly oblivious of the crowd sitting in chairs ringed around the table as he coolly dispatched such billiards luminaries as John Vermande, one of the best players in northern Indiana and southern Michigan; Ray Fisher, a Minnesota Fats-type character from nearby Mishawaka who weighed well over 200 pounds; and a highly rated player from Chicago known only as "The Greek," whom Gipp beat in a pocket billiards match at Hullie and Mike's during the winter of 1919. On March 3 of that year, Gipp dispatched Fisher, whom the *South Bend Tribune* described as "the best pool player in the South Bend area," as the *Tribune* reported the next day, adding that "Gipp has now become recognized as the best."

Gipp also engaged in a number of matches against George Hull, the Hullie of Hullie and Mike's, an excellent player and a big Notre Dame booster who often made bets on the Ramblers for the university students who patronized the restaurant in front. Out of Gipp's matches with Hull came a friendship that included visits by Gipp to Hull's home for dinners with his family and perhaps some inside information from Gipp to Hull, who bet heavily on Notre Dame football games.

"He was a handsome young man, unassuming and so nonchalant," Hull's daughter once recalled. "I was only about thirteen or so at the time, but I could see that he was much older-looking than the average college boy and much more mature. He was very shy, and I remember people who were introduced to him at our home invariably remarked later that they were surprised to find out he was really George Gipp."

Some of those people also would have been surprised at Gipp's dexterity with a pool cue. After leading Hullie and Mike's to victory over the Hotel Oliver—where, ironically, Gipp would eventually wind up as the "house" billiards player—in a two-match series, he won the South Bend three-cushion tournament before a crowd of several hundred at Hullie and Mike's in early January. His victim was none other than Elwin "Dope" Moore, his onetime roommate who had taught him the finer points of the three-cushion game. An account of the match the following day in the *South Bend Tribune*, obviously alluding to Gipp's football talents while blending football with golf, said, "Gipp's end runs were effective and Moore's putts were too short; hence we find the three-cushion billiards champion of 1920." The story did not give the size of Gipp's winning purse, but it was believed to have been substantial, perhaps even more than Gipp had bet on himself, which he no doubt had.

Even if Rockne actually was aware of Gipp's gambling and late hours, there was at least one vice, the coach often said, which he was not guilty of—chasing and staying out late with women. "There are a lot of girls who would like to go out with George," Rockne once said, "but he is much too committed to his football to do so." To Rockne, it was something of a noble trait for his players to stay away from women while playing football, even the female students at nearby St. Mary's College. Unfortunately for Rockne—no altar boy himself when he was a student-athlete—more than a few of his players consorted with females, both from St. Mary's and downtown, unbeknownst to the coach. Rockne and Dorais, like many players after them, were known to violate a campus rule that only permitted seniors to go into town on weekdays. Even at that, they had to be back on campus by 10 P.M. Well into his twenties by the time he was a senior, Rockne had no trouble getting a drink nor did Dorais since they were both well beyond Indiana's minimum drinking age; in Rockne's case, he could easily be taken for thirty or even forty.

As for Gipp, he was no doubt the most eligible, and coveted, bachelor in South Bend. His handsome visage appeared often in the city's newspapers and elicited a large number of letters from women eager to meet him, which were sent to him care of Notre Dame. Hunk Anderson said he was sure Gipp never answered any of them. That is not to say that he didn't go out with women. He did, but most of them were working girls he had met in downtown South Bend. One of them, whom he saw frequently, was a blonde manicurist who worked at a salon in the Hotel Oliver. That relationship never became serious, but one with a pretty brunette from Indianapolis would.

❧❦❧

For the second academic year in a row, Gipp's transcript for 1918–19 was blank, with neither any courses nor grades listed. At the top of his transcript, in longhand, was the notation, "did not take any examinations." Seemingly, that would have required Gipp to spend the summer of 1919 taking courses or else be expelled. But this was an era when some college football players enrolled in classes for the fall semester and perhaps attended a few and then dropped out of school after the last game of the season only to return to play again the following season. Gipp, at least technically, was always a student, since he at least signed up for courses and stuck around for most of the school year. At Notre Dame, that, it appears, made him eligible to play football (and, albeit rarely, baseball and basketball), even though he wasn't getting any grades. What he was doing, though, was helping to make Notre Dame a football power and making the university better known throughout the United States.

Back driving a truck and occasionally a taxi in Laurium, Gipp spent much of the summer of 1919 playing center field for the Calumet-Laurium Aristocrats in a strong semi-pro league of teams from Michigan's Upper Peninsula, whose games often drew thousands of fans and big league scouts, given the talent in the league. Gipp, far and away the best player on the Aristocrats and one of the best players, if not the best, in the league, had a sensational season and was largely responsible for the Aristocrats winning nineteen of twenty games and the league championship. Gipp led the league in batting with a .494 average, which included a home run in his last game of the season that traveled almost 500 feet, the longest ball ever hit at the Aristocrats home field in Calumet. Once again, major league scouts, most notably from the Chicago Cubs and the Chicago White Sox, salivated over Gipp's play, but, again, Gipp showed no interest when they tried to convince him to sign professional contracts, since he was determined to play two more seasons of football at Notre Dame. Whether Rockne had anything to do with Gipp's decision is unlikely since Gipp, as Rockne knew all too well, made up his own mind about everything.

A week after the Aristocrats' last game, Gipp returned to the Notre Dame campus, a week after classes had begun and two weeks before the opening game against Kalamazoo. With him was Percy Wilcox, a close friend from Calumet who had been wounded while serving with the Marines in France the year before. As he had done with Hunk Anderson and Ojay Larson, Gipp convinced Rockne—who knew nothing about Wilcox—to give him a scholarship, pointing out that, in addition to being a good halfback, Wilcox was an outstanding basketball and hockey player. Most likely to keep his star player happy, Rockne agreed to do so even though, as the coach was to find out, Wilcox was a far better basketball and hockey player than he was a halfback, although he was good enough to earn a monogram in 1920. That gave Rockne four players who had gone to high school in Calumet, Michigan, three of whom had been recruited by George Gipp, although Wilcox would not be eligible to play football until the following year.

By the fall semester of 1919 at Notre Dame, Gipp should have been a senior since he had enrolled in 1916. But not having received any grades during his first two years, he was, academically, a sophomore. However, he was listed as a junior on the team's roster and at that still had two more years of eligibility since the 1918 season did not count against eligibility. Thus if Gipp stayed around to play through the 1919 and 1920 seasons, he would have spent four years as a varsity player and one year on the freshman team. Not that that was a lot of eligibility in an era when star players like Elmer Oliphant and Chris Cagle played as many as eight varsity seasons at two different schools.

With a solid nucleus from the 1918 team along with nine lettermen who had returned from military service, Rockne knew that prospects were very bright so long as the returning war veterans were able to adjust to college life again and take football seriously after the carnage some of them had seen on battlefields in France during the Great War. For some it would be easy; for others very difficult, and understandably so.

11

GIPP'S BREAKOUT SEASON

IN ADDITION TO being the year the United States welcomed home most of its war veterans, 1919 was momentous for a number of other reasons: jobs were scarce and thus thousands of returning vets decided to attend college; the U.S. Senate blocked President Woodrow Wilson's effort to have the United States join the new League of Nations, which Wilson had helped establish; the Prohibition amendment was ratified, prohibiting the sale of alcoholic beverages throughout the nation at a time when many veterans were looking forward to their first beer in a long while; women finally won the right to vote, starting in 1920; Jack Dempsey knocked out Jess Willard to win the world heavyweight championship; Sir Barton became the first thoroughbred to win racing's Triple Crown; Babe Ruth, in his last season with the Boston Red Sox, hit more home runs than six of the other seven teams in the American League; and eight members of the Chicago White Sox baseball team were accused of conspiring to throw that year's World Series to the Cincinnati Reds and were later banned from the major leagues for life.

It was also the year that Father Cavanaugh relinquished the presidency at Notre Dame, which he had held since 1905. That was not necessarily good news for Knute Rockne, since Cavanaugh encouraged the growth of the Notre Dame football program because of the publicity it gave the school, while his successor, Father James Burns, although a former Notre Dame baseball player, was wary about the expansion of the school's varsity sports programs and more concerned about the university's academic reputation.

Father Burns, who had attended Cornell, Harvard, and Catholic University, and was the first Notre Dame president with a doctorate, also was confronted with a monumental housing problem, largely owing to an influx of several hundred war veterans, which was so severe that the university sought through newspaper advertisements to place around 500 students in off-campus rooms, an effort that proved successful. For many veterans going to college was a logical option because of the paucity of jobs as the country's economy soured. Unlike after World War II, there was no GI Bill, whereby the government paid for most if indeed not all of a veteran's college tuition. But at Notre Dame, tuition, along with room and board, remained relatively cheap—$120 a year for tuition, $350 for meals in the campus dining room, and from thirty to fifty dollars for a shared room. For those needing financial assistance, there were usually ample campus jobs. For Gipp, after a very brief stint as a campus waiter during the beginning of his freshman year, he more than covered school expenses with his gambling earnings in downtown South Bend.

For returning lettermen, including those who had served in the military, and promising recruits, a plenitude of scholarships or financial aid were available, although players had to work during the off season for their room and board and other necessary expenses. From the military, Rockne welcomed back such monogram winners as Slip Madigan, Joe Brandy, Frank Coughlin, Walter Miller, Dave Hayes, Fritz Slackford, Grover Malone, and Cy Degree, most of whom would become starters. Among the newcomers was twenty-three-year-old George Trafton, an Army veteran and an outstanding center who would only last one season because of his refusal to heed Rockne's order that he stop playing semi-pro football on Sundays. Trafton, nicknamed "the Beast" and once described by Red Grange as "the toughest, meanest, and most ornery critter alive," went on to become a charter member of the Chicago Bears for whom he played ten years after two seasons with the Bears' predecessor, the Decatur Staleys. Trafton was discovered by Rockne, who spent part of the war scouting service football teams.

Also discovered and then recruited by Rockne while playing for a service team was another lineman, Lawrence "Buck" Shaw, who after three years at Notre Dame later went on to be a head coach for four years in the All-America Football Conference and then eight years in the NFL. Others on the thirty-five-man squad were halfbacks Johnny Mohardt—a remarkable athlete and scholar who would later play five games for the Detroit Tigers of baseball's American League and five years with the Chicago Bears of the National Football League before attending medical school and becoming a physician—and Cy Kasper. Like Rockne, Mohardt and Kapser were products of Notre Dame's inter-hall football league, an intramural competition among the university's six residence halls, some of which had squads of as many as forty players. Most of the hall teams, whose games were played on Sundays, were coached by varsity players, and both Mohardt and Kasper had been recommended to Rockne by members of the varsity—as Rockne had been recommended to Shorty Longman by the Brownson coach at the time, Joe Collins, a varsity end. Rockne knew from firsthand experience how good some of the inter-hall teams were. In addition to providing players for the varsity, some of the inter-hall squads played, and beat, some small university teams in Indiana and Michigan. Missing from the 1919 squad, though, was a key player, center Ojay Larson. Larson had dropped out of school for a year because of a family situation in Calumet, but would return in 1920.

While he was particularly fond of the war veterans, Rockne also found that his bombastic rah-rah pep talks did not go over well with most of them. "I could [see] how some of them would smile when I launched into halftime talk, and so I had to change my approach to a certain degree," said Rockne, who realized that to many of the veterans on the team, football paled in significance to wartime experiences they had endured and that to try to equate a football game to action on a battlefield was absurd.

For the most part, there appeared to be no resentment generated by the war veterans toward players who, although of draft age, did not serve in the military. However, there was one unpleasant exchange that involved Gipp and Grover Malone, who had spent two years in the Army. It happened after a practice when Gipp picked up a towel that Malone insisted was his. When Gipp, claiming the towel actually belonged to him, refused to give it to Malone, Malone called Gipp a "slacker," a term usually used to denote someone who had gone out of their way to avoid going into service or even serving in Notre

Dame's Student Army Training Corps. While Gipp somehow had avoided induction when called by his Michigan draft board during the summer of 1917, he subsequently was rejected by both his draft board and by the SATC. As a result of the towel incident, Gipp and Malone did not speak to one another for at least several weeks, if indeed not for the rest of the season.

❧❧❧

For the second straight year, Gipp moved into Sorin Hall, this time to room with teammates George Fitzpatrick, a backup half-back just back from two years of military service, and Arthur "Dutch" Bergman, a swift 160-pound halfback whose brother, Alfred, was also a star halfback and Rockne's teammate. As was the case at most colleges of the era, football players tended to room together, a practice that was not always academically bene-ficial and was discontinued by many universities in later years, although many continued to do it into the twenty-first century. As both of Gipp's former roommates, Walter Miller and Elwin "Dope" Moore, had found out, he spent more nights in down-town South Bend than he did on campus. Of course that was also true of Moore, who introduced Gipp to Hullie and Mike's and some of the other more popular pool and poker hangouts in South Bend, and who was perhaps the most pernicious influ-ence Gipp was to encounter at Notre Dame.

By the fall of 1919 Gipp seemed to have become enamored with Notre Dame, its beautiful campus, the signature golden dome atop what is now the university's administration building, the school's struggle for recognition and respect, its growing sports traditions, its successful football program, and, of course, its head football coach, who tolerated, or rationalized, his nocturnal gambling in downtown South Bend, his haphazard academic record, and his chronic absences from classes and practices. Rockne was heartened, though, when, for the 1919–20 academic year, Gipp enrolled in Notre Dame's school of law and signed up for eight courses, seven of them law courses, although he was not studying for a law degree, which was not uncommon at the time. Well aware of Gipp's innate intelligence, his deep, soothing baritone voice, and his articulate way of expressing himself, Rockne said during the fall of 1919, "If he puts his mind to it, George could become one of the best lawyers in the country." But once again, Gipp rarely showed up for classes and received only three grades for the first quarter, none for the second or third, and two for the fourth. Moreover, he would spend even more time downtown than he had during his first three years at Notre Dame, making himself something of a local legend at pool tables at Hullie and Mike's, Goldie Mann's, the Hotel Oliver, in nearby Elkhart, and as far away as Chicago.

Gipp's skill as a billiards player was attracting him as much, if not more, attention among billiard fans in South Bend—especially those who bet on him to win a match—than his feats on the football field. Good looking, relatively clean-cut, and soft-spoken, Gipp did not project the image of a pool hustler, but, at times, he was, and won a lot of money in the process. He was more "Fast Eddie" Felson in the movie *The Hustler* than he was Minnesota Fats, his archrival in the film that starred Paul Newman and Jackie Gleason. Gipp's gambling routine, which included heavy smoking—about three packs a day, according to Hunk Anderson—and drinking and not much sleep, also was catching up with him, leaving him with sunken cheeks, an unhealthy looking pallor, and a hacking cough. Rockne must have noticed it, but if he ever brought it up with his transcendent star halfback, neither he nor Gipp ever said. And even if he did, given Gipp's diffident attitude and rebellious nature, it's unlikely that it would have prompted Gipp to change his lifestyle.

For all of his nightlife gambling, smoking, and drinking, and, some say, womanizing, Gipp somehow did not seem to let any or all of his vices affect his performance as a football player. Nor did the fact that Rockne indulged Gipp's frequent absences from both classes and practices have any effect on the team's morale, mainly because Gipp was well-liked by his teammates who knew from experience that he would perform and demonstrate leadership during Notre Dame's games. Even though he seemed to gamble more and sleep less during the 1919–20 academic year, Gipp had his best season yet in 1919, when Notre Dame won all nine of its games.

The opening game, at home against Kalamazoo, was a portent of things to come from Gipp. Generally low-key in his demeanor, Gipp surprised the standing-room crowd of more than 5,000 at Cartier Field by walking to midfield before the game with two footballs. He then turned to face one goal post and booted a 50-yard dropkick through the uprights as the crowd cheered. Gipp then turned around and sent another dropkick between the opposing goalposts. As he walked off the field toward the Notre Dame bench, the crowd gave him a thunderous ovation. They would cheer him even louder during the game. Despite his 62-yard field goal as a freshman, Gipp had attempted few field goals since joining the Notre Dame varsity in 1917, mainly, no doubt, because both Harper and Rockne eschewed field goal attempts and always went for touchdowns once Notre Dame was within 25 yards of an opponent's goal line.

Deciding to scout Nebraska, which would be Notre Dame's third opponent in 1919 and was favored to beat the "Fighting Irish," Rockne left the coaching to Gus Dorais, who had become his old teammate's assistant coach—the first one Rockne had—and also the head basketball and baseball coaches, after having been the head football coach at St. Joseph's College in Iowa. The game was hardly the cakewalk that Notre Dame expected it to be. Kalamazoo, a prohibitive underdog who had been crushed, 55–0, in a previous meeting two years earlier, battled the home team to a scoreless first half. Gipp appeared to have scored twice that half on runs of 75 and 68 yards, but both scores were nullified by penalties. After the second touchdown was nullified, an uncharacteristically agitated Gipp walked over to referee Walter Eckersall and said, "Listen, from now on, please whistle once for me to stop and whistle twice for me to keep going." Fortunately for Notre Dame, Gipp still managed to legitimately gain 148 yards on 11 carries—an astonishing average of more than 13 yards a carry—to lead Notre Dame to a 14–0 victory.

One of the Kalamazoo linemen victimized by Gipp was a friend from Calumet, Joe Mishica. After the game, Mishica recalled their boyhood together. "George was friendly, kind, and very personable to everybody," Kalamazoo's left tackle said. "While we were in high school, George would occasionally show up before practices, and, in his street shoes, both punt and drop-kick. I remember once I saw him drop-kick a football 100 yards.

One reason why he never played football for Calumet High was because he headed right for the poolroom after school." That explanation conflicted with the reason offered by school officials—that Gipp was always ineligible because of his numerous absences.

After the game, several Kalamazoo players charged that Eckersall and some other officials had favored Notre Dame throughout the game, contending that they constantly overlooked penalties by the Irish. That was plausible since Eckersall, a former All-American quarterback at Chicago and by 1919 a sportswriter for the *Chicago Tribune*, was a friend of Rockne's and was frequently invited to referee Notre Dame home games that he was covering. While this may seem strange by today's standards, at the time it was not at all uncommon for sportswriters like Eckersall to supplement their newspaper incomes by officiating college football games, including the ones they were covering. That, of course, raises the question of how such writers managed to write game stories without taking notes, which would seem to be impossible while officiating. As it was, the bigger a writer's name, the more big games he would be asked to officiate. In Eckersall's case, it meant a lot of Notre Dame games. When a writer found himself invited to cover quite a few of a popular team's games—and get paid by the team's school—he was likely, at least on some occasions, to penalize that team a lot less than its opponents, not to mention write glowingly of the team. Still, the fact that two long touchdown runs by Gipp were nullified by Notre Dame penalties seems to defuse the charges that the officials, including Eckersall, were favoring Notre Dame.

In failing to score, Kalamazoo became the first of three teams held scoreless by Notre Dame in 1919, when the Irish outscored its opponents, 229–47, with only one team, Purdue, able to score two touchdowns. In that game, because of Purdue's big and staunch line, Rockne had Gipp pass more than he ran. Though he only carried the ball 10 times, Gipp gained 52 yards on the ground. But he dazzled the Purdue crowd with the way he threw the stubby ball, completing 11 of 15 passes for a remarkable 217 yards and setting up most of the Fighting Irish touchdowns.

That 33–13 victory, along with triumphs over Nebraska, Indiana, and Army, all on the road, represented a significant achievement. Whereas only a few fans cheered Notre Dame on when Gus Dorais and Rockne led the visitors to a stunning 35–13 victory in 1913, the crowd of more than 5,000 at the 1919 game at West Point included hundreds—700, according to the *Notre Dame Scholastic*, the weekly student publication—of Notre Dame supporters, many of them former players, alumni, and current students, but including spectators from the New York area who would ultimately become the core of what would be called Notre Dame's "subway alumni" and whose ranks eventually would spread throughout the country.

Gipp's quick presence of mind accounted for the first of Notre Dame's two touchdowns against Army. With time running out in the first half and Notre Dame trailing, 9–0, while lined up at the Army one-yard line, Gipp, seeing the field judge prepare to fire his pistol ending the half, did not wait for quarterback Joe Brandy to call signals at the line of scrimmage as teams did in the pre-huddle era. Instead he yelled at center Slip Madigan. "Give me the ball. Hurry," he barked out to Madigan, and the talented center promptly did, whereupon Gipp bolted into the end zone as the field judge's pistol went off. There were no official game clocks in those days and the field judge had to rely on his watch, so it was an especially heads-up play by Gipp. The touchdown made the difference as Notre Dame prevailed, 12–9, after Walter Miller scored a touchdown in the third quarter after Gipp's runs and passes had again taken the visitors to Army's one-yard line.

Speaking of Gipp after the game, Army's captain and left end Alexander George said, "If you stop him on the ground, he goes to the air, and when you think he's going to pass he runs the ball down your gullet with a determination that eventually ends in a score. I've never played against anyone as good as he is."

The victory was literally profitable to the Notre Dame players who, collectively, had raised around $2,000 of their own that they wagered against Army, whose players also put up the same amount, in a winner-take-all bet, not uncommon among big-time college teams of the era. "George put up the most, about $400," Hunk Anderson recalled almost six decades later. "The student managers of both teams then gave the money to a shoe-maker right outside the West Point grounds to hold on to 'til after the game. It was a lot of money in those days, and we went home with all of it."

They returned with the cash, but not Gipp. With his share, Gipp, almost always a loner, apparently went out on the town in New York and maybe Chicago, too. If he returned to South Bend, none of his teammates saw him, not on campus or in any of his classes. After missing all of the team's practices the following week, and, of course, all of his classes (which was hardly unusual), Gipp turned up on Friday, the day before a home game against Michigan Agricultural, without divulging where he had been. A furious Rockne said that night that Gipp would not play in Notre Dame's last home game of the season. After a slow start, though, the pragmatic Rockne had second thoughts about punishing his star player and inserted Gipp into the game in the second quarter following a scoreless first period. Proving anew that he did not have to practice, Gipp played brilliantly, rushing for almost 100 yards and connecting on most of his 10 passes before a standing-room-only crowd of more than 5,000 at Cartier Field. The crowd was especially large for the time at a college game in the Midwest—if not the East—and it prompted an editorial in the *Scholastic,* which called for the erection of a football stadium on campus (which would not happen until eleven years later).

The year 1919 also appeared to have marked the first time that the Notre Dame football team was called the "Fighting Irish," as it was in the *Scholastic* account of the Notre Dame–Army game and the campus newspaper's accounts of several other games during the 1919 season, although some sportswriters insisted the nickname had been used earlier. Indeed even the *Scholastic* said the name, as applied to Notre Dame teams, had been around for "more than a score of years." At any rate, it was during Rockne's early years as the Notre Dame head coach that the name began to show up in newspaper reports across the country. Before long, it became one of the most famous nicknames in all of sports, even though some alumni contended that it was unrealistic to refer to the team as the Fighting Irish when the coach and star player were not only not Irish, but Protestant.

A number of Notre Dame players, using aliases, played in semi-pro games on some Sundays, which earned them as much as several hundred dollars a game, the equivalent of several thousand dollars today. Rockne, of course, had done the same and it is hard to believe that he did not know some of his charges were playing for money the day after Notre Dame games and thus risking injury. If he did, he was keeping quiet about it. So far as can be determined, Gipp only played in one such game, along with seven other Notre Dame starters, the day after the November 22 Purdue game, which had been a bruising encounter.

Along with the other seven players, including his three backfield teammates, Gipp was recruited to play in a game for the Rockford, Illinois, city championship by center Slip Madigan, who had been contacted by one of the team's coaches and general manager and told the Notre Damers each would be paid $400, a huge amount of money at the time. So after the train returning the Notre Dame team from Purdue arrived in South Bend, the eight players, carrying their football gear and apparently unnoticed by Rockne, slipped away and boarded a train for Chicago, and then, after midnight, another train for Rockford.

Wearing the uniforms of the players whose places they had taken and given aliases—Gipp's game name was "Baker"—the eight Notre Damers, using Notre Dame plays, led a team called the Grands to a 19–7 victory over the Rockford Amateur Athletic Club. That name was misleading since the Rockford AAC players, including a number of ringers from the University of Illinois, also were paid for playing in a heavily wagered-on game before a crowd of about 5,000. Since the Notre Dame ringers were not familiar to the Rockford fans, it's not hard to imagine that there were complaints from fans who had bet on the Rockford AAC team to win.

Suspicion was aroused in a story about the game in the next day's *Rockford Register Gazette,* which noted, "Local football fandom has been wandering through a maze of speculation concerning the identity of Grands football players who put over a victory on the AAC. It was no ordinary bunch of grid-iron talent that had been imported for the fray. That much was evident after the smooth working Grands backfield had been in operation for two plays. The backs played too well not to have been in operation all season." The story went on to say that not more than three of the Grands' players were from Rockford and that "AAC men insist that a regular (college) varsity backfield, the regular center and right end, was used." Not to mention two other Notre Damers. By then, the eight Notre Dame ringers were back in South Bend in time for their Monday morning classes—which Gipp quite likely missed—each richer by at least $400 (the equivalent of about $4,000 today), and as much as $800 if they had accepted the Grands' general manager's offer to double the winnings of those players who had bet on the Grands to win. Even for Gipp, who was accustomed to winning a lot of money at pool and poker tables and who undoubtedly had bet on the game's outcome, earning $800 was special. Certainly some good investigative reporting would have determined that the Grands team included one of the country's best halfbacks in George Gipp, along with seven other Notre Damers. But then maybe the fans and the local paper didn't want to cause too much of a fuss in fear that they'd never see good college football talent come through Rockford again.

⊶⊷

In mid-December 1919, the Notre Dame squad, along with Rockne, Dorais, and the university band, gathered in the dining room of the Hotel Oliver to celebrate the team's unbeaten season. The squad would also elect a captain for the 1920 season to succeed Pete Bahan, who had skippered the last two teams. Despite his missed practices and late arrivals for practice sessions, Gipp was elected by a margin of one vote over tackle Frank Coughlin. Gipp's election demonstrated the respect his teammates had for him, especially for his leadership on the field of play. Gipp may have been irresponsible in many ways, but, as Hunk Anderson was to say years later, "the guys loved him."

Something ever more special than being elected captain was about to happen to George Gipp before the 1919–20 academic year was over.

12

HEAD OVER HEELS IN LOVE

JUDGING BY KNUTE Rockne's comments about George Gipp, it's easy to get the impression that his wayward wonder was an ascetic, especially when it came to women. "He lived quietly, had few companions, (and) apparently cared nothing for female company, of which there's none whatever on the Notre Dame campus," Rockne was to write about his half-back in 1930. Of those four elements, only the fourth—that there were no women students at Notre Dame—was demonstrably true, although Notre Dame men were welcome guests at frequent dances at St. Mary's College, a fifteen-minute walk from the Notre Dame campus. But then Rockne was prone to stretch the truth, and, at times, even concoct stories—whether to inspire his players, assuage dubious administrators and faculty members, or impress sportswriters, all of which he succeeded in doing.

In Gipp's case, Rockne went even further, as he did when he once said, that "a check-up on his habits showed him with fewer than the usual faults of star athletes." If Gipp's lifestyle of spending endless nights shooting pool and playing poker for high stakes, chain-smoking, considerable drinking, missing most of his classes, chronically reporting to campus late for preseason practices, and skipping many practices during the season fell short of the standard, one is left to wonder what the "usual faults" of most star athletes of the era entailed and whether Rockne was feigning ignorance of Gipp's off-campus peccadilloes. But then Rockne, like many coaches, affected a macho image and liked his players to do so, too. In Rockne's perspective as a coach, it was a blessing that Notre Dame had no female students, since it meant the absence of what could be a major distraction for his football players.

As for Gipp apparently caring "nothing for female company," that was a stretch, too. A handsome and intelligent star athlete, Gipp was the object of a lot of women's affection, and it was unlikely that he would resist all of that female attention, especially since by the fall of 1919 he had his own room at the elegant Hotel Oliver, which he primarily used on weekends when the tempo in both billiards and poker picked up markedly. Most of his female interests were young working women in South Bend, including the manicurist at the Hotel Oliver with whom he was seen often even though he managed to keep such relationships private.

That changed, though, when he met a stunning brunette from Indianapolis named Iris Trippeer—who, at about twenty, was four years younger than Gipp—in South Bend while she was visiting a friend at St. Mary's in the winter of 1920. Indications are that he met her at a dance at St. Mary's, although the worldly Gipp hardly seemed likely to have been going to college dances, even though he was a very good dancer and liked to dance. However, Trippeer's granddaughter, Victoria Adams Phair, said in May 2010 that Trippeer had indeed met Gipp at a dance at St. Mary's, to which she had gone with a friend who was a student at the school. There, she and Gipp met and became smitten with one another. For all of his good looks and fame, Gipp had never met a woman like Trippeer, who, apart from her beauty, was highly intelligent, personable, and witty, as both Hunk Anderson and Victoria Adams Phair attested. Trippeer also was a mystery woman of sorts, and although she showed Gipp outward affection in public, she turned out to be as elusive in her way as Gipp was on a football field.

It would be a long-distance romance, and while, at least for Gipp, prolonged absences made his heart even fonder for Trippeer, the fact that she lived and worked in Indianapolis, about 125 miles from South Bend, meant they saw each other infrequently even as their ardor apparently intensified. Since neither had a car, when they did see one another it was after a train trip between the two cities.

Early in the burgeoning relationship, Gipp and Trippeer double-dated with Anderson and his wife-to-be, Marie Martin. On those dates, Marie Martin Anderson was to say, Trippeer was overly amorous with Gipp, which seemed to have annoyed Marie, accustomed as she was to the mores of the era that dictated propriety in social settings. While hardly resisting Trippeer's affectionate gestures, Gipp, Martin said, always remained a perfect gentleman, which was the persona he seemed to demonstrate in public, both on and off the football field. On one date, Martin noticed that Trippeer was wearing a gold football on a necklace and, when asked where she got it, Trippeer told her it was from Gipp. It turned out that Rockne had dipped into his own pocket to buy gold football charms for members of the undefeated 1919 team, and Gipp had given his to Trippeer. Martin's opinion of Trippeer differs from that of several of Gipp's friends who found her to be cultured, sophisticated, and demure—hardly the type to be clinging to a boyfriend in public. Perhaps Martin, though very attractive, may have been jealous of the attention the stunning Trippeer received when she was in her company. It is also possible Martin was envious of Gipp's courtly and sensitive demeanor toward Trippeer, contrasted with that of the earthy and far less polished Anderson's mannerisms.

As it was, Trippeer rarely came to South Bend. More often, Gipp visited her on weekends in Indianapolis, where she lived with her parents. Gipp never did meet Trippeer's parents though, apparently because she had told him that her father, a railroad brakeman, disapproved of her seeing Gipp because, from what he had heard and read, Gipp was a ne'er-do-well football player. As a result, Gipp and Trippeer were somewhat circumscribed during his visits to Indianapolis, confining their time to the Claypool Hotel, where he stayed while visiting Trippeer, and to downtown restaurants and clubs where they were able to dance. Gipp soon fell in love with Trippeer, and she in turn appeared enraptured with the handsome football star.

The romance flourished during occasional meetings through the winter and early spring of 1920, and they eventually became engaged. In the few times she came to South Bend, Gipp and Trippeer continued to double-date with Anderson and his fiancée. On one occasion when the four of them were together, Trippeer's ardor for Gipp came close to causing a serious auto accident, according to Marie Martin. Gipp, whose football exploits and good looks made him a favorite of a number of prominent South Bend business executives and others in the upper echelon of the city's social spectrum, had been invited to a party at a lakeside retreat of a businessman he knew. Gipp was told he was welcome to bring along friends, if he wished, to the businessman's house on nearby Diamond Lake in Michigan. Gipp asked Trippeer to come, of course, along with Anderson and Martin. Gipp drove the car, which he had borrowed from a friend, along a rutted dirt road. Trippeer snuggled up to him, impeding his driving on the unfamiliar road and eventually causing him to lose control, sending the car down an embankment and almost into a lake before Gipp was able to bring it to a stop. With the car mired in a ditch, Gipp and Anderson, despite the slippery terrain, managed to push the car up the embankment and back on the road, undamaged and operable. "Marie was pretty upset with Iris, feeling that she caused George to lose control," Hunk Anderson recalled. They finally made it to the party, where Gipp danced the night away with his beauteous girlfriend as partygoers, recognizing the Notre Dame football star, could not help but stare at the good-looking couple.

Gipp saw less and less of Trippeer during the spring, but if anything, their separation served to intensify Gipp's feelings. Gipp wrote to Trippeer often, but rarely got a response, and occasionally phoned her at her job as a secretary with the Indiana State Public Service Commission, which she tried to discourage him from doing since, she said, it incurred the wrath of her superiors.

For the cool and seemingly unflappable Gipp, who rarely if ever showed any emotion on or off the field, Trippeer's elusiveness was both puzzling and upsetting. Matters took a turn for the worse on March 8, when Father James Burns, the new Notre Dame president, wrote a letter to Gipp—who for some reason had gone home to Laurium—informing him he had been expelled. The letter, which began with "Dear Sir," read: "Due to the fact that you have been found to not be attending classes on a regular basis, or taking the final exams in your chosen major, it is the decision of this office to expel you from this university as of this date." Burns went on to say that if "in some time in the future" Gipp wanted to return to Notre Dame, his application would be considered. That it had taken Notre Dame almost four years to realize Gipp rarely had gone to class seemed odd. His professors certainly were aware of his chronic absenteeism, and so was Rockne. Some administration sources said the last straw came when word got back to the administration that Gipp had been seen patronizing a South Bend dance hall, which had been declared off-limits to Notre Dame students, apparently because the dance hall's hostesses tended to be more than just dance partners.

Burns's action was taken around the time Notre Dame was to begin spring football practice. As a result of Gipp's expulsion, the team no longer had a captain. Rockne filled that void by appointing Frank Coughlin, whom Gipp had beaten out for the captaincy by one vote at the team's post-season dinner three months earlier.

When he returned to South Bend, Gipp promptly moved out of Sorin Hall, where he hadn't spent much time to begin with, and into his room at the Hotel Oliver, while spending more time at Hullie and Mike's and continuing to write to Iris Trippeer. As word of Gipp's expulsion spread, the college football vultures went to work. Maybe Notre Dame no longer wanted one of the country's best halfbacks, but a lot of schools did. Gipp had barely finished Father Burns's letter when he began to receive scholarship offers—some of which included financial inducements—from such major football powers as Michigan, Pittsburgh, Detroit (now the University of Detroit Mercy), and West Point. In the latter case, Gipp received a letter from the head of the West Point Athletic Association saying he had been "recommended for appointment to the United States Military Academy," whose superintendent, ardent football fan General Douglas MacArthur, was reportedly the one who did the recommending. Apparently neither West Point nor any of the other schools trying to capitalize on Gipp's expulsion asked to look at his weak academic transcript and his attendance record at Notre Dame. Given the zeitgeist of the big-time college football world during the era, that was hardly surprising. Much like today, many of the country's college football powers cared far more about a player's playing statistics than his academic ones.

Gipp's expulsion was hardly undeserved considering how he had gone through two academic years without receiving any grades and had failed to take final examinations in any of his classes. Enrolled as a law student during his fourth academic year, Gipp had continued along the same truant path, rarely showing up for classes. Though Father Burns was well aware of Gipp's poor academic record, he did not take action until several of Gipp's professors complained to him about Gipp's absenteeism and failure to do assigned class work and to take examinations.

Very likely at Rockne's suggestion, a group of about eighty businessmen and civic leaders in South Bend signed a petition urging that Gipp be reinstated and sent it to Father Burns. The petition was hard to ignore since many of those who signed it had pledged support for the proposed expansion of Cartier Field and also supported Notre Dame's fund-raising program. "Increasingly, South Bend is taking pride in the splendid accomplishments of Notre Dame," the petition read. "The most spectacular of these are, of course, your victories upon the athletic field. Here George Gipp has been truly worthy of the University." Rockne also was to say that, at his request, Gipp was given a closed-door examination by several of his law professors, which ostensibly covered subjects he was taking, and passed with flying colors, and it was understood that he would complete a term paper by the start of the fall semester in September 1920. Such a deal seems highly unlikely, however, since it would smack of favoritism toward someone, his football talents notwithstanding, who hardly seemed to deserve such special treatment. And he was unlikely to get it from Father Burns, who, although a former Notre Dame baseball player, was a staunch disciplinarian, far more concerned with the university's academic reputation than its performance in sports. If his predecessor, John Cavanaugh, had wanted to turn Notre Dame into the "Yale of the West," Father Burns had taken that academic goal even further, saying, on his installation, that he wanted to see the school become the Yale, Harvard, and Princeton of the country's midland. Furthermore, giving a private test to an individual student by a panel of professors was not part of university policy. Yet Rockne insisted, in dramatic and hyperbolic fashion, that that's exactly what happened after Gipp asked him if he could take an oral examination to get re-admitted.

"Gipp claimed to have been ill and he got it on that account," Rockne was to write in one of a series of articles he wrote for *Collier's* magazine in 1930. "Gipp went into that examination room with the whole school and the whole city waiting on the outcome. Some of his inquisitors were no football fans. They were prepared to stop his scholastic run with tough tackling questions and blocking from the books. His professors knew that Gipp was not a diligent student. But he astonished everybody by what he knew when it came to cross-examination. He passed back into school, and there was general rejoicing. Not, however, by Gipp. Calmly, as usual, he accepted victory; but it was observed that he was once more irregular in attending class."

Rockne swore by that version. But more likely it was because of the pressure put on the administration by the South Bend petitioners that Father Burns yielded and Gipp was re-admitted as a student on March 29. In a letter to Gipp, addressed to his home in Laurium, where he had returned, Father Burns informed Gipp of his reinstatement. "It is my hope that you will take your obligations as a student in the law department seriously. And that you will attend classes on a regular basis, take exams given, and graduate with your degree."

It is entirely possible that Rockne had an influential hand in Gipp's reinstatement by letting Burns know that a number of major football powers, including a Catholic college, the University of Detroit, were trying to recruit Gipp, and reminding Burns how much he meant to the football team and the national attention its success drew to Notre Dame. Unfortunately, neither Rockne's apparent efforts to get his meal-ticket halfback reinstated nor a personal letter from the university president to Gipp seemed to have had an impact on the school's most famous athlete. As it developed, Gipp skipped more classes than he attended during the last two months of the spring semester, and again failed to complete his assignments or take any final examinations, even though some students claimed that they had seen Rockne accompany Gipp to campus in his car from the Hotel Oliver on some mornings, ostensibly so that he would attend classes.

Several days after his reinstatement, Gipp turned out again for the varsity baseball team, much to the delight of Gus Dorais, who was also the baseball coach. Hunk Anderson told of how scouts from the Chicago Cubs and the Chicago White Sox came to Notre Dame to see Gipp during a preseason intrasquad game. Aware of the scouts' presence, Gipp asked Anderson, who was catching for the other team, if he could tell him what the pitchers were going to throw to him, and Anderson agreed to do so. Gipp proceeded to belt about a half-dozen pitches over the fence, whereupon after practice the scouts both offered Gipp contracts for around $5,000 (about $50,000 by the second decade of the twenty-first century). Gipp took the contracts, but did not sign them, telling the scouts he wanted to think about the offers.

In his first game nine days after his reinstatement, on April 8 against Michigan Agricultural College, Gipp clouted a home run and walked with the bases loaded in the bottom of the tenth inning to bring home the winning run. Gipp played in Notre Dame's next two games, but then quit the team. Once again in baseball, as in varsity basketball, Gipp did not stick around long enough to get a monogram, though he had been a starting outfielder in three games. And again Gipp did not give a reason for quitting. Such formalities, it seemed, were not deemed necessary by the free-spirited Gipp, who may still have been smarting from his expulsion in March.

Even after the spring semester had ended, Gipp apparently continued to resent his expulsion, feeling that Notre Dame had not treated him fairly, especially in light of the attention he had helped bring to the school. His resentment grew to the point that during the late summer of 1920 he accepted invitations to visit both the University of Michigan in Ann Arbor and the University of Detroit, and for a while he was conflicted as to which one he favored. Pete Bahan, his fellow halfback on the football team and one of his few close friends on campus, had enrolled at Detroit for the following academic year after being expelled from Notre Dame for academic reasons. That Bahan had captained both the 1918 and 1919 Notre Dame teams showed how strict President Burns was about athletes' class attendance and their academic performances, as Gipp had learned first hand himself.

Given the virtually non existent eligibility rules that allowed football players to play as many as eight seasons at two schools, Bahan had been recruited by Detroit even though he had played three varsity seasons at Notre Dame, the maximum allowed at the time, at least for Notre Dame. He would play one additional year for Detroit and another at St. Mary's in California under Slip Madigan, the coach of the Galloping Gaels, with whom he had played at Notre Dame. Bahan, a very good runner, also captained St. Mary's in 1921, meaning he had been a football captain at two universities and had played five varsity seasons. So much for any interlocking eligibility rules.

In June, Gipp, along with Bahan, also a very good baseball player, was recruited to work and play baseball for a Buick plant in Flint, Michigan, which had several teams in a strong league consisting of a number of area factories whose level of play was close to that of a Triple-A circuit in the minor leagues. The "work" was hardly strenuous, essentially requiring Gipp and Bahan to do little more than show up at the plant each morning, according to Bahan, although Gipp would indicate to his paramour, Iris Trippeer, that it was arduous. Once again, Gipp had an excellent season, batting close to .400 while playing two games a week for the Buick team and a third game on Sundays in a General Motors league, and attracting the interest of a number of scouts. Before one home game in Flint, at the Buick team management's request, Gipp put on a drop-kicking exhibition, booting several balls more than 50 yards over the outfield fence. On another occasion, Gipp showed his dancing prowess at a Flint amusement park, winning a dancing contest (along with a gold watch) with a young woman he had met at the contest.

For Gipp, his partner was just that, a dancing partner. His one and only romantic interest remained Iris Trippeer, whom he got to see only once during the summer of 1920 when he took a train to Indianapolis, where he spent two days with the woman with whom he now was totally smitten. Meanwhile, Gipp wrote to Trippeer often, referring to her as his "little sweetheart," "honey," and "Iris of mine," while signing off as "yours only" and "always yours." In a letter dated August 27, 1920, Gipp wrote of "the sunny happy days we had together," and added "some day we'll have them all again forever this time and not just for a few sweet hours." Reflecting the influence his relationship with Trippeer had had on him, Gipp also wrote, "I've conquered every little habit, honey, and then, honey, you'll never have to doubt any more." Whether "every little habit" referred to his pool and poker playing, he never did say. Rockne, for one, would most certainly have hoped so.

In a letter a week earlier, Gipp told Trippeer about a bad cold and a routine that included "work, play ball, and then go to bed." Gipp went on to report he had received a letter from the University of Detroit, which, he said, was "going to send a man down to see me. Guess I won't stagger him a little when I tell him the price." That comment indicated that Detroit, like Michigan, was willing to pay Gipp for his services on the football field, not an uncommon lure at the time. In a curiously worded last sentence in the August 21 letter, Gipp wrote, "Iris dear I'm sorry but some day you'll know that I didn't mean any of the things that bring regrets to you."

Meanwhile, Gipp drew rave reviews in the *Flint Journal* for his play. In one story, sportswriter Harry Dayton called Gipp the best baseball player ever to play in the city. That was saying a lot, since the factory leagues included former major and minor league players, including Kiki Cuyler, who went on to an eighteen-year Hall of Fame career as an outfielder with the Pittsburgh Pirates, Cincinnati Reds, Chicago Cubs, and Brooklyn Dodgers. One of the Buick team's players, Joe Collard, raved about Gipp as a teammate: "George was a most likeable fellow, always smiling, very good-natured, and humorous. He was very deceptive in his movements, giving you the impression of not trying, but he had such fine coordination that he always seemed to do the job, getting under fly balls or stealing a base with nothing to spare."

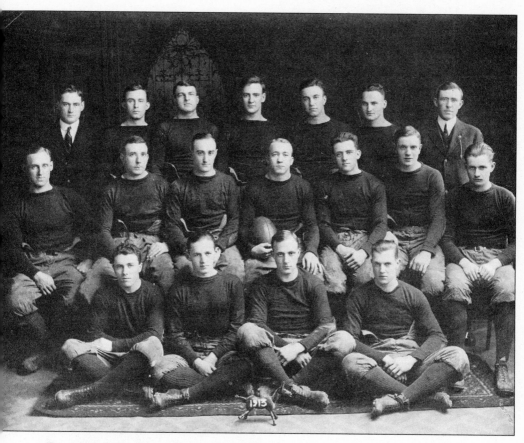

The 1913 Notre Dame team, with Captain Knute Rockne holding the football.

Knute Rockne, as a starting end for Notre Dame in 1913.

A middle-age-looking Knute Rockne as the 25-year-old captain of the undefeated Notre Dame 1913 football team.

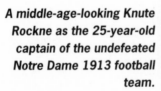

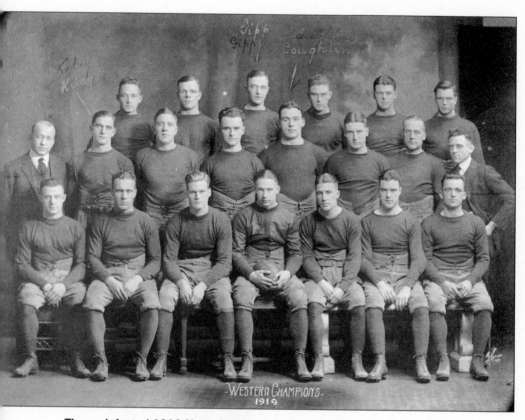

The undefeated 1919 Notre Dame team. George Gipp is third from left, top row.

George Gipp, who did it all — run, pass, punt, and drop-kick field goals and extra points.

George Gipp attempting a punt.

George Gipp carrying the ball during a game in 1919.

Gipp kneeling on the sidelines during a game in 1919.

George Gipp before a practice in 1919.

Outfielder George Gipp, top row right, with the 1920 Notre Dame Varsity baseball team.

Hunk Anderson, George Gipp's high school friend whom he convinced Rockne to give a scholarship to and who wound up as a star lineman at Notre Dame and with the Chicago Bears and head coach of both teams. Anderson, who succeeded Rockne as coach, is a member of the College Football Hall of Fame.

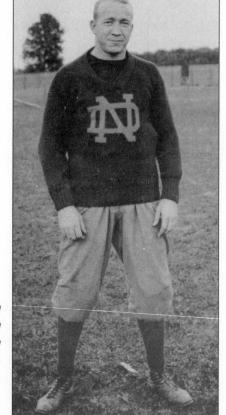

Knute Rockne before a practice session in the early 1920s.

Knute Rockne with his staff in the late 1920s. Former Notre Dame lineman and Rockne's eventual successor, Hunk Anderson, is on Rockne's right.

Knute Rockne admonishing his players during a practice session in 1921.

Knute Rockne before leaving on a trip with his Notre Dame team in 1920.

Knute Rockne delivering one of his patented pep talks before a Notre Dame game.

**Rockne with a special visitor to Notre Dame practice, the great Babe
Ruth of the New York Yankees.**

Fullback Elmer Oliphant played four years each of varsity football at both Purdue and Army, winning All American honors in basketball at both schools and named an All American in football at Army. Oliphant also starred in baseball, track, and swimming at the two schools.

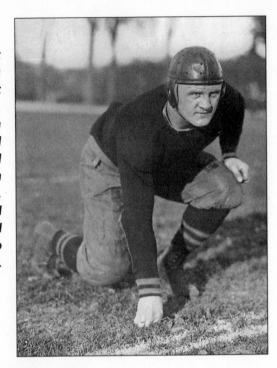

Halfback Chris Cagle played three years of football at Southwestern Louisiana and four years at Army, where he was an All American.

Halfback Harry "Lighthorse" Wilson played three years of football at Penn State and then four years at Army where he earned All American honors.

Elmer Layden, the 160-pound fullback for the fabled "Four Horsemen" who later became head coach at Notre Dame, attempts a punt.

The Notre Dame backfield immortalized by famed sportswriter Grantland Rice as "the Four Horsemen."

Rockne regarded Frank Carideo, Notre Dame's starting quarterback in 1929 and 1930, as the best quarterback he ever had.

Fullback Joe Savoldi in 1930.

Another story in the *Flint Journal* said that the legendary Jim Thorpe, the owner and star of the Canton Bulldogs of the fledging National Football League, had offered Gipp $200 a game to play for Canton, an offer Gipp apparently declined. If he was going to play professionally, it was going to be baseball for the Cubs or White Sox, and for more than $200 a week—but not until he was finished playing football at Notre Dame.

While at home, Gipp, bothered by a sore throat and shortness of breath, visited a doctor in Calumet, A. C. Roche, who told him that his tonsils were severely infected and should be removed. During his examination, Dr. Roche found that Gipp's blood pressure was very high—180 over 110—and deduced that Gipp's shortness of breath stemmed from possible rheumatic fever that he may have had as a child, but had not been detected. Despite the doctor's advice that he have his tonsils removed, a simple procedure for young people even during the early part of the twentieth century, Gipp declined the operation, explaining to Roche that he already was late for preseason practice and felt that a tonsillectomy would delay him further.

A few days later, in mid-September, Gipp boarded a train for South Bend to begin his fifth year at Notre Dame. Once again, Gipp's whereabouts became cloudy. One version is that he checked into a single room in the basement of Sorin Hall, while another had him move into Rockne's house for a while because he had very little money. Wherever he was staying, Gipp was notified on September 16 that he had been put on probation for failing to take final examinations at the end of the spring semester after he had been reinstated. Gipp immediately left campus to return home, thanks to a twenty-dollar loan from

Hunk Anderson at a time when Gipp was uncharacteristically short on cash after a losing streak at the poker tables. Eleven days later, for reasons never made clear, Gipp was reinstated, five days before Notre Dame's opening game against Kalamazoo. Again, Rockne's persuasiveness apparently had convinced Father Burns that with Gipp in the lineup Notre Dame had an excellent chance of going unbeaten and being declared the national champion—thus gaining the school immeasurable publicity and no doubt hundreds, if not thousands, of new applicants for the 1921–22 academic year. As it was, Gipp's academic troubles were getting Notre Dame the kind of publicity it did not want, although it did show that, unlike many other big-time football schools it would not tolerate lax academic behavior, even by a star athlete.

At any rate, Gipp finally agreed to return to Notre Dame in late September, only a few days before the game against Kalamazoo. It would be an unforgettable season, marked by glorious accomplishments and unimaginable sadness.

13

HEARTBREAK IN INDIANAPOLIS

BY THE FALL of 1920, when George Gipp was re-admitted to Notre Dame for the second time in six months, the country had undergone a number of major changes. Though jobs were still scarce, the United States had become the world's major economic power after Europe's long domination of the world economy had ended. South Bend, the home of several major defense manufacturers during the World War I, continued to thrive in the war's aftermath. The Studebaker plant in South Bend, which had produced trucks and personnel carriers for the Army during the war, now was turning out automobiles and trucks, while the Singer Sewing Machine Co. and other local factories quickly made the transition to peacetime manufacturing. As a result, more and more immigrants, mainly from Eastern Europe, found their way into the city seeking jobs at those plants.

Socially, too, the country had changed considerably. In addition to earning the right to vote, many women had shed many long-standing inhibitions by taking up smoking cigarettes, and, to the horror of the Women's Christian Temperance Union—a major force in the enactment of the Prohibition Amendment—drinking more than ever in the thousands of speakeasies that had sprung up in town after Indiana enacted its own prohibition law two years prior. As it was, it soon became apparent that the illegality of alcohol consumption had made it more alluring to many people, especially women who found it adventurous to circumvent what came to be called America's "noble experiment." Indeed, the empowerment of women as voters and the lure of alcohol marked the beginning of an era of "gin and jazz." And if women were shedding inhibitions, they were shedding even more on the stage, such as in the popular Ziegfeld Follies, begun by show business entrepreneur Florenz Ziegfeld, whose Broadway revues featured scantily clad chorus girls and dancers.

The year also marked the beginning of the so-called "Roaring Twenties," an era made for a handsome, young, and famous football star like George Gipp, who loved the lights of nights and more than an occasional drink, legal or illegal, as much, it seemed, as he did running for a touchdown or hitting a 400-foot home run. As word spread, albeit slowly, of Gipp's double life as a star halfback and skilled high-stakes billiards and poker player, his defiance of conventionality made him even more popular with much of the American public, both men and women, who felt that his aloofness and quest for privacy made him all the more attractive.

⚜

By 1920, Notre Dame had also become much more attractive. Where the university enrollment was only 700 at the start of World War I in 1917, it had grown four years later to a school of 1,821 students and 81 professors. And where as few as thirty-five players would turn out for varsity football before the war, more than fifty were on hand for the start of preseason practice in September 1920. With nine returning starters and a strong nucleus of past monogram winners and former freshman players, Notre Dame entered the 1920 football season more heralded than any other Notre Dame squad had ever been. The biggest loss had been that of Dutch Bergman, the fleet halfback and a three-year starter who had spent two years in the Army during the Great War and whose place would be taken by Norm Barry, a three-year letter-winner. As a student, Barry was a Notre Dame "lifer" who had been a minim, a prep, and a university student, all on the Notre Dame campus. Barry then went on to play for the Chicago Bears, the Chicago Cardinals, and the Green Bay Packers of the NFL, and in 1925 coached the Cardinals to the NFL title, all while attending law school.

Also gone from the 1919 team was left end Bernie Kirk, Gipp's favorite passing target, who had transferred to Michigan, where no doubt Fielding Yost had made Kirk an offer he found impossible to refuse. Rockne, who hadn't liked Yost to begin with, believing that he harbored anti-Catholic sentiments, never forgave Yost for luring Kirk to Ann Arbor, and most likely having tried to recruit Gipp away from Notre Dame, too. Rockne also felt, perhaps justifiably (as he would for years) that Yost, Bob Zuppke, and Amos Alonzo Stagg had conspired to keep Notre Dame out of the Big Ten Conference on the grounds that it recruited ineligible players and then subsidized them, which to a degree was true. But Yost, Pop Warner, Zuppke, Stagg, Jock Sutherland of Lafayette (and then Pittsburgh, where he would replace Warner in 1924) and a number of other well-known coaches were believed to have done the same, if not worse; in Rockne, they were up against one of their own. As professor Murray Sperber wrote in his voluminous and illuminating book about Notre Dame, *Shake Down the Thunder*, Rockne's "'ruthless side' allowed him to prosper in a very corrupt and cutthroat world—college coaching." Sperber went on to say that the Notre Dame coach "learned to swim with sharks, including Pop Warner, and not bleed."

⚭⚭⚭

By midseason, Gipp would almost be as famous as America's biggest sports icons—Heavyweight Champ Jack Dempsey, and Babe Ruth, who, in his first year with the New York Yankees in 1920, had hit an astonishing 54 home runs to break his own record of 29 set the previous season with the Boston Red Sox. Even thought he had been reinstated shortly before the season began, Gipp, now twenty-five but looking much older, had taken a single basement room at Sorin Hall on campus and had again signed up for six law courses. Keeping a promise he had made to Iris Trippeer, who had told him she was concerned about his post-football future, Gipp attended classes on a fairly regular basis at the start of the academic year, and would spend more time on campus during the fall semester than he had in the past. However, Gipp still kept his room at the Hotel Oliver, where he now received free lodging in exchange for being the hotel's "house man" in billiards, meaning that at any billiards competition in South Bend or elsewhere, he would represent the hotel. It hardly seemed like an arrangement conducive to attending six law courses on campus, and Rockne and Notre Dame officials could not help but know this. They read the South Bend papers, where Gipp's name cropped up for playing pocket or three-cushion billiards almost as often as for his derring-do on the football field. But so long as he showed up for most of his classes, no one seemed overly concerned, even though neither Rockne nor Father Burns liked the thought of the school's most famous student being a high-stakes pool shark and poker whiz. No longer would Rockne occasionally venture into South Bend some mornings to get Gipp out of bed at the Oliver and accompany him to campus in Rockne's car so that his star running back would remain eligible to play.

In large measure because of Gipp's growing fame, Cartier Field had been expanded by 3,000 seats to bring the capacity to 8,000, which was relatively large for the era, even at a school that now had a national reputation in football. While Notre Dame students could still attend home games for 50 cents, outsiders paid $1 for general admission seats, $1.50 for reserve seats, and $3 for box seats. College football games on the high level that the Fighting Irish had now reached were a far cry from 1913, when Notre Dame had upset Army at West Point. With almost every team using the pass more often as an offensive weapon, the game was now far more open, college bands played before and during games, and cheerleaders performed acrobatic feats, albeit not as spectacular as today, on the sidelines. Those features, along with the festive atmosphere that prevailed on crisp fall afternoons, made big-time college football a major pastime, rivaling base-ball and horse racing, which along with boxing were the country's most popular sports for media and spectator attention on Saturday afternoons.

Given his heavy schedule, Gipp rarely got to see Iris Trippeer during the 1920 football season, although she did come to several of Notre Dame's home games, sitting with Rockne's wife, Bonnie, and spending Friday and Saturday nights at the Rockne's home, according to Trippeer's granddaughter, Veronica Adams Phair. However, a somewhat cryptic letter he wrote to Trippeer on September 24 of 1920 indicated he had gone to Indianapolis to see her, and, strangely enough, while in the Indiana capital had written to her. In a letter whose envelope bore an Indianapolis postmark, Gipp wrote, "Iris, I didn't know that he knew that I had been told or I certainly wouldn't have stayed last night, but I thought that I was supposed to be ignorant so just had to stay. Guess I was dumb alright. Wish that I had known that last night. Thought of coming out to-day because it might have helped matters, but was afraid of pulling a 'boot.'"

Gipp did not say who the "he" alluded to in the letter was, but it may have been Trippeer's father, who still did not want to have his daughter seeing a college football player, no matter how famous he was becoming. Later in the letter, Gipp perhaps indicated that another romantic interest may have come into her life when he wrote, "Some day the happiness that is due you shall come. I know it will Iris because you deserve it. The average has to be even some day so think of all the happy days that must come to balance the dark ones." That sounded ominous, but then in the same letter Gipp suggested that the romance might still be on when he said, "Would have liked to have talked to you today but I'll call you tomorrow from S. Bend. Good-bye dear and keep the proud little chin up as the champion should." Gipp then closed with "Always yours, George." So far as is known it was the last letter Gipp ever wrote to the love of his life.

⤜⟡⤏

One of the additions to the 1920 Notre Dame team was an unlikely one—twenty-eight-year-old Chet Grant, a 135-pound quarterback and all-around athlete who had spent two years as a lieutenant in the Army and who would back up Joe Brandy. Grant had been a sportswriter for the *South Bend Tribune* and a semi-pro quarterback when Jesse Harper recruited him in 1915 at twenty-three, even older than Rockne and Gipp when they entered Notre Dame in their early twenties. After World War I, he returned to the *South Bend Tribune* as a reporter for a year before re-enrolling at Notre Dame in the fall of 1920.

Bright, quick-witted, and an elusive runner, Grant had worked as a part-time sportswriter with the *Tribune* at night while playing on the freshman football team in 1915 and the 1916 varsity football, basketball, and track teams. In addition to returning to Notre Dame in 1920, Grant resumed his reporter's job at the *Tribune*, where he covered Marion County Courthouse, usually before attending classes and then practices. How he managed to do it no one seemed to recall, including Grant. To say the least, that combination, along with his relatively advanced college age, made him a most unusual student-athlete, who would finish his football career at the age of twenty-nine in 1921, when he would be the starting quarterback for the Fighting Irish, and later would serve as an assistant coach under Rockne and Elmer Layden.

In 1946 and 1947, immediately after World War II, Grant managed the South Bend Blue Sox, one of the teams in the All-American Girls Professional Baseball League, which became the subject of the popular 1992 film *A League of Their Own*. Then, in 1948, Grant managed the Kenosha, Wisconsin, team on the same circuit. (The league was organized in 1944 as an alternative to baseball's watered-down major leagues, all of whose teams had lost most of their starting players to the military, and did surprisingly well before going out of business following the 1954 season.) Later, Grant became the curator of the International Sports and Games Research Collection in the Hesburgh Library at Notre Dame—named for Father Theodore Hesburgh, perhaps the university's most liberal president when he served from 1952 to 1987—where Grant worked into his late eighties.

Of Gipp as a teammate, Grant said, "He was a man of great poise and intelligence, a glamorous figure and a gentleman, but also a quiet, private person." That was quite a tribute, since Grant admitted that he did not particularly like Gipp, apparently because of his indifference to practice sessions and classwork, which in those respects made him the antithesis of Grant.

With Gipp eligible to play once again, Arch Ward, a sportswriter for the *South Bend Tribune* and recent Notre Dame graduate who would go onto become a nationally known columnist for the *Chicago Tribune*, wrote in advance of the opening game, "Notre Dame fandom is fizzing and foaming like an uncorked bottle of pop in anticipation of another glorious gridiron campaign." Hyperbolic writing? Yes, but typical of the gee-whiz school of sportswriting of the era. That Gipp had broken an untold number of rules at Notre Dame and at best had been an occasional student during his second and third years mattered not at all to most of the student body, alumni (both actual and "subway") and South Benders who had vested interests in Notre Dame's success, both academically and in sports.

For the third time in four years, Notre Dame's opening day opponent was Kalamazoo, which had not scored at all in the first two meetings. The largest crowd ever to see an opening-day Notre Dame game—about 5,000 spectators—turned out on a mild day for a three o'clock start. On hand, too, was Rockne's favorite and handpicked referee, Walter Eckersall, who would once more be doing double duty by both officiating and covering the game for the *Chicago Tribune*. Again, Kalamazoo offered little resistance as Notre Dame routed the visitors 39–0 (in six contests between 1917 and 1923, Notre Dame outscored Kalamazoo by a combined score of 284–0), allowing Rockne the opportunity to give ample playing time to the second team—his so-called "shock troops," who were probably better than many starting college teams.

Though he played little more than half of the game, Gipp ran 16 times for 183 yards, an average of more than 11 yards a carry. The game marked the debut of Roger Kiley, who would turn out to be an outstanding end. Early in the game, Gipp launched a long pass to Kiley, which he dropped. "I felt like running right out of Cartier Field and all the way home to Chicago," Kiley said more than a half century later. "The great George Gipp throws me a pass for the first time, and I drop it. When I went back into the huddle, George didn't say a word to me, but told

Joe Brandy, the quarterback, to call the same play, and he did, and this time I caught the pass and a couple of others during the game. After the game George asked me to come early to a practice the following week so we could get better acquainted. That's the way he was, whether you were a veteran player and a new guy like I was."

Another rout followed the next Saturday on an unseasonably warm afternoon at Cartier Field when Western Michigan was crushed, 41–0, with Gipp gaining 123 yards on only 14 carries (nearly a 9-yard average). A week later, though, Notre Dame found itself in an underdog role against a strong Nebraska team in Lincoln. But even though Gipp had a sub-par game by his standards, gaining just 70 yards on 15 carries and completing only 6 of 20 passes, the Irish prevailed on a rainy Saturday afternoon, 16–7. After the game, Nebraska's All-American tackle Clarence Swanson said Gipp was the best all-around back that he had ever played against.

Returning home to play before the largest crowd ever to watch at Notre Dame home game—around 7,000—Notre Dame had to come from behind in the second half to turn back a much heavier intrastate opponent, Valparaiso, 28–3. In that game, Rockne did something extraordinarily rare—and which he would often do in future seasons—starting his outstanding second unit, which played the entire first quarter and most of the second period as Valparaiso took a 3–0 halftime lead. To Rockne's way of thinking, this enabled his starters to look for weaknesses and strengths in their opponents and also let the shock troops soften up the opposition for the regulars. With the first unit playing the entire second half, the Irish, again led by Gipp's passing and running, scored 28 unanswered points, 14 of them on two touchdowns by Gipp and two drop-kicked extra-points. On his first touchdown run, Gipp electrified the crowd when he burst off left tackle and carried four would-be tacklers into the end zone. He was equally dazzling on his second touchdown when, dodging and twisting, he literally eluded the entire Valparaiso defense during a 39-yard scoring run.

Good as that performance was, it actually amounted to a warm-up for the Army game the following Saturday at West Point, when George Gipp would play the greatest game of his life against an undefeated Army team, which had given up only two touchdowns through their first five games, one more than Notre Dame had yielded in four. Army's opposition, though, had been the weakest it had been in years—Union, Marshall, Middlebury, Springfield, and Tufts. None of those opponents were in the class of Nebraska, which Notre Dame had beaten, or Syracuse, Boston College, and other such strong teams the Cadets had played in the past. The softer schedule was not of Army's choice, but was the result of more and more major football powers opting not to play the Cadets due to their inclination to use outstanding players who had played elsewhere for years.

After a twenty-two-hour train trip, a Notre Dame squad of twenty-three players arrived at West Point in late morning on Friday, October 29, and held a brief workout. The next morning, by pre-arrangement, Hunk Anderson once again met with the manager of the Army team for breakfast, after which each of them gave an off-campus shoemaker about $2,000 to hold as a winner-take-all pot.

In their advance stories, many sportswriters played up the head-to-head meeting between Gipp and Army's star running back, Walter French. Like Elmer Oliphant before him, French, only five feet seven inches tall and weighing around 155 pounds, had been an All-American at another school before coming to West Point. In French's case, it was at Rutgers University, where he had won letters in football, basketball, and baseball. That Army still recruited such stars after they had played as many as four years at other schools made it increasingly difficult for the Cadets to book top-flight opponents, who felt that using such experienced players gave Army a huge advantage. That did not seem to matter to Notre Dame, which was still having difficulty booking games against football powers in the Midwest and, of course, found that playing Army had attracted national publicity to the university.

A capacity crowd of about 10,000, including about 500 Notre Dame fans, packed the bleachers at West Point's Cullum Field—Michie Stadium would not open until 1924—on a gray and chilly afternoon. Also on hand were sportswriters from major newspapers in the Northeast, and as far west as Chicago, including two of the country's most famous writers, Grantland Rice and Ring Lardner, once a sportswriter for the *South Bend Tribune* but by 1920 a celebrated writer for the *Chicago Tribune*. Lardner would achieve his greatest acclaim as a short-story writer, but also had a passion for Notre Dame football. Asked in advance of the Army game what Notre Dame's strategy should be, Lardner had a succinct answer: "Give the ball to Gipp and let him decide what to do." Before the game, Gipp gave Rice, Lardner, the other writers, and the crowd a portent of what was to come when, while practicing drop-kick field goals, he went to midfield with four footballs. As he had done before a few other Notre Dame games, Gipp then turned toward one goal post and calmly drop-kicked two balls through the uprights. He then turned to face the other goal post and nonchalantly did the same with the other two balls as the West Point cadets and others in the crowd cheered.

To paraphrase the great entertainer of the era, Al Jolson, they hadn't seen anything yet.

As expected, Gipp and French were the central figures in the game. Both teams scored two touchdowns in the opening half, and their star running backs were largely responsible for both. A 40-yard run by French was the key play that led to the game's first touchdown by the Cadets, while Gipp ran back the ensuing kickoff 38 yards and then gained another 23 yards rushing and 25 yards on a pass to end Roger Kiley as Notre Dame tied it at 7–7 on a 5-yard run by halfback Johnny Mohardt. A 57-yard punt return by Gipp, followed by a 38-yard touchdown pass to Kiley and Gipp's second drop-kicked extra point gave the Fighting Irish a 14–7 lead early in the second quarter.

Shortly thereafter, the diminutive French caught a Gipp punt, raced 60 yards for a touchdown, and kicked his second extra point to tie the game at 14. Just before the end of the half, the redoubtable French booted a 15-yard field goal to give Army a 17–14 lead in a game that had lived up to all expectations, particularly the brilliant play of Gipp and French. The Army lead could have been even larger as a result of a Gipp gamble that failed late in the half. With the ball inside the Notre Dame 10-yard line on fourth down, quarterback Joe Brandy called for

Gipp to punt. But Gipp had other ideas, knowing that Army, expecting a punt, would be vulnerable to a pass, even a long pass. He then told left end Roger Kiley, but not Brandy or anyone else, "When I get the ball, you tear down the left side, and I'll pass it."

In punt formation on the Notre Dame goal line, Gipp took the snap from center, and instead of punting, did indeed fire a 45-yard pass to a wide-open Kiley, who, for what is believed to be the only time in his distinguished career, dropped the ball. "That was gambling, absolute gambling," Rockne was to say, "and proved to me that Gipp was a gambler."

That remark indicated that Rockne was guilty of naivete or was speaking with tongue in cheek. In fact it wasn't until after Gipp had played his last game that Rockne said he had belatedly learned that Gipp was indeed a gambler. That, almost everyone agreed, was hard to believe since the coach was anything but naive.

Fortunately for Notre Dame, Gipp's unsuccessful gamble did not cost it, since Army was unable to capitalize on its excellent field position after the incomplete pass and had to be content with a 17–14 halftime lead.

As the players left the field for the halftime break, Rice turned to Lardner and said of Gipp, "He's really something special." Whereupon Lardner, who had watched Gipp play often, replied, "I think he's just getting started."

In the Notre Dame locker room, Rockne proceeded to give what Hunk Anderson would say many years later was one of his best halftime pep talks. Before a game, a Rockne pep talk often would include such rallying calls as "Go get 'em. Hit 'em and knock 'em down. Then hit 'em again. Then knock 'em down and make 'em stay down!" At halftime, though, Rockne tended to be caustically critical of individual players whom he felt had either made crucial mistakes or were not going all-out in their blocking and tackling, which to Rockne were far and away the most important aspects of football. As he spoke during halftime of the 1920 Army game, Rockne, still fuming from Gipp's pass from the Notre Dame goal line late in the half, spotted his star left halfback in a corner puffing on a cigarette. "And you there, Gipp," he said in a voice dripping with sarcasm, "I guess you don't have any interest in this game."

"Look, Rock, I've got 400 bucks bet on this game, and I'm not about to blow it," Gipp replied, evoking laughter from his teammates and even a grin from Rockne.

Ring Lardner was right—Gipp was even better in the second half, when he more than atoned for the ill-advised pass to Kiley, slashing through and around the bigger Army line and completing all three passes he threw. Following a scoreless third quarter, Notre Dame took a 21–17 lead early in the final period when a 10-yard run by Mohardt punctuated a touchdown drive highlighted by Gipp's dazzling running.

On its next possession, Gipp ran back a French punt 40 yards to the Notre Dame 47. Gipp then connected on passes to Kiley and captain Frank Coughlin to put the ball on the Army 8-yard line, from where fullback Chet Wynne scored the game's final touchdown, making the score 27–17. With less than three minutes left and a Notre Dame victory virtually assured, Rockne took out Gipp, who by then had gained 150 yards rushing on 20 carries (an average of 7.5 yards) and completed 5 of 9 passes for

123 yards, a total of 273 yards. In addition, Gipp had run back punts and kickoffs for 112 yards to give him an overall offensive total of a remarkable 375 yards, and had played brilliantly on defense. Indeed, Knute Rockne was to say years later that Gipps was also a "master of defense."

"I can say of him what cannot, I believe, be said of any other football player—that not a single forward pass was ever completed in territory defended by George Gipp," Rockne said in praise of his star's defensive play.

Many years later, Roger Kiley, by then an eighty-five-year-old federal judge in Chicago, vividly remembered the crowd's reaction as Gipp headed toward the Notre Dame bench near the end of the Army game. "I have never seen an athlete get the acclamation George received when he walked off the field that day," Kiley said. "He was tired and pale, and his face was a little bloody, and the crowd at West Point stood up although nobody applauded. It was thrilling. Awed silence."

After the game, Gipp was showered with plaudits by Army players and from sportswriters. "Gipp just would not be stopped," Army end Donald Storck said. "Whatever he did, it was with little effort, but with grace and agility. His long-legged gallops through our line were as difficult to stop as might be those of an antelope in an open field. His long strides made his deceptive speed difficult to time, with the result that most of the time we were tackling air."

The writer for *The New York Times* also used an antelope as a metaphor in the lead of his story, which read, "A lithe-limbed Hoosier football player named George Gipp galloped wild through the Army on the plains here this afternoon, giving a performance which was more like an antelope than a human being." The *New York Herald* rhapsodized, "This man Gipp could do everything with a football that there was to be done. He proved an all-round star of the first magnitude. They do not come any better."

The *New York Morning Telegram* story said of Gipp, "All he did for his team was hit with a nice slashing drive that brought many gains, skim the ends in great style, punt beautifully, throw forward passes when they accomplished most, and essay an occasional dropkick."

After dressing, Hunk Anderson hurried over to the shoemaker's shop in nearby Highland Falls to collect $4,200, the total of the team's wager and the money bet by the Army team. Gipp's share alone was $800 (about $8,000 by the second decade of the twenty-first century). Even for the high-stakes poker and billiards player from Michigan's Upper Peninsula, that amounted to a sizable payday.

Considering how he had powered his way through and around the Army defense, Army center Frank Greene said he was stunned upon seeing Gipp later. "Several of us saw Gipp in the shower room after the game and were shocked to see how emaciated he was," Greene said. "He was literally down to skin and bones, and we discussed it later in the squad room."

Were all of the late nights and his overall lifestyle finally catching up to Gipp? His teammates were used to his facial pallor and occasionally gaunt look. But the observations by Greene and his teammates were especially telling.

With Rockne's blessing, Gipp and the rest of the Notre Dame team went out on the town in Manhattan that Saturday night before leaving Sunday morning for South Bend, where the team would be greeted shortly after midnight on Monday by more than 1,000 Notre Dame students and townspeople. Gipp, no lover of crowds, retreated to a rear car of the train, from where he alighted and joined Bonnie Rockne, the coach's wife, who was cradling her baby son on the station platform, to watch the late-night festivities, which included a brief talk by Rockne in which, as usual, he downplayed his own role while crediting the Notre Dame victory entirely to his players, who, of course, knew better.

That same Sunday, sports sections across the country featured the Notre Dame victory and the heroics of Gipp, by then regarded by journalistic giants such as Grantland Rice, Ring Lardner, and Damon Runyon as the best football player in the country, playing for one of the nation's best teams. Further, the victory over Army not only focused more attention on Notre Dame but also boosted the spirits of tens of thousands of Irish Catholics throughout the country—many of whom had never set foot on a college campus but had become enamored of a team and a university with which they now had a common bond. These newfound followers of Notre Dame football would come to be known as the school's "subway alumni," since so many of them were from New York City and travelled by subway to and from Army-Notre Dame games at Yankee Stadium. Indeed, from the Gipp era on Notre Dame's football team would become their team, even if most of them had never been near Indiana. For the most part, that allegiance and rooting interest could be attributed to the team's colorful, innovative coach and its handsome star halfback—both Protestants, no less—and, of course, its nickname. Though he welcomed the backing of the "subway alumni," Father Burns and some faculty and alumni members found the name "Fighting Irish" offensive. Burns also felt that the nickname would mislead many prospective students and their parents into thinking that the university was exclusively Irish and Catholic. While the majority of the roughly 1,500 students were Catholic, the names on the football team's roster showed that only fifteen of the thirty-five players could be classified as "fighting Irishmen." That same proportion had existed since Rockne's days as a player. As the nickname took hold, Burns realized that it was not meant to signify that all of the players were Irish and Catholic and relented in his opposition, aware, too, that "Fighting Irish" was a lot better than Papists, Catholics, or Harps.

❧❧❧

For all of the euphoria across the Notre Dame campus in the aftermath of the latest victory over Army—Notre Dame's third in a row with Gipp in the backfield—the school and the city of South Bend were abuzz over their upcoming first-ever homecoming game, against Purdue, which would draw hundreds of alumni back, including former players such as Louis "Red" Salmon, the star running back from Notre Dame teams of the turn of the century, who, until Gipp, had been regarded as the school's most illustrious football player. The night before the game, almost the entire Notre Dame student body, about 1,500 students, marched to the Hotel Oliver to serenade the Purdue team, who was staying there. Players from both teams spoke at the rally, during which chants of *Gipp! Gipp! Gipp!* were shouted.

Alas, but not surprisingly, Gipp was not on hand for the rally. A few cynics suggested that he might have been inside the hotel, which, of course, was one of his favorite playpens, shooting pool or playing poker for high stakes. In fact, though Gipp still had a room at the hotel, he usually had the good sense to spend nights before home games on campus in his rarely occupied bed in Sorin Hall.

Though bruised and still sore from the pounding he had taken at West Point, Gipp—described in an advance story by Arch Ward in the *South Bend Tribune* as "the Babe Ruth of the gridiron"—put on a dazzling display against Purdue before a standing-room crowd of roughly 12,000, about 4,000 more than the enlarged capacity of Cartier Field. For the second week in a row, Gipp totaled well over 200 yards on offense, rushing 10 times for 129 yards, an average of almost 13 yards a carry, and completing four of seven passes for 128 yards—a grand total of 257 yards—as Notre Dame routed the Boilermakers 28–0. Red Salmon, who had been keeping tabs on Notre Dame players since 1900, said after the game that Gipp was "the greatest player ever to play for the old school."

Purdue players also had high praise for Gipp. "Many times I was sure I had him, but then ended up with empty hands," guard Cecil Cooley said. "I remember looking around after he had evaded me and seeing him going down the field weaving, side-stepping, hesitating, speeding up, and twisting like a young colt that had just got out through an open gate."

By that stage of the season, no other college player in the top tier of college football was producing such glittering offensive statistics, and the Associated Press was by now taking note and carrying stories of his achievements on its newswire to newspapers and radio stations throughout the United States. By then, almost everyone had heard of Gipp's exploits, albeit not at the pool or poker tables. Sportswriters, far more restrained at the time, tended to overglorify famous athletes while divulging hardly anything about their lifestyles, no matter how scandalous, unless it was in a positive vein. (Babe Ruth was a classic example, as was the belligerent racist but great baseball player, Ty Cobb.) Despite his frailties, Gipp was angelic by comparison. Some sportswriters led readers to believe that he was an incarnation of Frank Merriwell, the fictional star all-around athlete at Yale whose exploits were chronicled in magazines, newspapers, and so-called dime novels by the writer Gilbert Patten, who used the pen name Burt L. Standish, aimed at young male readers. The only problem with that analogy was that Merriwell, in Standish's words, "never drank, never smoked, and exercised regularly," in addition to solving mysteries and righting wrongs, all while he was an outstanding student at Yale. Apart from his athletic feats, Gipp, by contrast, was hardly a role model in that he drank, smoked, and gambled, all to excess. The only similarity between the real Gipp and the fictional Merriwell was that both were college athletes.

Notre Dame, which had scored 28 points in each of its one-sided games against Valparaiso and Purdue, was expected to face a far more difficult in-state foe when it met Indiana University in its seventh game of the season in Indianapolis. Since losing its opening game to Iowa, Indiana had beaten four Big Ten rivals—Minnesota, Northwestern, Purdue, and Wisconsin—along with DePauw, by far the toughest schedule any of Notre

Dame's opponents had played. Gipp looked forward to the trip to Indianapolis, since it meant he would see Iris Trippeer again. He had seen her briefly the week before when she went to South Bend to spend part of the homecoming weekend with Gipp. While en route to Indianapolis on Friday afternoon, Gipp told Hunk Anderson he felt a chill and had been coughing a lot. After arriving in Indianapolis and checking into the Claypool Hotel with his teammates, Gipp went out for a walk and found himself besieged by Indiana fans, many of whom recognized him from photos of him in store windows advertising the Notre Dame game. "Wherever Gipp went, he was followed by a host of admirers," Gene Kessler was to write in the next day's *South Bend Tribune*. "Gipp started up Illinois Street, and police thought it was an Indiana parade."

A few hours later, Gipp's sense of elation turned into a devastating sadness. According to Anderson, Gipp met Iris Trippeer on the hotel's mezzanine, their usual rendezvous. It was, Gipp felt, to be a highlight of the trip to see Trippeer, who had accepted his proposal of marriage earlier that fall. As Gipp approached to kiss Trippeer, she turned her head away. Obviously nervous and ill at ease, Trippeer then said, "I've got something to tell you, George. I got married."

"You what?" a stunned Gipp replied. "How could you? And why didn't you tell me this was going to happen last week when you were in South Bend?"

Engulfed by a combination of anger, sadness, and a sense of betrayal, Gipp realized that Trippeer, despite proclaiming her love for him as recently as a week ago, had been seeing someone else. "I can't believe you could have done this," Gipp said as Trippeer, her head in her hands, began to sob. Whereupon the distraught Gipp, no longer the cool, poised, and supremely confident football star who had been pursued by so many women, but now a jilted lover, walked away and back to his room, leaving a sobbing Iris Trippeer sitting on a love seat on the Hotel Claypool mezzanine. Suddenly, the game against Indiana was the furthest thing from his mind, and for the first time in his life George Gipp felt alone and helpless on what would turn out to be worst night of his young life.

❧

In an effort to get Trippeer off his mind, Gipp went from bar to bar and pool room to pool room that Friday night, trying to place bets on Notre Dame while hoping no one would recognize him; since he wore a cap and pulled-up aviator's jacket collar, only a few people did. But even though he offered as many as 14 points to Indiana bettors, he found no takers. Desperate to get a bet down, Gipp finally began to identify himself and offered that he would personally outscore Indiana, a type of bet he had made in the past. So far as is known, Gipp still found few takers before giving a friend from South Bend $100 (the equivalent of $1,000 in 2010) to bet on Notre Dame, giving Indiana a "spot" of 15 points, meaning the Fighting Irish would have to prevail by more than 15 points for Gipp to win his bet. Finally, still distraught over his meeting with Iris Trippeer, Gipp returned to the Hotel Claypool about eleven o'clock, the curfew that Rockne had set, and went to bed, more deeply hurt and angry than he had ever been.

14

THE LAST GAME

AFTER A RESTLESS night, made particularly uncomfortable by his lingering cough and his distress over the breakup with Iris Trippeer, Gipp had breakfast at the Hotel Claypool with his teammates, Rockne, and Walter Halas (Rockne's new assistant coach and brother of George Halas). He then took a taxi to the Indianapolis train station to pick up his sister, Dorothy, a schoolteacher in Evansville, Indiana, who was known as Dolly. Gipp's brother, Alexander, the oldest of the eight Gipp children, had attended the Army game at West Point, but so far as is known neither of his parents had ever watched Gipp play football at Notre Dame or for that matter ever visited the school. But that was hardly unusual in an era when parents of modest circumstances, as was the case with Matthew Gipp and his wife, Isabella, rarely visited their children when they were at a distant college, which Notre Dame was from Laurium, Michigan. At any rate, Dolly Gipp would be the second family member to watch her famous brother play.

Gipp had told only one person, Hunk Anderson, about the surprise breakup of his relationship with Iris Trippeer. After greeting and hugging his sister on her arrival at the Indianapolis train station and chatting about her life in Evansville, the conversation turned to Gipp, whereupon he told her how Trippeer, whom he had told family members about, shocked him by saying she had gotten married. Stunned and aware that her brother obviously had been hurt, Dolly Gipp hugged him as they stood on the station platform and expressed her sorrow over the strange turn of events. Gipp then hailed a taxi and returned to the Claypool Hotel, where he checked his sister into her room before leaving to join his teammates, who were about to leave in their uniforms, no less, for Washington Park stadium. His sister's presence and the knowledge that she was going to watch him play football for the first time lifted Gipp's spirits, which had been dashed the night before, and made him all the more determined to play well. And besides, there was that $100 bet he had on Notre Dame.

⚜

By game time, about 15,000 spectators had jammed into Washington Park stadium to watch Notre Dame take on a strong, heavier Indiana team, which was a prohibitive underdog to its in-state rival. Notre Dame students, the school band, and other fans of the Fighting Irish accounted for more than a thousand members of the crowd, none of whom knew that George Gipp would be playing with a broken heart and, by game's end, several serious injuries.

To the delight of its screaming fans, Indiana scored on a field goal in the second quarter and a touchdown in the third period, while holding Notre Dame scoreless throughout, to take a 10–0 lead into the final quarter. As Hunk Anderson was to say, the Hoosiers used a stunting defense, "screwed us up and gang-tackled Gipp." One of the gang tackles in the second period dislocated Gipp's left shoulder and rendered him virtually ineffective and on the bench for much of the bitterly fought game. Finally, early in the fourth quarter, the Fighting Irish reached the Indiana one-yard line. After two plunges had failed, Rockne turned to the bench and asked an injured Gipp, "George, can you put the ball in the end zone?"

"I'll try, Rock," a usually confident Gipp replied, knowing he would be hard-pressed just to catch a snap from Ojay Larson, one of the first centers to snap the ball with one hand.

Re-entering the game to a huge ovation from the Notre Dame fans, Gipp, still writhing in pain from his dislocated shoulder, tried to burst off left tackle on third down only to be gang-tackled again for no gain. But on fourth down, on what would turn out to be perhaps the most crucial play of the game, Hunk Anderson, the left guard, and captain Frank Coughlin at left tackle, opened up a hole in the Indiana defense that they had been unable to create on the previous play, and Gipp bolted through it for a touchdown, banging into the goalpost on the goal line as he did. Gipp then drop-kicked the extra point to cut the Indiana lead to three. In South Bend, several hundred Notre Dame rooters let out a collective roar as the Gridgraph, a lighted gridiron facsimile in front of the *South Bend Tribune* building, which received play-by-play descriptions of the game from Western Union, recorded the Notre Dame touchdown and Gipp's conversion.

Shortly after Gipp's ensuing kickoff, Notre Dame fullback Chet Wynne recovered a fumble on the Indiana 28-yard line, which had been forced by Anderson's bone-rattling tackle. Three plays later, from the 15-yard line, Gipp completed a 10-yard pass to right end (and future Holy Cross coach) Eddie Anderson, who reached the one-yard line before being tackled. Quarterback Joe Brandy then drove across the goal line to give Notre Dame a 13–10 lead. Gipp, having difficulty catching the snap from center, missed the extra point. That miss could have been crucial, as Indiana's Elliot Risley's field goal attempt with several minutes left in the game sailed just wide. After the Fighting Irish had run out the clock, hundreds of Notre Dame students swarmed onto the field to engulf the Irish players, while the school band struck up what would eventually become the best-known fight song of all time, "The Notre Dame Victory March." Meanwhile, Gipp, in severe pain both because of his dislocated shoulder and what he would eventually discover was a broken collarbone, boarded a bus that took the players back to the Claypool Hotel to change and shower. Dressing for a game at a hotel and then showering there later was not uncommon at a time when not all stadiums had locker room facilities, as was the case at Washington Park. In Gipp's case, because he could not raise his left arm, he needed the team's student manager, Joe Donaldson, to help him undress, shower, and then dress again before having dinner with Hunk Anderson and Ojay Larson. While with Anderson and Larson, Gipp, his left arm in a sling, complained of a sore throat, which prompted his boyhood friends to ask a team aide to get some medication from a nearby drugstore.

The next morning, Gipp had breakfast with his sister at the Claypool Hotel. After convincing her he would be all right, Gipp made arrangements for her to be driven to the train station. Later, Rockne told Gipp he had made arrangements for his star halfback to be examined in Chicago by a specialist who was a friend of the coach, and also had made a hotel reservation for him. In addition, according to Dorothy Gipp, Rockne also had changed Gipp's ticket so that when the train carried the team back to South Bend that Sunday afternoon, Gipp would remain on the train until it reached Chicago.

What happened during the three days Gipp was in Chicago is unclear. Several published accounts said Gipp had mainly gone to Chicago at the invitation of former teammate Grover Malone to work with drop-kickers on the Loyola Academy football team that Malone coached. Since Malone had called Gipp a slacker the year before and Gipp was unable to drop-kick because of his injuries, that seemed unlikely, although, admittedly, Gipp could have given the kickers a verbal lesson. Also dubious were reports that Gipp and Malone spent the three days carousing at a number of speakeasies. That, too, seemed far-fetched unless the pair had made up since Malone's slacker charge. The third version, provided by Rockne, is that Gipp did indeed see an orthopedic specialist who confirmed that he had both a dislocated shoulder and a broken collarbone. Rockne also said that Gipp had had dinner on Monday night with several members of the Chicago Notre Dame Alumni Society, which was making arrangements to honor Gipp at a game the following Saturday against Northwestern in Chicago, the first meeting between the two schools since 1903. At any rate, Gipp, his left arm still in a sling, returned to South Bend by train on Wednesday and took a taxi to Sorin Hall to rest up for at least the next few days.

Visiting Gipp there to see how he was, Anderson recalled that Rockne asked Gipp if he was up for the trip, and Gipp said he thought he was. "If you're not sure, why don't you stay home and rest," said Rockne, who also noticed that Gipp coughed often and that his voice was hoarse. "Are you sure you're OK?" Rockne asked. "If you're not, I won't use you."

"I'm not great, Rock, but I'm OK," Gipp replied with a smile. "If I don't feel jake, I won't play."

Gipp naturally did not practice Thursday or Friday before the Notre Dame team—which was heavily favored to win despite Gipp's uncertain status—left by train late that afternoon for the two-hour ride to Chicago, followed by a half-hour bus trip to Evanston, a Chicago suburb. Not only were Gipp's shoulder and collarbone still hurting, but what had become a persistent cough and sore throat had gotten worse, and he had a temperature of 102. Even though the Chicago alumni group had designated the game day, November 20, "George Gipp Day," Gipp was sure he would not play, not just because of his injuries, cough, and sore throat, but also the forecast of cold, rainy weather.

"I don't think I can make it," Gipp told Anderson, who also had a series of injuries, the night before the game at the Auditorium Hotel in Chicago. Once again, Gipp, coughing often and with his sore throat seeming to worsen, had a restless night. As predicted, the weather at Northwestern Field was raw and windy with a cold mist. A capacity crowd of more than 20,000 was on hand, including about 4,000 fans who had gobbled up the Notre Dame allotment in one day and had traveled by train to the game on a chartered twenty-five car special. Few, if any, knew what bad condition Gipp was in. Cynical as he was, Gipp knew that it was a special day for him, and thus, despite his cough, sore throat, and shoulder and collarbone injuries, he suited up. Knowing that he might not be up to playing, Gipp entertained the crowd briefly before the game by drop-kicking about 6 practice field goals almost 50 yards through the goal post uprights, evoking cheers from both the Notre Dame and Northwestern fans. Watching from the sidelines, Rockne beamed while recalling how he had discovered George Gipp doing just that—booting eye-popping dropkicks as the coach was walking across the Notre Dame campus four years earlier.

As expected Gipp did not start, and heavily favored Notre Dame soon showed it could survive without their best player, who remained huddled in a heavy, hooded parka on the sideline. Once again, Rockne started his second string—his shock troops—which played Northwestern to a scoreless first period. With the first team on the field, minus Gipp, Notre Dame scored twice in the second quarter to take a 14–0 halftime lead. But after Northwestern scored in the third quarter to narrow its deficit to seven points, chants of "We want Gipp! We want Gipp!" reverberated through much of the crowd. Capitalizing on an interception in Northwestern territory, Notre Dame scored later in the period to pull ahead, 21–7. By midway through the fourth period, the chant for Gipp grew even louder. By then a cold wind was blowing in from Lake Michigan and the field was frozen. On the sideline, Gipp was coughing sporadically and still running a fever. But hearing the growing chants for him, the normally stoic Gipp, who in the past had seemed oblivious of a cheering crowd, was moved. Given his condition and with only one other game remaining on the Notre Dame schedule, he knew this was probably his last game, and that, moreover, he owed it to the crowd to play no matter how briefly. Finally, he shed his parka, walked over to Rockne and said, "Put me in Rock. We can't disappoint them."

Rockne by now had no intention of putting Gipp in the game, what with his condition, the cold weather, and the frozen field. Then, too, Notre Dame was doing all right without him. Looking at his pale and obviously still injured star, Rockne shook his head. Again, Gipp asked to go in. Realizing all that Gipp had meant to Notre Dame football, and that this was, indeed, probably his last game, Rockne said, "All right, George, but, remember, don't run with the ball." Not that Gipp wanted to. Before the game, he found that when he raised his right arm to throw a pass, the pain in his left shoulder was excruciating.

As the *Notre Dame Scholastic* reporter wrote in his game story, "Pandemonium broke loose when Gipp went into the fray at the beginning of the last quarter." With the ball on Northwestern's 35-yard line, quarterback Joe Brandy, who had been told in advance by Rockne not to call any running plays for Gipp, called for a pass. On his first play from scrimmage, Gipp, at tailback, took the snap from center and, enduring the pain, fired a pass to right end Eddie Anderson at the 15-yard line. Anderson then outran two defenders for a touchdown that gave Notre Dame a commanding 27–7 lead.

On Notre Dame's next possession, which started at its own 45-yard line, Gipp outdid himself when he connected with halfback Norm Barry on a 55-yard touchdown pass (which traveled 40 yards in the air) to make it 33–7, which turned out to be the final score. Again, the thousands of Notre Dame fans roared with delight. On the Notre Dame sideline, Rockne, knowing that Gipp was not well, felt guilty about yielding to Gipp's entreaties to put him in the game.

In another memorable, albeit brief, performance, an ailing Gipp had completed five of six passes for 129 yards, including two touchdowns. After his second touchdown pass, Gipp, in defiance of Rockne's instructions, told Brandy that he wanted to field the ensuing kickoff, obviously to give the crowd a chance to see him run at least once. Seeing Gipp as the deep back on the kickoff, Rockne was furious, fearful that he might be hurt even worse than he already was. Sure enough, the kick, a high, soaring, but short end-over-end boot that hit the ground and bounded toward Gipp; either Northwestern guard Graham Penfield or quarterback Charles Palmer, who both were closing in on Gipp, could have downed the ball. Instead, Gipp stunned Rockne when he fielded the ball with the intention of running it back. But after he had gone only a few yards, Penfield and Palmer, aware that Gipp was playing hurt, grabbed him and, in a beau geste maneuver, gently pulled him down to the frozen grass.

Francis Wallace, a Notre Dame student and part-time sportswriter for the *South Bend News-Times,* who would go on to a successful career as a sportswriter in New York and author of more than a dozen books, said some forty years later that the gesture by the Northwestern players "was the finest thing I have ever seen on a football field." And by then, Wallace had seen hundreds of college and professional football games.

After the game, Penfield, an all-Big Ten guard, raved about Gipp's touchdown pass to Anderson. "It was one of the best passes I've ever seen thrown," he said.

Only Michigan Agricultural College, scheduled five days later on Thanksgiving Day in East Lansing, stood between Notre Dame, its second straight unbeaten season and possible recognition as the national champion of college football. With his left arm back in a sling on the train ride to South Bend, Gipp hardly looked like a man who only a few hours before had thrown two long touchdown passes. Asked by Anderson how he felt, Gipp said, "The shoulder and collarbone still hurt quite a bit, but my throat is getting worse and worse," he said. "I really don't feel good at all, Hunk."

Back on the Notre Dame campus, Gipp spent most of the weekend in bed at Sorin Hall. Reading the South Bend and Chicago papers Sunday morning, Gipp was moved anew by the crowd calling for his appearance against Northwestern and the cheers he heard when he went into the game, which grew even louder when he threw his two touchdown passes. "That crowd was great," he said to Anderson at one point.

"Hey, you're actually human," Anderson responded with a smile. "You really were touched by that, weren't you?"

"Yes, I was," Gipp replied. "It made me feel good."

Little did Gipp or Anderson realize that the Northwestern game had been George Gipp's last hurrah.

On Monday night, Gipp, though feeling increasingly weak, and his teammates and coaches were honored at a banquet at the Hotel Oliver that was sponsored by the University Club, an organization of South Bend businessmen. The affair, which attracted more than 400 people, had all the trappings of a football game, most notably the Notre Dame band and the team's cheerleaders. Chet Grant recalled many years later that about midway through the banquet, Gipp turned to him and asked to use his handkerchief, and then, after telling him he didn't feel well, excused himself and left. "To me, it was obvious that he was a sick man," Grant said.

Some cynics at the table, unaware of Gipp's sore throat and prolonged coughing spells, presumed he might be going elsewhere in the Oliver in search of action at a pool or poker table. As it was, Gipp did go elsewhere in the Oliver—to bed in the room he had kept there for more than a year, far sicker than Chet Grant or anyone else realized.

Anderson offered another version of the story. He said he had noticed that Gipp had not touched his dinner at the banquet. "Are you all right, George?" Anderson asked, aware that Gipp had been coughing on and off for more than a week and looked even palen than usual.

"I feel awful, Hunk," a haggard-looking Gipp replied. "My throat feels like it's on fire, and I think I have a fever."

Anderson then put his hand on Gipp's head and was stunned by how hot it felt. "George, you're hotter than hell. You better tell Rock right away," Anderson advised his longtime friend and teammate.

According to Anderson's version, Gipp then approached Rockne at the dais and told him how bad he felt. After delivering a brief talk, an alarmed Rockne called nearby St. Joseph Hospital and made arrangements for him to be admitted.

"Don't worry, Rock, I'm going to be OK," Gipp told his coach before leaving the banquet hall to go to his room at the Oliver.

"I'm sure you will, George," Rockne replied. "I'm sure you will."

A short while later, a hoarse and haggard Gipp hailed a cab outside the Hotel Oliver and told the driver to take him to nearby St. Joseph Hospital. It was the beginning of a drama that would capture the attention of much of the nation for the next three weeks.

15

GIPP'S FIGHT FOR LIFE

SICK AS HE was, Gipp walked into St. Joseph Hospital unaided and was brought to a private room, where his temperature was immediately taken. It was 104 degrees, nearly six degrees above normal. A prominent South Bend doctor who certainly knew who Gipp was quickly diagnosed his condition as tonsillitis, hardly, it would seem, a cause for alarm and something which he had been warned about only three months earlier. The doctor, James McMeel, was the president of the Indiana State Medical Association and later became head of the American Medical Association, so Gipp appeared to be in good hands. As a precaution, however, Doctor McMeel called in an associate, Doctor Thomas Olney, for a second opinion and Olney concurred with McMeel on the tonsillitis diagnosis.

An initial concern of both doctors was streptococcus, an infection of the throat commonly known as strep throat, which is more serious. It then became apparent to the doctors that George Gipp had been a sick man when he played, even though briefly, against Northwestern on a bitterly cold and raw day in Evanston three days earlier. The question probably rose in their minds as to why Gipp, coughing constantly and with an elevated temperature, had not been checked out by a doctor before the game. As it was, the football team had no team doctor. Indeed, Rockne, despite his limited medical knowledge, also acted as the team trainer, which was not unusual at the time.

Gipp was immediately put on a liquid diet and prescribed aspirin to keep his temperature down; a mixture of borax, glycerin, and honey was used to swab his inflamed sore throat. Neither penicillin nor antibiotics were options, since they had not yet been devised.

That Tuesday afternoon, Rockne and Anderson visited Gipp at the hospital and found him in good spirits but looking haggard and frail. Doctors assured them, however, that Gipp was merely suffering from tonsillitis, and that his prognosis was good. Both Rockne and Anderson were further encouraged when they returned to see Gipp on Wednesday and were told that his temperature had lowered to a point where it was almost normal and that he seemed to be doing all right. Following the brief visit, Rockne, Anderson, and the rest of the Notre Dame football team left by train for East Lansing to face Michigan Agricultural College on Thanksgiving Day in the final game of the season. Gipp was much on the minds of the players, who were encouraged, though, when Rockne told them that Gipp appeared to be doing well and that he was on his way to a complete recovery. Ironically, in a story that appeared in the *South Bend Tribune* on the day Gipp was taken to the hospital, Arch Ward wrote that Gipp would play against the Michigan Aggies "should the going get too tough for his mates." Ward, of course, did not know that Gipp's Notre Dame career had ended the previous Saturday when he threw two touchdown passes while playing with a separated shoulder, a broken collarbone, and severe sore throat.

By game time on Thanksgiving, Gipp's hospitalization had made it onto the Associated Press wire and into newspapers across the country. Even without Notre Dame's greatest runner, the Fighting Irish easily beat the Michigan Aggies, as they were called, 25–0, to complete their second straight unbeaten season. Gipp's replacement at left halfback, Dan Coughlin, gave a good imitation of Gipp when he ran back the opening kickoff 80 yards for a touchdown, and Rockne played his second unit more than half of the game.

Gipp's condition remained stable through the Thanksgiving weekend. His fever had lowered, raising hopes that he was out of the woods. But then on November 29, six days after he had been admitted to the hospital, pneumonia set in, and doctors said that the next forty-eight hours would be critical. At that point, his parents were notified, and his mother, his brother Matthew, and his sister Dorothy arrived in South Bend to be at Gipp's bedside. Rockne also hurried to the hospital, both to see Gipp and to tell Mrs. Gipp that he had made arrangements for her to stay with George Hull, the co-owner of Hullie and Mike's, and for the two children to stay at his own home. Hunk Anderson was to say that Mrs. Gipp, who was a Methodist, told her son that she preferred having him moved to another hospital because the nuns who worked at St. Joseph and the priests who visited him made her nervous. However, still according to Anderson, Gipp told her he felt that he was getting very good care and did not want to be moved, whereupon, apparently, she did not press for him to be transferred.

To assist the South Bend doctors who had been tending to Gipp, Rockne and administration officials at Notre Dame arranged to have two eye, ear, and throat specialists from Chicago come to St. Joseph for consultations and to stay by his bedside around the clock. By now, fearful that Gipp's heart may have been failing, doctors began to administer digitalis to stimulate the organ. A blood transfusion also was deemed necessary, and blood from Anderson, who had been determined to be a compatible donor for his boyhood friend, was transferred to Gipp in a direct transfusion.

"George Gipp's condition was pronounced grave by attending physicians last night," the *South Bend Tribune* reported in its editions the following morning, November 30. "A decided change for the better or worse is anticipated before another night has passed."

The news cast a pall of gloom over the campus, where students and faculty had been led to believe that Gipp was merely suffering from tonsillitis. Students, faculty members, and others at the university converged on Sacred Heart Church (now Sacred Heart Basilica) on the Notre Dame campus to pray for the most famous athlete in the school's history as they would do in subsequent days. The hospital's announcement, carried throughout the country by the Associated Press, both stunned and saddened tens of thousands of Notre Dame alumni and football fans who had come to idolize the sensational halfback from the small, Midwestern Catholic school, which had been virtually unheard of a decade prior. By now, in an unprecedented vigil, scores of students gathered each day on the sprawling lawn of St. Joseph Hospital, directly outside of Gipp's second-floor room, to pray for the school's most famous, and most enigmatic, athlete.

In the next few days, Gipp's condition improved. Gipp, who had lapsed into a coma, was conscious again by December 2, and doctors said he apparently had overcome his pneumonia. Though his condition was still listed as critical, they also said they expected Gipp to recover. By December 4 Gipp's sixty-six-year-old father, Matthew, who had not been well himself, had arrived from Laurium to see his son. Told that his condition had improved, Matthew Gipp returned home the following day. Meanwhile, visitors from outside the family were allowed to see Gipp, who, though obviously having lost a considerable amount of weight, appeared alert and in good spirits. Among the visitors were Rockne, several of Gipp's teammates, Father Patrick Haggerty (a priest at Notre Dame who had become a regular caller and seemed to have established a close relationship with Gipp), and Father James Burns, the Notre Dame president who had expelled Gipp nine months before for failing to attend classes, but then reinstated him a month later. Another visitor was Johnny Evers, the second baseman in the legendary Tinkers-to-Evers-to-Chance double-play combination for the Chicago Cubs, whom club president Bill Veeck had dispatched to sign Gipp for the 1921 season when Evers was to take over as manager of the Cubs. Gipp, who had received a contract from the Cubs the previous summer, was still too ill to consider such a proposal, but Evers's visit heartened him, according to Anderson, a daily visitor to his best friend's room. Gipp was even more heartened when Rockne told him he had been named to Walter

Camp's All-America team at fullback, becoming the first Notre Damer selected to a Camp first team by the legendary football pioneer.

"How does that make you feel being the first player from Notre Dame to make Camp's first team?" Rockne asked Gipp with a smile.

"That's jake with me," Gipp replied.

In naming Gipp to his All-America team in *Collier's Weekly* magazine, Camp wrote, "In the backfield, Gipp of Notre Dame gets the first place on account of his versatility and power, able as he is to punt, drop-kick, forward pass, run, tackle—in fact do anything that any backfield man could ever be required to do and do it in well-neigh superlative fashion." Some Notre Damers and others thought that Camp was again showing a bias for Eastern players when he put Gipp at fullback, rather than at his normal position of left halfback, a spot that went to A. C. Way of Penn State. However, the prestigious Helms Athletic Foundation did pick Gipp as a first-team All-American at left halfback and also selected him as the College Football Player of the Year, the equivalent at the time of today's Heisman Trophy, which was first awarded in 1935.

By the end of the first week of December, Gipp felt well enough to get out of bed for the first time to walk around. During one of Anderson's visits, he told Notre Dame's star guard that he was thinking of becoming a Catholic.

"What the hell do you want to do that for?" asked Anderson, a Protestant, as were both Gipp and Rockne (although Rockne would eventually convert to Catholicism, his wife's religion).

"Look, Hunk, my problems aren't over, and I want to make sure when I die I go to the right place," Gipp responded, according to Anderson's recollection of their conversation. "I think the odds are better if I hold the right cards."

"George was barely able to talk," Anderson told the author more than a half century later. "He said to me, 'Hunk, I don't think I'm going to make it.' I tried to encourage him, and told him he'd been in tougher battles, which was probably not true. But he said to me, 'Not as tough as this one, Hunk. I think I've kicked my last dropkick.'"

It is more than likely that, although Gipp was not religious, he probably had heard at Notre Dame that salvation was not an option outside the Catholic church, a contention that the church had promulgated at the time. Though his father was a deacon in the Baptist church in Laurium, Gipp had drifted away from the family's religion in his late teens and had adopted a fatalist attitude toward life, to the point of telling friends that he did not expect to live long. To which friends like Hunk Anderson would respond, partially in jest, by saying that if he continued his lifestyle of smoking, drinking, eating irregularly, and getting very little rest, he probably would not.

According to Victoria Adams Phair, the granddaughter of Iris Trippeer, Knute Rockne—apparently unaware that Trippeer had been married recently and thus had ended her intense relationship with Gipp—sent Trippeer a telegram in early December telling her about Gipp's dire condition and saying that Gipp wanted to see her. Even though Trippeer had married another man, she quickly took a train from Indianapolis to South Bend to see Gipp at the hospital, according to Phair. "She told me years later that she did go to see George Gipp," Phair said in 2010. During the visit, Phair said, Gipp gave Trippeer the miniature gold football that Rockne had given all of the players on the 1919 team, who had finished the season undefeated. Phair said Trippeer then wore the gold football on a charm bracelet every day until she died of cancer in 1973, when she was seventy-three years old.

"She told me George Gipp was the only man she ever loved," Phair said during one of our 2010 conversations. Phair, the daughter of one of Trippeer's two sons, said Trippeer divorced her husband, Jack Adams, in the 1940s and became a successful interior decorator. "My sister and I took care of her the last two years of her life, and she was gorgeous till the end," Phair said.

However, no one else seemed to recall Trippeer visiting Gipp at St. Joseph Hospital. Also, her granddaughter's version of Gipp giving Trippeer the gold football is at variance with the account by Hunk Anderson's wife, Marie, who said she had seen Trippeer wearing the pendant when she and Hunk were on a double-date with Gipp and Trippeer earlier in 1920.

One woman did definitely turn up frequently outside the door of Gipp's room, but apparently was not allowed to see him, even though she claimed to be a former sweetheart. Hunk Anderson recognized the woman and said he thought she was the manicurist at the Hotel Oliver whom Gipp had dated before falling in love with Trippeer, and may have dated her again after their breakup.

By December 7 calls went out on the Notre Dame campus for blood donors. Hunk Anderson immediately offered to donate again, but was turned down since he had given blood the week before. In the next two days, around 150 Notre Dame students offered to donate blood to their stricken campus hero, and ten were placed on standby in the event another transfusion was deemed necessary. Then on December 10, the *South Bend Tribune* reported that Gipp had "regained the strength lost yesterday. His condition was improved, and he once more showed signs of recovery. However, the following day, Anderson said, he was visiting Gipp along with Gipp's mother and two of her children when Gipp told him, "Hunk, I don't think I'm going to make it. But thanks for everything."

His boyhood friend and Notre Dame teammate was stunned, even though Gipp had lost considerable weight—perhaps as much as forty pounds—and was extremely pale. "Up until then, I thought George was going to pull through," Anderson said years later, "but after hearing what he said, I began to think the end might be near."

By, Monday, December 13, the doctors and nurses at St. Joseph Hospital thought so, too, as Gipp lapsed into and out of a coma. Anderson cut classes to be at the hospital all that day. Gipp's mother and other members of the family who were in South Bend were summoned to the hospital early in the evening and, a short while later, Rockne arrived at the hospital and was led into Gipp's room, where the family had gathered. Regaining consciousness for a short while, Gipp apparently spotted Rockne and said something to Doctor McMeel, who by now had spent most of every day of the last three weeks at Gipp's side. Doctor McMeel thereupon waved to Rockne, indicating that Gipp wanted to see him. Rockne then walked to Gipp's side and bent down to talk to him. The scene was dramatized in *Knute Rockne:*

All American, in which Gipp is portrayed by eventual President Ronald Reagan and Rockne by Pat O'Brien. In the film, Rockne is alone with Gipp at the time, but recounting what he was to say years later, Rockne indicated someone else was with him at Gipp's bedside.

"It's pretty tough to go," Rockne quoted either someone else or himself saying at Gipp's bedside. "What's tough about it?" Gipp replied with a smile while looking "up at us," according to Rockne's account in the series he—or a ghostwriter—wrote for *Collier's* magazine. Rockne said that Gipp then turned to him and said, softly, "I've no complaint. I've got to go, Rock. It's all right. I'm not afraid." It was then, according to Rockne, that Gipp, in what would become the most famous rallying cry in sports history, whispered, "Sometimes when things are going wrong, when the breaks are beating the boys, tell them to go out and win one for the Gipper. I don't know where I'll be then, Rock, but I'll know about it, and I'll be happy."

The only problem with that account is that no one seems to recall anyone being with Rockne when he saw Gipp for the last time. Nor did anyone recall Gipp ever having been called the "Gipper." However, Hunk Anderson did say years later that he and his fellow Calumet High School pals and Notre Dame teammates Ojay Larson and Perce Wilcox, occasionally called their fellow Calumet alumnus Gipper. "Rock occasionally called George that, too," Anderson said. Anderson said the nickname was first used by Joe Swetish, who managed a baseball team that Gipp and Anderson played on back in Laurium. Recounting a particularly good game Gipp had had, Swetish, referring to his star outfielder, told an acquaintance, "The Gipper had a round-tripper," employing baseball slang for a home run. "After that a lot of the guys on the team started calling George 'Gipper,'" Anderson recalled while conceding that apart from him, Rockne, Larson, and Wilcox, he didn't recall anyone else ever using "Gipper."

⌖

After putting a hand on Gipp's forehead and saying good-bye, an ashen-faced Rockne left Gipp's room. Family members, having been told that the end was near, then gathered around Gipp and remained for the rest of the evening as Gipp continued to lapse in and out of a coma. During the evening, Father Pat Haggerty made his fifth visit of the day to Gipp's bedside, and, with Gipp conscious again, prayed over him.

In the early hours of the next morning, Tuesday, December 14, with Gipp now in a deep coma, Father Haggerty—at Gipp's prior request, he was to say later—gave Gipp conditional baptism and conditional absolution, which in effect converted him to Catholicism. A few minutes later, Father John O'Hara, Notre Dame's prefect of religion (who would become president of the university in 1934 and later the archbishop of Philadelphia) administered the last rites of the Roman Catholic Church to the fallen football star. At approximately 3:30 A.M., Doctor McMeel felt for Gipp's pulse once more, then turned to Gipp's mother, his brother Matthew, and his sister Dorothy, put his head down, and then announced softly that Gipp was dead. The date was December 14, 1920. Coincidentally, and almost hauntingly, eighty-nine years later St. Joseph Hospital—by then known as the St. Joseph Regional Medical Center—would close on the same date, December 14, that its most famous patient had died.

George Gipp, who had come to Notre Dame as an unknown in the fall of 1916 and by the fall of 1920 had become one of the best-known athletes in the United States, was twenty-five years and ten months old when he died. Shortly after Doctor McMeel's announcement, a nurse at St. Joseph, by pre-arrangement with the Hotel Oliver, called the hotel and told the night clerk that Gipp was dead. The clerk then pulled a master switch on and off three times to let the staff know that Gipp, the hotel's best-known resident, had died.

No other Notre Damer had ever been, or ever would be, so honored in death.

In what could have been a fitting epitaph for Gipp, Father Charles O'Donnell, who would become president of Notre Dame in 1928, said shortly after Gipp died, "He was an enigma that we never solved."

16

A HEARTFELT FAREWELL

A PALL OF GRIEF settled across the Notre Dame campus on the morning of Tuesday, December 14, as word of George Gipp's death during the night spread from dormitory to dormitory, from classroom to classroom, and into the university's dining halls. Scores of students, faculty, administrators, and staff workers converged on Sacred Heart Church close by the administration building to pray for Notre Dame's most revered sports star, whose exploits on the football field had lifted their spirits and whose fame had enhanced the reputation of the school. American flags on campus flew at half-staff, as did the flag at the Marion County Courthouse in downtown South Bend. As on the Notre Dame campus, Gipp's death was the main topic of conversation downtown, where he had spent as much, if not more of his time, and had become extremely popular.

The death of Notre Dame's first first-team All-American football player, whose spectacular 1920 season had made him a national sports icon, was front-page news in many American papers the afternoon of the day he died (it was an era when afternoon newspapers still flourished in the United States). Among them was the *South Bend Tribune* whose headline read, STUDENT BODY PLANS ITS FINAL TRIBUTE TO IDOL. Meanwhile, tributes of sympathy poured into Notre Dame's administration building from across the country in an unprecedented degree. Many of the tributes expressed a sense of shock and incredulity over how a great athlete, in the prime of his career, and after having enjoyed his best season as a football star, could have been stricken and then died two weeks later. That shock was understandable, since Gipp initially had been diagnosed with tonsillitis, hardly a life-threatening affliction, but the cause of death given by the hospital was a streptococcus infection that presumably had set in after Gipp had been admitted to St. Joseph Hospital on November 30.

Among those hit hardest by Gipp's death was Knute Rockne, who of course had discovered Gipp's football talents on the Notre Dame campus. Both during Gipp's time in the hospital and in the aftermath of his death, Rockne indulged in self-flagellation, feeling that he should not have acceded to Gipp's request to send him into the Northwestern game on a frigid day in Chicago when Rockne knew his star halfback was not well. Since Gipp already had complained of a sore throat for more than a week before the Northwestern game, and, at that, played less than a quarter in the game, doctors who treated Gipp at St. Joseph Hospital said they were convinced that Gipp's participation in the game had no bearing on his illness or his death. Nevertheless, Rockne felt a heavy sense of guilt.

The grief hit home to the Rocknes, since Gipp had been a frequent dinner guest at their home on St. Vincent Street, which Knute and Bonnie had moved into following their marriage in July 1914. Their oldest son, William, then five years old—the Rocknes had two other children, Knute Jr., who was two, and Mary Jean, who had been born that year—was thrilled whenever Notre Dame's biggest star visited the Rocknes, which made the youngster the envy of his friends.

Responding to a telephone request from the *South Bend Tribune,* Rockne sat down at a desk in his study and began writing a statement about Gipp, who, though only six years younger, had in a way become a surrogate, if somewhat incorrigible, son—and whose death, he realized, had left a huge void in his life. Writing on a long white legal pad in longhand, Rockne wrote, "George Gipp was the greatest halfback who has ever represented Notre Dame, and his unquestionable ability was surpassed by a grit which featured in all his work on the gridiron and was the marvel of his attending physicians. The outstanding feature of his character was a deep affection for his mother, and in his death I feel a keen personal loss."

It was a heartfelt tribute, and as he read what he had written, Rockne began to cry. He then called the *Tribune,* read the tribute over the phone, and drove to his office on campus, knowing it would be a very busy, and very emotional, day.

By noon, only eight and a half hours after Gipp had died, his open coffin was on display at the McGann Funeral Home on North Michigan Street. Closed coffins were a rarity at the time, but more than a few people who knew Gipp well were stunned at how emaciated he looked, and felt that it would have been better if his coffin had been closed. Some reports said Gipp had lost eighty pounds while he was on his deathbed, which would have left him weighing around 100 pounds when he died. The owner of the funeral home, Lewis McGann, said in fact Gipp had lost only twenty pounds while he was at St. Joseph Hospital.

Nearly 1,000 people paid their respects between noon and 10 A.M. the following day. Appropriately enough, given Gipp's penchant for spending late hours in downtown South Bend, his coffin was on view throughout the night. Among those who extended condolences to Gipp's mother, his brother Alexander, and his youngest sister Dorothy were university president James Burns, more than a score of former players, almost all of his thirty-four teammates, Knute and Bonnie Rockne, assistant coach Walter Halas, numerous city officials and civic leaders, prominent South Bend businessmen, and an estimated 500 Notre Dame students who were given fares for the streetcar that ran to and from the Notre Dame campus. Also paying their respects were numerous friends—and billiard- and poker-playing cronies—from Hullie and Mike's, Goldie Mann's, the Hotel Oliver, and other establishments where Gipp had made hundreds of acquaintances over the last four and a half school years.

Wakes at the time tended to be as much social gatherings as opportunities to pay respects to the dead and to extend condolences to family members. But the wake for Gipp was solemn, and remarkably quiet given the throng of mourners passing in and out of the funeral home and past Gipp's coffin. At times, as many as 300 people were lined up outside waiting to view the body of Notre Dame's greatest player, many of them still stunned by his death at such a young age.

By then, almost all of the mourners had read the front-page story in the *South Bend Tribune* about Gipp's death, which included plans for a service the next day. The story also included a statement from Frank Coughlin, captain of the 1920 Notre Dame football team, in which he said, "George Gipp was a man among men, brilliant and unassuming; and has endeared himself to the heart of every Notre Dame student by his athletic prowess, magnetic personality, keen mind, and his great love for the old school. He will forever be remembered as a friend, a student, an athlete, and a gentleman, for to know him was to love him."

Maybe Coughlin was stretching it a bit to say that Gipp would be remembered as a student, but, still, it was a heartfelt and pretty accurate description of perhaps the most unusual student-athlete Notre Dame had ever had and who, indeed, would forever be remembered.

⁂

The next morning, December 15, with classes canceled for the day and snow falling, hundreds of students and other mourners packed Sacred Heart Church to attend a mass for Gipp, which was celebrated by Father James Burns, the university president. From the church, most of the mourners went by automobile or streetcar to the McGann Funeral Home, where Gipp's mother, his brother, and sister bade him farewell. An eerie quiet hung over the normally bustling industrial city, which had virtually come to a halt. Some stores and other businesses closed for the day so that their employees could attend the service or watch the ensuing procession through the heart of the city to the train station. Scores, perhaps even hundreds, of children, were kept out of school so that they could watch the farewell to South Bend's most famous athlete and, unbeknownst to most, perhaps the best pool-shooter in the city's history.

A large crowd had gathered outside the funeral home by the time Gipp's coffin was carried out and placed in a hearse to begin the short trip to the New York Central train station. Despite the snowstorm, thousands more lined the route of a procession, which included a police escort; Gipp's teammates, with ten of them lined up in formation with one position—Gipp's left halfback—empty; members of the Notre Dame Monogram Club (who had won letters in various varsity sports); almost the entire Notre Dame student body of 1,500; scores of faculty and other staff members; the hearse; and then three cars carrying family members, President Burns, and other Notre Dame dignitaries. Walking alongside the hearse were the pallbearers, all starting members of the football team. On one side were the three players from Calumet whom Gipp had recommended to Rockne—Hunk Anderson, Ojay Larson, and Perce Wilcox; on the other side were Frank Coughlin, Norm Barry, and Joe Brandy. At the train station, Gipp's coffin was placed in the baggage car of a New York Central train bound for Chicago on the first leg of a train trip that would end in Calumet.

In what was believed to have marked the first time that the term "Gipper" appeared in a newspaper, *South Bend Tribune* sportswriter Arch Ward wrote that as the hearse reached the train station, "the students bared their heads to the snow as the body of their Gipper went on to its appointed end." It would, by most accounts, be another eight years before "Gipper" would appear in print again, and when it did, it would mark the launching of a legendary expression that would become the most famous sports quotation in American sports history.

Two hours after its departure from South Bend, the train carrying Gipp's body arrived in Chicago at one o'clock in the afternoon, where, according to an Associated Press account, almost 10,000 people had gathered, hoping, apparently, to see the coffin. Following a four-hour layover, the train, carrying members of Gipp's family and his six teammate-pallbearers, departed for Calumet, arriving there at eight o'clock in the morning. A crowd of perhaps as many as 500 people—a large turnout for a small town—met the train and watched the coffin be carried from the baggage car onto a hearse and then taken to the Gipp family home on Hecla Street in nearby Laurium. On Saturday, Gipp's coffin was taken to the Calumet Light Guard Armory, where about 300 people paid their respects as Gipp's coffin lay in state from 10:30 a.m. until 2 p.m., when a service was conducted by a Baptist and Congregational minister. That, of course, meant that in a span of forty-eight hours, Gipp, never a religious person, had been mourned in death at both Catholic and Protestant services. As was the case in South Bend, business came to a halt in both Calumet and Laurium during the funeral service, and a church bell tolled in the nearby town of Red Jacket as a procession formed to head for Lake View Cemetery in Laurium.

Three days of unrelenting snow had left roads in the Calumet area impassable; thus, having a hearse bear Gipp's coffin five miles from the armory was out of the question. As a result, the coffin, covered by a blanket, was placed on a sled, which two horses then pulled five miles through the snow to a hillside in the cemetery overlooking Lake Superior. There, gravediggers had burrowed through snowdrifts as high as five feet to excavate a grave for the onetime Calumet High School dropout who many people had perceived as a directionless and cavalier young man not apt to amount to anything significant in life.

Gathered around the grave at the cemetery were Gipp's parents: four of his siblings; the two ministers; Gipp's six teammate pallbearers; a group of baseball teammates from Laurium and Calumet, along with other longtime friends; and members of the Calumet American Legion Post, which gave Gipp a military burial ceremony that included a twenty-one-gun salute. Why Gipp, who seemed to go out of his way to avoid serving in World War I, was given a military funeral was never made clear; like so much of his life, it was both incongruous and inexplicable. The service ended with a brief prayer by one of the ministers and then a few parting words by Gipp's ailing father, after which the coffin was lowered into the grave.

George Gipp's premonition of dying young, so often expressed to Hunk Anderson and other close friends, had been borne out, and during a snowstorm he had been laid to rest, more than 200 miles from Notre Dame, where, in large measure because of his almost filial admiration for a direct opposite in Knute Rockne, he had found at least a modicum of direction and purpose, along with the affection of his classmates and football teammates, plus nationwide acclaim for his stardom in a sport he had never intended to play.

How good was Gipp? Rockne would be asked that often in the years to come, and the answer would always be the same: "I have seen them all, and I consider George Gipp superior to both Jim Thorpe and Red Grange."

There could be no greater tribute.

17

THE FOUR HORSEMEN

FEELINGS OF SHOCK and emptiness permeated the Notre Dame campus on Thursday, December 16, the day after George Gipp's memorial in South Bend and the shipment of his body to Laurium, the day before the start of the Christmas break. No one could recall the scope of such grief following the death of anyone else in the Notre Dame family over the years. "Neither the death of Father Morrisey nor of Father Zahm affected the students," wrote Father Arthur Hope, a professor and historian at Notre Dame, referring to two popular educators at Notre Dame—Andrew Morrisey, the school's president at the turn of the twentieth century, and John Zahm, a professor at the university in the early part of the same century. "But the death of George Gipp was another matter."

Similar tributes appeared in the *Scholastic,* the monthly campus magazine, and the *Dome,* the university's yearbook. An article in the *Dome* in the spring of 1921 recalled that, in the aftermath of Gipp's great performance at West Point only six weeks before he died, at least one newspaper had described him as the "Lochinvar of the West," a reference to a heroic figure in "Marmion," a poem by Sir Walter Scott, "while others had portrayed Gipp as 'a demigod of football.'" That the writer of the *Dome* article did not explain the significance of the literary Lochinvar indicates, perhaps, that he assumed that the school's students were familiar with Scott's Poem.

Newspapers, both on sports and editorial pages, paid tribute to Gipp. Many dwelled on the irony and sadness of Gipp dying during the same month that he was named to every All-America team. Eight years later, W. O. McGeehan, a highly respected sports columnist for the *New York Herald Tribune*, described Gipp as "the greatest triple-threat man I ever saw in action." McGeehan went on to write, "I do not ever expect to see on a football field as dynamic, as colorful a figure as this George Gipp of Notre Dame." Some years after that, Arthur Daley, the sports columnist for *The New York Times* starting in 1942—the *Times* had only one sports columnist until the 1960s—wrote, "It has been a long parade of superstars who have marched through that capital of the gridiron world (Notre Dame), but at the head of that parade and greatest of them all was Notre Dame's beloved Gipper."

Sadly, though, controversy and rancor between the university and the Gipp family would develop, mainly over Gipp's putative conversion to Catholicism and the cost of his medical bills and funeral. To the chagrin of the university, it would be a controversy that would attract national attention.

The doctors who had been summoned to attend Gipp, including the two specialists from Chicago, had billed Notre

Dame for their services, whose costs ran into the thousands of dollars. At first Father Burns, the university president, thought that the Gipp family was obligated to pay part of the costs. But when they realized Rockne had contacted the specialists in Chicago, Burns agreed that Notre Dame should pay all of the medical expenses, which amounted to around $4,500. Gipp's brother Matthew, who had been at his side when he died, apparently paid for Gipp's casket and for other funeral expenses. However, Burns and other Notre Dame officials said the university, along with many of his classmates, also paid about $500 to defray the costs of shipping Gipp's body from South Bend to Michigan and sending six of his teammates to the funeral in Laurium.

The university was forced to divulge those expenses after reports circulated that the Gipp family had had to pay all of Gipp's hospital and funeral expenses. One of those who made such a charge was Fielding Yost, the football coach at Michigan, a devout Methodist and Rockne's *bete noir*, whom Rockne had in the past labeled as anti-Catholic. Rockne had long felt that Yost's bias and negative comments about Notre Dame had been instrumental in the repeated rejection of the university's application to join the Western Conference, which later became known as the Big Ten. For Rockne, having Notre Dame join the Big Ten was virtually a moral imperative. Playing Big Ten schools like Northwestern and Purdue was fine, but Rockne resented the implication that Notre Dame, as an institution, wasn't in the same class academically as schools in what many still called the Western Conference. Rockne, a Lutheran who converted to Catholicism in 1925, justifiably could not understand whatever bias did exist toward Notre Dame, whose student body in 1920 was about twenty percent non-Catholic. Nor could Rockne's predecessor as coach, Jesse Harper, who was also a Protestant. "I was the head coach at Notre Dame for five years, and during four of those years my captains, who were elected by the other players, were Protestants," Harper said. "I found that the religious beliefs of a man were never important at Notre Dame. They take a man for what he's worth." Years later, Harper and others who had been connected with Notre Dame were pleased to note that, in one of Notre Dame's most memorable victories, in 1935, star halfback Bill Shakespeare, a Protestant, threw a touchdown pass in the final minute of play to Wayne Milner, a Jew, to upset Ohio State. And then, of course, there was Gipp, the son of a Methodist father and Baptist mother.

When reports that Notre Dame felt the Gipp family was responsible for Gipp's medical and funeral bills came to the attention of Grantland Rice, the *eminence gris* of sportswriters and a close friend of Rockne, he wrote a column criticizing the university for not paying for Gipp's funeral expenses, and that, as a result, Gipp's parents "had to mortgage their small home to pay the charges." Since Rice's column was nationally syndicated, and because he was highly respected in journalistic circles, those allegations were damaging—at least for a while—to Notre Dame's prestige. Rockne himself was upset over what he considered unfair charges against Notre Dame. A week after Gipp's death, the coach wrote a letter of sympathy to Gipp's parents in which he said Gipp would be a paradigmatic figure for all future Notre Dame football players and would be missed by all of Notre Dame's students and that he himself would greatly miss the greatest player he had ever coached.

In the aftermath of Gipp's death, the question naturally arose as to whether, somehow, his life could have been saved. The consensus of medical experts was that it apparently could not, but that strep throat, as streptococcus is commonly known, is easily controllable. "Had antibiotics been available, Gipp's streptococcus infection could have been cured," said Doctor Charles Higgs-Coulthard, the chairman of the Family Practice Department at the Saint Joseph Regional Medical Center in South Bend. That is now the case, as it has been for more than seventy-five years as a result of antibiotics and penicillin. "In my sixteen years of practice, I've never heard of anyone dying from strep throat," Doctor Higgs-Coulthard said.

∽◦∽

Strangely enough, Gipp's youngest sibling, Dorothy, may have written a friendly letter in late December to Iris Trippeer, Gipp's former fiancée, who apparently had jilted him and married another man three months before his death, unbeknownst to Gipp. In the typewritten letter, whose authenticity has been difficult to establish, Dorothy Gipp discusses Gipp's reputed conversion to Catholicism, which, she purportedly wrote, "is quite a well-discussed subject here—and elsewhere too, I imagine." By "here," she apparently referred to Gipp's hometown of Laurium, which, surprisingly, she misspells "Larium." "If it were not for those other Calumet & Larium [sic] boys at Notre Dame, we could deny it openly at South Bend, but it seems that it would make it hard for them—so I understand it," she wrote of her brother's supposed religious apostasy. Her reference to "boys" appears to be to Hunk Anderson, Ojay Larson, and Perce Wilcox, all of whom were from Calumet and were pallbearers for Gipp's coffin both in South Bend and in Laurium. That Miss Gipp, a schoolteacher who grew up in Laurium, would misspell the name of her hometown seems somewhat surprising.

❧❦❧

Among the many encomiums to Gipp was a long, unbylined piece in the *Notre Dame Scholastic* that described his memorial service in South Bend as "a tribute which some of the Caesars had not received." Later, the writer, apparently referring to Gipp's off-campus lifestyle, said, "There were things in his character we did not understand, and there were others in which he may have fallen short of our ideal." It was one of the few instances where anyone lamenting Gipp's death had alluded to his pool and card playing, and his deficiencies as a student. Overall, the tributes from those who knew Gipp well focused mainly on his popularity among his teammates and other students, his low-key persona, his determination to play in crucial situations while injured, and his trustworthiness and honesty.

"Let me give you the human side of Gipp as I knew him," said Arthur "Little Dutch" Bergman, one of Gipp's former roommates, who later became the head football coach at Catholic University in Washington. "No man is a hero to his valet, they say, and that goes double for a roommate, yet you couldn't help admiring George. He was the soul of generosity. Though he came from a poor family, money meant nothing to him. I've seen him win $500 in a crap game, and then spend his winnings buying meals for destitute families. No wonder he was idolized by the South Bend townies."

On the first anniversary of Gipp's death, another former teammate, Ed DeGree, by then a junior, wrote of Gipp in the *Notre Dame Scholastic*, "Notre Dame men, especially those who knew him best, his teammates, coaches, and fellow students, were given the privilege of knowing him not as George Gipp the All-American, but as George Gipp the man. George Gipp was a true gentleman and friend of splendid character and high ideals. Notre Dame shall always cherish his memory and point with mingled pride and sorrow to George Gipp as a man well worth emulation."

Those comments added to the martyrdom of Gipp and seemed to dispel the perception by some people, including at least a few in the Notre Dame family, of Gipp as an indulgent hedonist and loner who defied social mores and team rules and was indifferent about the Notre Dame football team—and the baseball and basketball teams, too—and his teammates.

❧

Gipp's final statistics, which reflected his great versatility, were both glittering and remarkable. His rushing average of 8.1 yards per carry in 1920 and his career average of 128.4 total yards a game for a non-quarterback still stood as school records in 2010, while his career record of 2,341 yards rushing in 27 games stood for 58 years until Jerome Heavens broke it in 1978. No records were kept for passing at Notre Dame during Gipp's career, but it was generally conceded that he was probably the best long passer in the country, deadly accurate as long as 50 yards with the oblong ball of the era, which made long-range passing difficult. "Until Sammy Baugh came along, Gipp was the greatest long-range passer of all time," said Dutch Bergman, referring to the star halfback from Texas Christian whose exploits with the Horned Frogs and the NFL's Washington Redskins in the 1930s and 1940s established him as one of the best, if indeed not the best, passer in the game's history. Perhaps Gipp's most astonishing achievement, though, for which no records have ever been kept, was not allowing a completed pass in his territory over a four-year, twenty-eight-game period when Gipp played both offense and defense. And then, of course, there was Gipp's 62-yard dropkick field goal as a freshman in 1916. No Notre Dame player has ever kicked a longer field goal by placement, which is acknowledged to be a lot easier than by drop-kicking, a method that went out of style in the 1930s.

❦

Even without Gipp, indisputably the greatest back he would ever have, Rockne kept on winning. Still underpaid at less than $10,000 a year compared with the likes of Fielding Yost, Pop Warner, and a number of other high-profile coaches, but earning more than double Notre Dame's most highly paid profes-sors, Rockne arranged Notre Dame's longest schedule ever for 1921—11 games. With a veteran team that included a virtual fraternity of future coaches in linemen Eddie Anderson (the team captain), Hunk Anderson, Clipper Smith, Harry Mehre, and Tom Lieb; quarterback Frank Thomas; fullback Chet Wynne; and the squad's best back in Johnny Mohardt, the Fighting Irish ran their winning streak to twenty games before losing to Iowa, 10–7, in the third game of the season. In that game, Duke Slater, an outstanding Hawkeye tackle who played without a helmet, as only a few players still were doing in 1921, endeared himself to the Fighting Irish late in the game by his gentleness. Bearing down on Chet Grant, the 135-pound Notre Dame quarterback, after Grant had fielded a punt, Slater grabbed the diminutive Grant—whom he outweighed by more than 100 pounds—and pulled him gently to the ground. Francis Wallace, at the time a student sports aide for Notre Dame, said years later that had Slater hit Grant with full force, "Grant could have been annihilated." Instead, Wallace recalled years later, it was one of the most sportsman-like gestures he had ever seen on a football field. Like Roger Kiley and Norm Barry, Slater also became a judge in Chicago—in his case one of the first black Superior Court judges in the city.

Following the loss to Iowa, Notre Dame recovered to win its last eight games to finish at 10–1, while starting a new winning streak of fourteen games, which would end with a scoreless tie at Army in 1922. Before the second game of the 1921 season, against Indiana in Indianapolis, Rockne was said to have invoked George Gipp's name for the first time. Before the opening kickoff, Rockne supposedly claimed that rough play by the Hoosiers in the 1920 game had resulted in dislocating Gipp's shoulder and could have hastened Gipp's death. Whether that was the reason the Irish beat Indiana, 28–7, is unlikely, although the allegation, true or speculative, was typical of Rockne, who was not averse to stretching the truth or fabricating an anecdote to inspire his charges.

For years, Rockne, exerting the clout he had amassed at Notre Dame, had resisted overtures for games from other

Catholic schools such as Georgetown, St. Mary's, John Carroll, and Marquette. His position was that by playing those schools it could divide the loyalty that Catholic fans throughout the country had amassed for Notre Dame, mainly because of the stronger opposition it played, its nickname, its charismatic coach, and the great George Gipp. That Rockne and Gipp were both Protestants did not matter. Notre Dame actually had played Marquette 5 times, but that was from 1908 through 1912 when Notre Dame was still a relatively unknown school and certainly not yet a football power. Somehow Rockne had tentatively acquiesced in 1919 to play Marquette in 1920, but then, as he sometimes was wont to do, decided to play a better-known school instead. Marquette officials subsequently complained to the Notre Dame administration, and Rockne was in effect forced to schedule Marquette in 1921. Angered over Marquette's athletic director having gone over his head to get a game with Notre Dame, Rockne got even by never scheduling the school again, although he did agree to play three other Catholic schools between 1922 and 1930—St. Louis, Detroit, and Loyola of New Orleans. Charming and likeable as he was, Rockne was quick to take umbrage and never forgot a slight, as Marquette was to find out.

Perhaps the most notable aspect of the 1921 season was Notre Dame playing three games within the span of eight days. After beating Army on Saturday, November 5, the team remained in the New York area, staying and practicing at the Bear Mountain Inn near West Point, and then made its New York City debut on the following Tuesday, Election Day, by routing Rutgers,

48–0, before a crowd of less than 12,000 at the Polo Grounds, home of baseball's New York Giants and New York Yankees. Despite the short period of time between the games, Rockne had accepted an offer from Rutgers—which Notre Dame had never played—to play at the Polo Grounds because it would attract the attention of New York's dozen newspapers and Notre Dame alumni in the metropolitan area, along with hopefully adding to its growing "subway alumni" who had no connection with the school. Returning home the following day, the players were able to return to their classes on Thursday and Friday before demolishing the Haskell Institute, a school for native Americans, 42–7.

While playing two games in the New York area in four days did attract considerable media attention, it wasn't a financial windfall. Notre Dame received less than $7,000 ($70,000 in 2010) as its share for the two games, but train travel, hotel, and food expenses resulted in a net profit of less than $3,000. Because of the newspaper coverage, however, Rockne thought the trip was well worth it for Notre Dame.

Much as he appreciated what George Gipp had done for his first three teams—from 1918 through 1920—Rockne hoped that never again would he have to depend so much on one player. That certainly was the case starting in 1922 when four undersized backs—Don Miller, Elmer Layden, Jim Crowley, and Harry Stuhldreher, who together averaged 158 pounds, light even by the standards of the 1920s—joined the varsity. Two years later, they would be immortalized by Grantland Rice following a Notre Dame victory over Army in their only meeting at the Polo

Grounds in what is considered the most memorable, and best, lead ever written by a sportswriter under deadline pressure:

> *Outlined against a blue gray October sky the Four Horsemen rode again. In dramatic lore they are known as Famine, Pestilence, Destruction, and Death. These are only aliases. Their real names are Stuhldreher, Miller, Crowley, and Layden.*

Rice, a colorful and literate writer prone, like many sportswriters of the era, to hyperbole, was referring to the Four Horsemen of the Apocalypse in the New Testament of the Bible. Hyperbolic? Yes. But this was not only the Golden Age of Sport, but the Golden Age of Gee-Whiz sportswriting. Although Rice also tended to deify some athletes and overly dramatize some games, he wrote far more elegantly than many of his star contemporaries. He was also better educated than most, having received a degree from Vanderbilt University in his native Tennessee, where he played football. Later, as a young sportswriter for the *Nashville Tennessean*, he clearly demonstrated his talent for elegant writing when he wrote a poem about sportsmanship that was to become a classic:

> *"For when the One Great Scorer comes*
> *To write against your name*
> *He marks—not that you won or lost—*
> *But how you played the game"*

Copies of the poem, which made it into *Bartlett's Familiar Quotations,* were to be hung up in locker rooms and other venues where athletes gathered as a reminder that the way one played was far more important than the outcome of a sporting contest.

Years after the Rice lead, which immortalized the Four Horsemen, George Strickler, the Notre Dame student press aide who handled the football team's public relations in 1924, said that he had seen the movie, *The Four Horsemen of the Apocalypse*, starring the silent screen star Rudolph Valentino, at Washington Hall on the Notre Dame campus the night before the team left for the Army game at the Polo Grounds. At halftime, Strickler said he was talking to Rice, Damon Runyon, and some other sportswriters in the press box during which several of the writers raved about the precision of the Notre Dame attack. After mentioning he had only recently seen the movie, Strickler said to the writers, "Just like the Four Horsemen."

"Rice was the only one who picked up on it," said Strickler who went on to become the publicity director of the fledging National Football League and then assistant sports editor of the *Chicago Tribune*. "In later years, my appreciation of Granny (Rice's nickname) as a writer and a reporter grew as I recalled that others had the same opportunity to pick up a chance remark and build it into a classic, but missed it entirely."

But then, of course, none of the other writers, good as some of them were in the Golden Age of Sportswriting, was Grantland Rice.

When Strickler saw Rice's story on the front page of the *New York Herald Tribune*—which wasn't inclined to put sports stories on page one—he got an idea, which would lead to a classic sports photo. He immediately wired South Bend to arrange to have four horses and a photographer on campus Monday afternoon, by which time Strickler and the rest of the Notre Dame party would have returned to South Bend. Unbeknownst to Rockne, Strickler then had the four horses trot onto Cartier Field during a practice session.

"Rock gave me hell in a polite way," said Strickler, who had explained to the coach what he had in mind. "He thought it was a swell idea, but he objected to the timing that barged unannounced into his practice."

Eventually Strickler managed to get Crowley, Layden, Stuhldreher, and Miller, all in uniform and clutching footballs, onto the horses, who were more accustomed to pulling ice and coal wagons than being mounted, and the photos were taken by a South Bend photographer whom Strickler had called on Sunday. Within an hour, Strickler sent the best of the photos to the Associated Press and other wire services and by the next day the shot of the Four Horsemen astride four horses appeared in sports pages across the country.

For at least a few minutes while the photos were being taken, Notre Dame's formidable linemen were neither amused nor appreciative of Strickler's stroke of genius. But if Rice's lead had led to the Notre Dame backs being crowned the "Four Horsemen," a comment by center Adam Walsh led to a nickname for him and his fellow linemen. While watching the photo shoot, Walsh turned to a few reporters and said, "We are the seven mules who do all the work so these four fellows can gallop to fame." Thereafter, the Notre Dame line became known as the "Seven Mules." That nickname stuck, but was far overshadowed by the one Grantland Rice had bestowed on Crowley,

Layden, Miller, and Stuhldreher, which ultimately became the most famous, but not necessarily the best, backfield in football history, thanks also to George Strickler's prescient photo idea. Playing the triple-threat position of left halfback, as Gipp had done, Layden was the best runner among the "Horsemen," but not in Gipp's class. Strickland was another example of Rockne's tendency to hire bright and creative student press aides at a time when few colleges had sports information directors. Strickler's predecessors were Francis Wallace and Arch Ward, both of whom became nationally known sportswriters. Ward, who like Wallace also worked on South Bend newspapers, later became the sports editor for the *Chicago Tribune*, where, in the 1930s, he created both the Major League All-Star game and the College All Star game, which, until the 1960s, matched a group of recent college graduates, most of whom had been All-Americans, against the defending National Football League champion. Later press aides included Paul Butler, who became the chairman of the Democratic National Committee, and J. Walter Kennedy, who after a career in public relations that included tours of duty as sports information director at Notre Dame and publicity director for the Harlem Globetrotters basketball team, became mayor of his hometown of Stamford, Connecticut, and later commissioner of the National Basketball Association, for which he had served as its first publicity director in the mid 1940s.

Two years before their immortalization as the Four Horsemen, Crowley, Miller, Layden, and Stuhldreher were members of the first Notre Dame team to play in the Deep South, when the Irish met Georgia Tech in Atlanta on October 28, 1922. Because Atlanta was the headquarters of the Ku Klux Klan, one of whose main targets was the Catholic Church, Rockne warned his players that it was entirely possible they could receive a verbally hostile, or even worse, reception in the Georgia capital. Before the game, Rockne let loose with his most vigorous pep talk of the season, telling the players that they were about to play the best team in the South, who would be playing for the honor of Southern football. "We're a young and green team, but I want you to show what you can do for me and for yourselves and for Notre Dame," he said in his customary and dramatic staccato style of speaking.

Then came the bombshell. Pulling a telegram out of his pocket, Rockne suddenly became emotional and appeared barely able to talk. "I want to read this to you," he said solemnly, staring down at the telegram. "PLEASE WIN THIS GAME FOR MY DADDY. IT'S VERY IMPORTANT TO HIM. The telegram is from Billy who's very sick and in the hospital." The players were stunned. Six-year-old Billy Rockne often came to practices and home games, and the players regarded him as their mascot. Jumping from their stools in the locker room, they let out a collective roar and raced onto the field, where, ignoring anti-Irish and anti-Catholic taunts from a crowd of about 15,000, easily defeated Georgia Tech, 13–3. When the team returned by train to South Bend the following day, among the several hundred on hand were Bonnie Rockne and little Billy, who was jumping up and down on the station platform. "You never saw a healthier kid in your life," Jim Crowley was to say sometime later. Once again, as he was prone to do when he thought desperate measures were required, Rockne had not only stretched the truth, but had pulled a fast one, and it appeared to have paid off. Was there resentment?

Not at all. Even sophomores like Crowley, Layden, Miller, and Stuhldreher had heard about Rockne's tendency to deal in apocrypha, and they would hear it again before their careers at Notre Dame were over.

Having allowed only 10 total points in its first five games, Notre Dame was heavily favored the following Saturday to beat Indiana, which was making its first appearance in South Bend. Fans of the Hoosiers, who had arrived from Bloomington in chartered trains, along with large Notre Dame alumni groups, resulted in an overflow crowd at Cartier Field. Prohibition may have been in effect in Indiana for four years, but it was not apparent before, during, or after the game in South Bend, which had more speakeasies in 1922 than it had bars before Indiana had gone dry in 1918. Notre Dame would win the game easily, 27–0, its fourth shutout victory in six games. After blanking Carnegie Tech (now Carnegie Mellon), 19–0, for its fifth shutout, the Irish would lose their only game of the season, to Nebraska, 14–6, in Lincoln in the season's final game. Again in 1923, Notre Dame's only loss would be the Cornhuskers, 14–7, again in Lincoln, where, after the team's arrival, Rockne had flashed the front page of the *Lincoln Star*, which, above a story on the next day's game carried a headline that read HORRIBLE HIBERNIANS ARRIVE TODAY. Rockne was furious, but neither the headline nor the coach's fiery pregame talk would be enough to lift the Fighting Irish to victory. However, the Four Horsemen and the Seven Mules would get even in a big way during their final game against Nebraska, a 33–6 demolition of the Cornhuskers the following season, when Notre Dame would win all ten regular season games and then beat Stanford in its only Rose

Bowl appearance to cap a national championship season. At the time, the Rose Bowl had New Year's Day all to itself in football; it was the first and, during its early years, only bowl game in the country.

During the Four Horsemen's three varsity seasons at Notre Dame (college players were limited to three years of varsity play at the time), the Fighting Irish won 28 games, lost two, and tied one, while winning the national championship in 1924 when the Four Horsemen were seniors. Crowley, Layden, and Stuhldreher were named consensus All-Americans in 1924, as were Adam Walsh and tackle Rip Miller. Only Crowley—called "Sleepy Jim" because of his heavy eyelids, which gave the impression that he was perennially tired—played in the NFL, appearing in two games with his hometown Green Bay Packers and one with the Providence Steam Roller in 1925. All of the Four Horsemen later became head coaches: Miller at Georgia Tech (before becoming a lawyer and then the United States attorney for northern Ohio); Layden at Duquesne and Notre Dame, where he later served as athletic director; Crowley at Michigan State and Fordham (where he coached the famous "Seven Blocks of Granite" line that included Vince Lombardi); and Stuhldreher at Villanova and Wisconsin, where he also served as athletic director.

Crowley, Layden, and Stuhldreher all would become successful business executives, while Layden would serve as commissioner of the NFL from 1939–1946. After serving in the Navy during World War II, Crowley became the first commissioner of the new All-America Football Conference in 1946, and the next year was part owner and the coach of the league's Chicago Rockets. Crowley later became the manager and sports director of a television station in Scranton, Pennsylvania, and then commissioner of the Pennsylvania State Athletic Commission. Throughout their lives, though, each of the foursome would be forever linked to their collective designation as the "Four Horsemen of Notre Dame." Speaking of her husband's legacy as one of the Four Horsemen, Mary Stuhldreher was to say, "No matter where he speaks or what he says, he is always remembered as the quarterback of the Four Horsemen."

Remarkably, Rockne did virtually no recruiting and had nothing to do with Crowley, Miller, Layden, and Stuhldreher coming to Notre Dame. Miller was merely following in the footsteps of four older brothers who had played at Notre Dame, including Gerry, a backup halfback on the same team Don starred on; Crowley was steered to South Bend by Curley Lambeau, his high school coach at East Green Bay High School, who had played with Gipp; Layden was recruited for track and baseball by Walter Halas, who was coaching both sports at Notre Dame at the time and who had coached Layden in high school in Davenport, Iowa; and Stuhldreher merely had followed in the footsteps of a brother, Walter, who already was at Notre Dame.

Rockne conceded that it was mere coincidence that the legendary foursome had arrived at Notre Dame at the same time. But then, of course, Rockne was prone to stretching the truth. "How it came to pass that four young men so eminently qualified by temperament, physique, and instinctive pacing complement one another perfectly and thus produce the best coordinated and most picturesque backfield in the recent history of football—how that came about is one of the inscrutable achievements of coincidence of which I know nothing, save that it's a rather satisfying mouthful of words." Rockne always insisted that he did no recruiting on his own, relying on alumni, especially former players, to steer promising high school and prep players to Notre Dame, or just hoping that outstanding young players would apply to the university. Again, when he said that, Rockne seemed to be spinning a yarn.

The "Four Horsemen" were probably not the best Notre Dame backfield, even up until that time. The 1920 backfield of Gipp, Joe Brandy, Chet Wynne, along with Johnny Mohardt and Norm Barry, who alternated at right halfback, was at least equal and perhaps, because of Gipp, even better, as was the 1929 and 1930 unit of quarterback Frank Carideo, Marchmont "Marchy" Schwartz, Marty Brill, and Joe Savoldi (who was replaced by Larry "Moon" Mullins midway through the 1930 season), which Rockne felt was his best ever. But those outstanding backfields would became overshadowed by the Four Horsemen, who had achieved sports immortality, primarily as a result of Grantland Rice's prose and George Strickler's offhand comment about a movie he had seen shortly before the 1924 Notre Dame–Army game at the Polo Grounds in New York.

Fortunately, the focus on the Four Horsemen in the early 1920s and the outstanding teams they were part of overshadowed several ugly incidents in South Bend. Though a northern state, Indiana had by 1924 become a hotbed of Ku Klux Klan activity, most of which had been previously confined to the South. By the middle part of the decade it was estimated that approximately one of every three men in Indiana were members of the ardently anti-Catholic Klan. During a number of klavens held in South Bend, much of the Klan's venom was directed at Notre

Dame, the pope, and Catholicism in general. On several occasions, hundreds of Notre Dame students confronted and clashed with robed Klansmen during Klan gatherings in downtown South Bend until the skirmishes were broken up by police officers, many of whom appeared more supportive of the Klan than the students. Fortunately, by the fall of 1929 the Klan's influence in Indiana had waned considerably, and Knute Rockne's biggest concerns were how he could possibly top another unbeaten season and a serious health issue.

18

WIN ONE FOR THE GIPPER?

AS ROCKNE'S TEAMS continued to win and his fame and popularity grew, he became more attractive as a potential head coach to a number of major universities. Starting in the mid-1920s, overtures reportedly were made to Rockne by Iowa, Northwestern, Wisconsin, Michigan State, and Princeton. General Douglas MacArthur, who as the superintendent at West Point once tried to recruit George Gipp for Army after Gipp had been expelled, albeit briefly, from Notre Dame, in the spring of 1920, apparently had his eye on Rockne as a coach of the Cadets as well. In a letter to Red Blaik, who had played for Army and who later became the coach at West Point, MacArthur wrote in 1924, "Had I stayed at West Point, I intended introducing new blood into our coaching system, and Rockne was the man I had in mind."

Apparently the most serious offer to Rockne—at least at the time—came from the University of Southern California. While in Pasadena for the Rose Bowl in January 1925, Rockne met with representatives of USC to discuss the possibility of him becoming the Trojans' coach. Once an offer was made, the word got back to Notre Dame president Matthew Walsh, who knew Rockne had signed a ten-year contract in 1922, the year Walsh succeeded Father James Burns as president of the university. Despite that contract, Rockne in December 1925 signed an agreement to coach at Columbia, which by then had high hopes of elevating its football team to the elite level of Yale, Harvard, and Princeton, who still dominated the college game.

Columbia said it had offered Rockne $25,000 ($250,000 in 2010) a year for a three-year period, two and a half times what he was getting paid at Notre Dame, and which probably would have made him the highest paid football coach in the country. When news of the agreement appeared in New York newspapers, and eventually papers around the country, Rockne was embarrassed and furious at Columbia for releasing the news prematurely. Swayed to a large degree by friends who were Notre Dame alums, Rockne managed to back out of the deal. Saving face as it were, Columbia announced it had withdrawn its offer to Rockne when it learned he was under a long-term contract, which Rockne later claimed Columbia had known about all along.

By 1925, Rockne's relationship with Father Walsh and other administration officials at Notre Dame, who had begun to exert greater control over the school's sports program through the school's Faculty Board of Control, had begun to exasperate him. What led Rockne to accept the Columbia offer was a decision by the faculty board to cancel the 1926 game against Nebraska following anti-Irish chants and a demeaning halftime show during the 1925 game in Lincoln. Rockne thought the cancellation was overkill and deprived Notre Dame of a big-time rival. Already having seen how a number of Big Ten schools had built huge stadiums, including one at Michigan that could hold 85,000 spectators, Rockne was upset at the reluctance of Notre Dame to consider building a stadium at least half that size, rather than continuing to expand Cartier Field, which now held 12,000 spectators, puny by comparison. But Walsh and the faculty board, determined to improve the school's academic reputation and not to have Notre Dame perceived as a football factory, said the school had other priorities, such as new class-rooms and dormitories. For his part, Rockne was able to note that during the 1924–25 academic year, Notre Dame football had generated almost $300,000 in revenues, and that after oper-ating expenses more than $200,000 went into the university's general fund. That a varsity sports program could raise that much money for campus projects was extraordinary, and Rockne knew it. He also knew that although he was still the athletic director he had little to say about where the sports program's allotment, around $100,000, would go. Despite his problems with the faculty board, Rockne stopped looking elsewhere and ignored what coaching offers were extended to him during his remaining years as football coach at Notre Dame—with one exception.

❧❧❧

With the Four Horsemen and Seven Mules gone, the 1925 season was memorable for two reasons. First, with a team consisting primarily of sophomores (freshmen still were not allowed to play varsity sports), Notre Dame lost two games for the first time since Rockne became head coach in 1918, and indeed the first time since 1914. Secondly, Army ended a seven-game winless streak against Notre Dame by crushing the Fighting Irish, 27–0, before a crowd of about 70,000 in the first game between the two schools at two-year-old Yankee Stadium. (However, Notre Dame would rebound to beat Army in four of their next five meetings and lose only two of its nineteen games in 1926 and 1927.) It was also in 1925 that Rockne converted to Catholicism, and received his First Holy Communion, one of the first rites that a Catholic takes, on Saturday, November 21, the day of a home game against Northwestern.

That conversion may have influenced the play of the Fighting Irish that afternoon—at least in the second half, according to fullback Rex Enright, the team's best runner, who later became the head coach at South Carolina. "We were losing ten to nothing at the half, and our failing Rock on that particular day was heartbreaking," Enright said. "I'm sure this had a great influence on our play in the third quarter when we scored two touchdowns and won the game."

But then, the players may have been trying too hard for their coach in the first half. Or perhaps they were motivated by his sarcastic halftime scolding. "We expected him to come in and let us have it, but we waited and waited and waited, and no Rockne," tackle Joe Boland recalled. "Then suddenly, only three minutes before the second half kickoff, he burst in and said, 'Fighting Irish, are you? You look like peaceful Swedes to me. You can have the honor of dandling your grandchildren on your knees and telling them that you had the honor of playing on the first team at Notre Dame that quit.' After he walked out, we almost broke down the door going out on the field and took the kickoff and went 75 yards, all on the ground, for a touchdown. Then a little while later, we scored on another long drive without a single pass."

In 1926, Notre Dame appeared to be on its way to a possible unbeaten season after winning its first eight games, seven of them shutouts. In the second to last game, against Carnegie Tech in Pittsburgh, Notre Dame was a heavy favorite, and Rockne decided to turn over the coaching reins to Hunk Anderson who, along with former teammate Tom Lieb, had joined Rockne as assistant coaches. Rockne, meanwhile, would go to Chicago to see the Army–Navy game. He had been talked into doing so by his new agent, Christy Walsh (now also the ghostwriter of Rockne's weekly syndicated column), who had arranged for publicity photos to be taken of Rockne, Pop Warner, then the coach at Stanford, and Yale coach Tad Jones. It turned out to be one of Rockne's biggest mistakes, and, although Anderson followed Rockne's instructions, his absence may indeed have cost him an unbeaten season. Anderson was a great line coach, but not in Rockne's league—hardly anyone was—as a head coach, especially on game day.

Rockne's decision to let Anderson take over while he was in Chicago proved a potent motivating tool for Carnegie Tech's part-time coach Chicago judge Wally Steffen. Before the game, Steffen, seizing on what he felt was a golden opportunity, told his players, "Rockne thinks you're so bad that he's gone to Chicago to see some real football players in the Army–Navy game."

Steffen's pep talk was all the Tartans needed as they proceeded to upset Notre Dame, 27–17. When Rockne got word of the final score at Soldier Field, he blanched, incredulous at the result and furious at himself for having gone to Chicago rather than coach his own team. The Irish had a chance to finish on a winning note the following Saturday against Southern California at the Los Angeles Coliseum, but with two minutes to play, the Irish trailed, 12–7. Rockne shocked everyone at that point when he sent seldom-used, fourth-string, 145-pound, ambidextrous quarterback Art Parisien into the game. Rockne's theory was that the USC defense would be confused by a quarterback who could pass with either hand. He was right, and, with time running out, Parisien threw a touchdown pass—with his left arm—to half-back Butch Niemiec that enabled Notre Dame to win, 13–12, and finish the season at 9–1. Despite that heroic achievement, Parisien, then one of the few Notre Dame football players from New England—in his case, Haverhill, Massachusetts—felt he would still not see much action with the Irish the following season and transferred to Boston University. Meanwhile, elated as he was over the dramatic victory over USC, the loss to Carnegie Tech the previous week would haunt Rockne for much of the off-season.

Despite the embarrassment of the Carnegie Tech loss, Rockne was pleased to have Anderson and Lieb join the Notre Dame coaching staff. After graduating with a degree in engineering, Anderson had gone from being a 170-pound guard at Notre Dame to a 190-pound professional lineman. Following four years as the head line coach at Notre Dame, Anderson, a Rockne favorite, became the head coach at St. Louis University. In 1930, he would return to Notre Dame as Rockne's assistant, and then serve as head coach from 1931 through the 1933 season. After three years as the head coach at North Carolina State, Anderson served as line coach with the Detroit Lions and the Chicago Bears of the NFL. From 1942–1945, Anderson was the head coach of the Bears while George Halas was in the service during World War II. It was an opportune time to be with the Bears, who won the NFL title in 1940, 1941, and 1943, and finished as runner-up in 1942. Anderson was a co-coach with Luke Johnsos of the 1943 championship team. "Hunk was the best defensive coach in the history of the NFL," said Halas, the Bears' founder and longtime coach. Anderson is also credited with devising the "blitz," wherein a defensive back or a linebacker bolts through a hole in the offensive line, and other novel defensive schemes.

Anderson, elected to the College Hall of Fame as a guard, was one of about a dozen of Gipp's Notre Dame teammates who went on to coach on the college or professional level, many of them with distinction at major universities. Four other Gipp teammates, three linemen and a quarterback, were elected to the College Football Hall of Fame for their distinguished coaching careers: Eddie Anderson, who coached at Holy Cross, Iowa, and DePaul and later became a prominent surgeon; Edward "Slip" Madigan, who turned tiny St. Mary's College in northern California into a nationally known school when he coached the Galloping Gaels to a victory over a powerful Fordham team that included Vince Lombardi in 1930 and also recorded victories over West Coast football powerhouses like California, UCLA, and Southern California; and Lawrence "Buck" Shaw, who after a College Hall of Fame coaching career at Santa Clara and the University of California became the first head coach of the

San Francisco 49ers and later coached the Philadelphia Eagles, whom he took to an NFL title in 1960, their last to date. Shaw also became the first head coach at the Air Force Academy; and Frank Thomas, who became a College Hall of Fame coach at Alabama and whose order to punt as a quarterback with the Notre Dame freshman team in 1916 Gipp defied and instead kicked a 62-yard field goal.

One other Gipp teammate, halfback Norm Barry, spent three years playing in the NFL, two with his hometown Chicago Cardinals and one with the Green Bay Packers while at the same time attending law school. After coaching the Cardinals in 1925 and 1926, Barry became a superior court judge in Chicago. End Roger Kiley, also a Chicago native, played one season with the Cardinals and then coached at Loyola University in his native Chicago before becoming a state and then federal judge in his hometown.

Former Gipp roommate Dutch Bergman coached both Catholic University and the NFL's Washington Redskins, while Harry Mehre, Jim Phelan, Joe Brandy, and Chet Wynne, also teammates of Gipp, each coached on the college level. Curley Lambeau, of course, became the founder and a player and coach with the Green Bay Packers. Other coaches who had played for Rockne in the 1920s included Lieb, Frank Leahy, Edgar "Rip" Miller, Frank Carideo, Marchy Schwartz, and Noble Kizer. All were disciples of the Rockne system and spread his coaching style and enthusiasm for football and his players across the country in the coming decades.

"We were everywhere, but there was only one Rockne," said Schwartz, an All-American running back in 1929 and 1930, who was an assistant coach at Notre Dame before becoming the head coach at Stanford in 1942.

Among other Gipp teammates who did well after graduating from Notre Dame was Dave Hayes, a five-foot eight-inch, 160-pound end from Manchester, Connecticut, who hopped several freight trains to get to South Bend in 1916 and played alongside Gipp as a freshman that year. Like many of his teammates, Hayes went off to war in 1918 and, after being wounded in action in France in 1918, returned to Notre Dame the next year. Upon graduating in 1921, Hayes, who held several part-time jobs while at Notre Dame, presented a check for $250 to President Burns toward a university building fund. "I came here broke on a freight train, Father," Hayes told Burns, "and I'm leaving the same way." As it turned out, Hayes became successful in business in the Hartford area. Several years later, Hayes's young son died while holding onto the miniature gold football that Rockne had given to all members of the undefeated 1919 team. Hearing about the tragedy, Hunk Anderson, then the Notre Dame coach, sent his own gold football to Hayes with a letter of condolence. It was the same miniature football that Anderson's then fiancée, Marie Martin, asked Anderson for—only to be rebuffed—after she claimed to have seen Gipp's then girlfriend, Iris Trippeer, wearing one that Gipp had apparently given to her in early 1920.

❧❧❧

Having outgrown Cullum Field at West Point, Notre Dame and Army decided to move their rivalry to New York in 1923. The first game was played before a near-capacity crowd of around

35,000 at Ebbets Field in Brooklyn, then the home of the Brooklyn Robins of the National League, who later became the Dodgers. The second game, played in Manhattan on October 18, 1924, at the Polo Grounds, the home park of the New York Giants baseball team, attracted a larger crowd, a capacity gathering of 55,000. An even bigger crowd of about 65,000 turned out for the third New York City game, and the first at Yankee Stadium in the Bronx. Those large crowds, which mainly seemed to be made up of Notre Dame supporters—perhaps because of the city's large Irish population—were an indication that the school's "subway alumni" was continuing to grow. (Notre Dame administrators preferred to use the somewhat derogatory term "synthetic alumni.") From that game in 1925 through 1946 every game between Army and Notre Dame was played at Yankee Stadium with crowds of upward of 80,000, except for the 1930 game, which was played at Soldier Field in Chicago before an estimated 110,000 spectators.

The 1946 game, though it ended in a 0–0 tie, is regarded as a classic, since it matched the country's two best teams, including the eventual national championship Cadets, who were led by the great backfield tandem of All-Americans Felix "Doc" Blanchard and Glenn Davis—the fabled "Mr. Inside" and "Mr. Outside"—while the Notre Dame lineup included All-Americans Johnny Lujack, the Irish quarterback, and fullback and defensive end Leon Hart. After 1946, the schools met only twice more in New York—at two-year-old Shea Stadium in 1965 and at Yankee Stadium in 1969. In their only other games in the New York area, Army and Notre Dame played twice at Giants Stadium in East Rutherford, New Jersey, in 1983 and 1995. A scheduled meeting between the two schools in November 2010 was to be their first in New York since 1969 and the first at the new Yankee Stadium. It was also to be the fiftieth meeting between the two schools.

Strangely enough, the most storied game between Army and Notre Dame did not come about from the game itself, but became immortalized by a legendary oration by Knute Rockne. With a 4–2 record and what Rockne regarded as his weakest team ever, Notre Dame came into the 1928 game at Yankee Stadium on November 10 as a prohibitive underdog to an undefeated Army team before a capacity crowd of 78,000. Before the game, Rockne, by then the most famous football coach in the country, gave what is generally regarded as the most famous pep talk of all time. Or at least that is the legend.

Walking into the Yankee Stadium locker room following the pre-game practice, wearing his trademark fedora and tan over-coat and looking somber, Rockne, as usual, drew the attention of his players, even without saying a word. Once their spellbinding coach started talking, though, all forty players, along with some of his friends—including New York's flamboyant mayor, Jimmy Walker; Ed Healey, a former All-American at Dartmouth; and a leading heavyweight boxer, Gunboat Smith—sat and stood mesmerized and enrapt, according to at least several eyewitnesses, as Rockne began to talk. "You've all heard of George Gipp, I presume," he said softly. Naturally, they had, even though they'd been in grade school when Gipp played. After recounting Gipp's great talent, his sudden illness near the end of his final season, his hospitalization, and his deathbed struggle, Rockne said, again softly, "You may not have heard what he told me that night, which I'm going to tell you now." What none of them knew was that, according to Rockne, the day before he died Gipp had asked a final favor of Rockne: that he ask "the boys" on a day when things aren't going right for the team to "win one for the Gipper. I've never told any team of that request before, but I've told you now."

Rockne then turned and, without another word, walked out of the locker room. For a few moments, the players sat on their stools in silence, most of them with their heads down. Then, suddenly, they let out a collective cheer and raced for the locker room door. Among them was Lawrence "Moon" Mullins, a sophomore fullback. "You can imagine the effect of that talk on me, a sophomore, going out to look at Army for the first time," said Mullins who became a coach at Kansas and Loyola University in New Orleans and then a lieutenant commander in the Navy during World War II. "As we rushed out for the field, I passed Walker, Healey, and Smith, and I saw tears in the eyes of each one. Three men from three totally different spheres of life, all affected the same as we Notre Dame kids."

Some sources claimed Rockne's "win one for the Gipper" talk was made at halftime of the game. But a number of others who were present when Rockne delivered his most inspirational talk agreed with Mullins. They included Ed Healey, a part-time assistant Notre Dame coach at the time, and Francis "Frank" Wallace.

"Rock was terribly disturbed on the day of the game," said Healey, a College Hall of Fame tackle at Dartmouth and later a Pro Football Hall of Famer with the Chicago Bears. "About five minutes before game time, he spoke to the team. He prefaced his remarks on the terrific Army team. Finally he recalled standing beside the deathbed of Gipp and told of reaching out his hand and listening to the dying athlete say, 'Coach, when the going gets tough, especially against Army, win one for me.' There was no one in the room that wasn't crying, including Rockne and me. Then there was a moment of silence, and all of a sudden those players ran out of the dressing room and almost tore the hinges off the door."

Two years later, Rockne, in an article ghostwritten for him for *Collier's* magazine, provided what became the oft-quoted classic "win one for the Gipper" request that the coach said Gipp had made while dying at St. Joseph Hospital in South Bend. The same quote would be included in Rockne's autobiography, which was published in 1931.

Still, there were doubters, especially among former teammates, that Gipp had ever asked Rockne to ask one of his teams to "win one for the Gipper" when prospects were bleak. Among them was Hunk Anderson, the last player to visit and talk to Gipp before he died. "I doubt very much if he would have said that," Anderson told the author shortly before he died in 1978. Anderson and some others who knew him best said it would have been out of character for Gipp, even on his deathbed, to have made such a request to Rockne. It would have been more plausible and likely, some of them said, if Gipp had asked Rockne to put $500 on the Irish to win when Notre Dame was an underdog but had a good chance to win. But there were a few of Gipp's teammates who thought it possible that Gipp did indeed intone the immortal exhortation. "I didn't believe it for a long time," Chet Grant, also interviewed in the late 1970s, told this writer, "but I now think it's entirely possible that he said it." So did President Ronald Reagan, who was to say that, while filming the movie *Knute Rockne: All American,* Rockne's wife, Bonnie, told him that her husband had noted in his diary that during his deathbed conversation with the coach, Gipp had indeed asked that the team "win one for the Gipper."

Despite their motivation, stoked even higher by Rockne's eloquent oration, the Notre Dame players still had to face an undefeated Army team who was favored by two touchdowns and was expected to win the national championship. One thing Notre Dame had in its favor was a "friendly" referee in Walter Eckersall. But if Notre Dame was to win, it would have to stop All-American halfback Chris "Red" Cagle. Like Elmer Oliphant, Harry "Light Horse" Wilson, and a number of other Army stars before him, Cagle had played varsity football elsewhere—in his case at Southwestern Louisiana—and now was in his third of four seasons at West Point, where, as at Southwestern Louisiana, he was an All-American. That Army used players who had played as many as four years of college football elsewhere is why it became a pariah to many schools who refused to play the Cadets. Even Navy temporarily put an end to its hallowed rivalry with Army in 1928 and 1929 because it adhered to the conventional three-year varsity eligibility system but Army did not.

The Irish did stop Cagle in the first half, and even reached the Army 2-yard line before losing the ball on a fumble by full-back Fred Collins in what turned out to be a scoreless first half. In the third quarter, Cagle led Army on a drive that ended in the game's first touchdown. But later in the period, in front of the overwhelmingly pro-Notre Dame crowd of 78,000, the Irish drove 52 yards to tie the score on a 1-yard plunge by halfback Jack Chevigny. After crossing the goal line, Chevigny tossed the football into the air and exultantly called out, "That's one for the Gipper!" As Army had done, Notre Dame missed the extra point attempt, leaving the score knotted, 6–6.

With tension mounting, and Notre Dame obviously playing with a fervent intensity, the Irish undertook their last offensive drive late in the fourth quarter. With the ball at the Army 35-yard line, Rockne sent in the seldom-used end Johnny O'Brien. At this time the rules forbade an incoming player from talking to the quarterback, or anyone else, for that matter, so as not to relay a play from the coach. But halfback Butch Niemiec knew exactly what he had to do. On the next play, Niemiec rolled out to his right as O'Brien sprinted down the left sideline, cut inside (faking out five-foot nine-inch safety Bill Nave), and then cut back towards the sideline. From the 40-yard line, Niemiec fired a high and long pass to the speedy six-foot two-inch O'Brien, who caught the ball on the 2-yard line, juggling it slightly as he crossed the goal line to give the Fighting Irish the lead as the crowd erupted with a roar that could be heard across the Harlem River. Again, the Irish missed the extra point, and it was 12–6, Notre Dame.

Army now had one last chance. Notre Dame's kickoff inexplicably went to Cagle, one of the great Army runners of all time, and he ran it back 62 yards to the Irish 31-yard line on the home-plate side of Yankee Stadium. On the next play, Cagle darted and dashed to the Notre Dame 10, but then staggered off the field exhausted to cheers from the entire corps of West Point cadets. His substitute, Dick Hutchinson, completed a pass to the Irish 4-yard line, then plunged to within a yard of the goal line on fourth down and referee Eckersall blew his whistle ending the game. The Fighting Irish had prevailed, 12–6. The pro-Notre Dame crowd exploded with cheers, and hundreds of Irish supporters burst onto the field, tearing down the goalposts a foot away from where the game had ended. For his game-winning catch, O'Brien would go down in Notre Dame football lore as "One-Play O'Brien." That was uncharitable, since O'Brien had already caught several other passes that season. But he had caught only one against Army; thus the sobriquet.

The next day, over drinks at the Ritz-Carlton Hotel in Manhattan, Joseph Byrne, a Notre Dame alumnus and Rockne friend, told Frank Wallace about Rockne's "win one for the Gipper" oration in the Notre Dame locker room. A few hours later, Wallace typed out his story for the Monday editions of the *New York Daily News,* quoting Rockne as having said that, on his deathbed, Gipp had requested of Rockne that, "when the time came, he wanted me to ask a Notre Dame team to beat the Army for him."

"It was not a trick," Wallace went on. "George Gipp asked it. When Notre Dame's football need was greatest, it called on its beloved 'Gipper' again." Rockne's written account two years later of what Gipp had said to him on his deathbed differed slightly from Wallace's written account, using the "win one for the Gipper" exhortative quote for the first time. Still, Wallace had essentially broken the "win one for the Gipper" story. After reading Wallace's story, Harry Schumacher, a copy editor in the sports department of the *Daily News,* realized that the story deserved a striking, catchy headline, and he wrote one that fit the bill. GIPP'S GHOST BEAT ARMY, Schumacher's headline read, followed by a sub-head that said, "Irish Hero's Deathbed Request Inspired Notre Dame."

"When the *Daily News* hit the streets a few hours later, the story of George Gipp soon became an American legend, as common to sports fans as a familiar fairy tale is to a sleepy-eyed youngster," Jimmy Breslin, who later became a columnist for the *Daily News,* was to write years later. "The Gipp myth gained fantastic momentum through an era of newspaper sportswriting that saw athletes likened, in print, to Greek gods. Out of this came the legend of 'The Gipper.'"

In fact, Gipp had already become a legend at Notre Dame, as Breslin pointed out, but Wallace's story, which attracted national attention, expanded his legendary status and anointed him with the nickname of "The Gipper," far and away the most famous and evocative nickname in sports history. Indeed, forty-six years later, in 1984, the *New York Daily News* would refer to then President Ronald Reagan exhorting members of the United States Olympic team by quoting him in a front page headline that read, "Ron Tells U.S. Olympians before the Summer Olympics in Los Angeles, 'DO IT FOR THE GIPPER,'" a reference to Reagan's portrayal of George Gipp in the 1940 movie about Knute Rockne.

The year 1928 was especially significant to Notre Dame for another reason besides their upset of Army. It was also the year in which a Roman Catholic ran for president on a major party ticket for the first time. Because of his stature and popularity, and perhaps because he had converted to Catholicism three years earlier, Rockne was asked by some prominent Democratic leaders to campaign for New York Governor Al Smith, whom

Rockne had met and liked—perhaps because they had much in common, even though Smith was a native New Yorker and Rockne a Norwegian immigrant whose family had settled in the Midwest. However, Rockne, very likely at the suggestion of Notre Dame administrators, chose not to campaign for Smith, although he supported him in the election, which he lost to Herbert Hoover the week before the Army game.

⁂

Ironically, while the 1928 Army–Notre Dame game would best be remembered for Rockne's recitation of a young athlete's dying wish, a number of players in the game would die young, most of them tragically so. Chris Cagle, who averaged 6.4 yards a carry during his four seasons at West Point, went on to play five seasons in the NFL with the New York Giants and then the Brooklyn Dodgers. While living in New York, Cagle, then thirty-seven years old, fell down a subway stairwell on December 26, 1942, and died of a fractured skull. Jack Chevigny, after serving as an assistant to Rockne and then becoming the head coach at Texas, was killed at Iwo Jima in 1945 while leading a unit as a forty-year-old Marine captain during World War II. Eight years earlier, in 1937, Johnny O'Brien, who caught the winning touchdown pass in the game and later served as an assistant to Elmer Layden, was killed in an auto accident. Then in 1954 Fred Miller, captain of the 1928 team who later became the president of his family's Miller Brewing Co. in Milwaukee, was killed along with his son, Fred, when his private plane crashed. Miller had served as an assistant coach to Frank Leahy, who succeeded Layden in 1940. None of the four had reached the age of fifty. Nor, of course, had

George Gipp, who had died at twenty-five. And then, of course, Knute Rockne would also die much too early.

Unfortunately, Notre Dame was unable to extend its three-game winning streak and lost its last two games. The first of those losses was to underrated nemesis Carnegie Tech by three touchdowns at Cartier Field, where the Irish hadn't been beaten since 1905; and the second was in Los Angeles to USC by two touchdowns. Thus, Notre Dame finished with a record of 5–4, Rockne's worse mark since becoming head coach in 1918. Besides ending Notre Dame's twenty-three-year long winning streak at home, the loss to Carnegie Tech was also jarring, since the Tartans, so called in honor of the school's Scottish-born founder, Andrew Carnegie, were coached on a part-time basis by Walter Steffen, a Chicago judge.

Among the sportswriters on hand for the Carnegie Tech game was well-known *New York Herald Tribune* sports columnist W. O. McGeehan, who, though he had written glowingly about George Gipp, had expressed doubt, seemingly in jest, as to whether Notre Dame actually had a campus and suggested that the football team—because of all of its long-distance traveling—spent the football season living in sleeping cars aboard trains. Following the Notre Dame upset of Army, McGeehan decided to travel to South Bend to cover the Carnegie Tech game and to check out the school's campus or at least see if there really was one. When Rockne got wind of McGeehan's train trip, he invited him to stay at his house, which McGeehan did. On his return to New York, McGeehan wrote that Notre Dame "is no place of mystery and no recruiting camp, but just an American university with some fine traditions and some very human undergraduates." McGeehan even got to look at some of the university's financial records and concluded that much of the money made from football went toward the building of dormitories and classrooms on campus. Rockne and the mandarins at Notre Dame couldn't have been happier over McGeehan's prose relating to the university. Also, the columnist never again referred to Notre Dame teams as "Knute Rockne's Wandering Irishmen," as he had in the past.

❧❧❧

Despite the upset of Army, and the fact that the team still ended with a winning record, some disgruntled alumni apparently felt that Rockne, at the age of forty, should be replaced, not only because of the four defeats but due to his growing number of outside interests. Whether Rockne had heard such rumors or not, he did consider an offer at the end of the 1928 season from Ohio State. It was tempting since it meant that Rockne would be coaching a team in the Big Ten and thus would have a shot at beating two coaches who had refused to play Notre Dame—Fielding Yost of Michigan, whom he disliked intensely, and Bob Zuppke of Illinois. Rockne's demands apparently had been met, but then the deal unraveled when it became public during a coaches' meeting in New Orleans, whereupon Rockne backed out of what had been a tentative agreement. According to Francis Wallace, who was close to the coach, top executives at Studebaker wanted Rockne to stay in South Bend, and, indeed, shortly after Rockne's second thoughts about going to Ohio State, the company hired Rockne to travel around the country to deliver speeches motivating Studebaker's sales force. The charismatic coach turned out to be so good at it that Studebaker not only kept raising his salary, but eventually named a car for Rockne.

Nevertheless, Rockne came close to leaving again the following June, when, upset over two appointments that had been made within the athletic department without his knowledge, he sent a wire to the new Notre Dame president Charles O'Donnell from one of his coaching camps asking him to accept his resignation. Another reason for his ostensible intent to quit was O'Donnell's refusal to re-admit a promising halfback who had flunked out the year before. In a subsequent letter to O'Donnell, Rockne also said he felt that there were a group of professors and some other staff members at Notre Dame who had been conspiring against him, resentful of his success and the attention the football team had received. Unwilling to lose Notre Dame's renowned coach, O'Donnell made a number of changes that mollified Rockne and convinced him to stay. It would be the last time Rockne would consider any outside coaching offers. The main reason could have been his new association with Studebaker.

June 1929 was even more notable for another reason; it marked the last graduation of a minims class, the students from first through the eighth grade who had been a part of Notre Dame since its founding in 1842. The prep school, which included students from the ninth through the twelfth grades, had closed seven years earlier, in 1922, when its last senior class graduated. (Freshman and sophomore years had been eliminated in 1920, and the junior year in 1921.) While the minims and "preps," as they were called, shared the same campus, they attended classes in separate buildings. During Notre Dame's early years, the minims and preps outnumbered the college students, but they were a small minority by the time the grade and prep schools were closed.

⁂

From his worst team, in terms of records at 5–4 in 1928, Rockne's 1929 unit was probably as good as any he ever had, winning all nine of its games, all of them on the road, which prompted many sportswriters to restamp the Irish as the "Ramblers" once more. After years of trying, Rockne had finally persuaded the top administrators at Notre Dame that a new stadium was desperately needed to attract major football-playing schools, and, of course, produce more money for the university. Since construction was well underway, the Fighting Irish were unable to play at home, but would play three games at Soldier Field in Chicago, only eighty-five miles away, where the team had a huge fan base and which was less than a two-hour train ride from South Bend.

Fortunately for Rockne, he would have one of his best backfields ever, if indeed not the best, in Frank Carideo, Joe Savoldi (at least for a while), and halfbacks Marchmont "Marchy" Schwartz, who had spent the first part of his freshman year at Loyola of New Orleans but left when he found out that many of the football players rarely went to class, and Marty Brill, a rare transfer from the University of Pennsylvania, where he felt his running and outstanding blocking talents had not been appreciated. Ethnically, they was hardly the "Fighting Irish." Of the four backfield men, two, Carideo and Savoldi, were Italian; and two, Schwartz and Brill, were Jewish. A year later, Rockne, in what would be considered a gross faux pas decades later, told a

San Francisco sportswriter that Schwartz was particularly smart "from the Jewish blood in him."

Indelicate ethnic comments such as Rockne's on Marchy Schwartz were hardly unusual in sports stories in the 1920s, and rarely drew complaints from readers. Brill's backup at left halfback, Clarence Kaplan, also was Jewish, as was guard Norm Hewitt, a mainstay of a strong line, but Rockne refrained from attributing their intelligence to their religion. As Rockne, ever the promoter and visionary, saw it, that backfield quartet would help produce a lot of victories and would no doubt attract Italian and Jewish fans, which they did. Rockne's greatest loss was his line coach and right-hand man, Hunk Anderson, who had become the head coach at St. Louis University. Anderson's replacement, though, was an excellent one in Tom Lieb, who had been a teammate of Anderson's in 1921 and had returned to South Bend in 1929 after serving as an assistant coach at Wisconsin.

Rockne's other "coaches" were his quarterbacks, in whom he had supreme confidence. "All Rockne quarterbacks called their own plays," Carideo, a two-time All American and probably his best quarterback, recalled. "Rock simply trained us to think the way he did and react the way he would to a changing situation. The best way to put it, without sounding immodest, is that Notre Dame quarterbacks were an extension of Knute Rockne himself. For example, he would say to us, 'I want you to be cocky at all time. At all times! And without a let-up. For several reasons. First of all, it shows the other team that you have complete confidence, and you know exactly what you're going to do next. That there's no doubt in your mind.'"

Rockne also disavowed huddles, where he thought debates and disagreements could occur. He wanted only the quarterback to talk between plays. "'I'm not asking you to put on phony airs,'" Carideo quoted Rockne as having told him, and probably other quarterbacks, too. "'You're just playing a role. It isn't you personally that I want to be cocky. It's you the Notre Dame quarterback. But be wise enough to know a limit. Don't get your teammates soured on you.' That was Rock's way." Rockne hardly had to tell Carideo to be cocky; it was one of his trademarks.

❧❦

Playing on the road in 1929 proved to be no disadvantage whatsoever, although three of the games were decided by one touchdown, and one, against Southern California at Soldier Field, by a single point. What appeared to be a disadvantage, though, was Rockne's health. In the week before the second game of the season, against Navy in Baltimore, Rockne was diagnosed with phlebitis. A blood clot had developed in his right leg and there was a danger of it going to his heart. Doctors convinced him not to make the trip to Baltimore that Saturday or to Chicago for the Wisconsin contest a week later. They also told him that rest and the immobilization of his ailing leg were the only way to cure the phlebitis. The garrulous and outgoing Tom Lieb turned out to be an excellent choice to fill in for Rockne, especially against Wisconsin, whose system he knew so well. During the weeks leading up to all of Notre Dame's games during the 1929 season, Rockne conducted practices from a platform erected at Cartier Field, from where he bellowed instructions to his players and coaches through a megaphone. And before each game, he carefully charted what he wanted Lieb to do. Lieb may have been in charge on the sidelines of most of the 1929 games, but Rockne was still calling the shots, and even calling the Notre Dame locker room before games to talk to his starting players.

When word of Rockne's illness spread across the country, the now famous Notre Dame coach received hundreds of get-well letters and telegrams from fellow coaches, former players, alumni, and the legion of Fighting Irish subway alumni. Though he was still incapacitated and confined to a wheelchair, there was no way Rockne was going to miss the fourth game, in Pittsburgh against Carnegie Tech, which had beaten Notre Dame in their last two meetings. Wheeled into the locker room about fifteen minutes before the game was to start, Rockne sat quietly for several minutes while his players alternately looked at him, uneasily, and at each other, unsure of what he was going to say and, more importantly, concerned about his health. Off to one side, Rockne's doctor, Maurice Keady, turned to Francis Wallace and said, "If he lets go and that clot dislodges and hits his heart or his brain, he's got an even chance of not leaving this dressing room alive." Wallace, who had become a close friend of Rockne, blanched.

Finally, with just about everyone in the locker room in a collective state of discomfort, Rockne spoke. "A lot of water has gone under the bridge since I first came to Notre Dame, but I don't know when I ever wanted to win a game as badly as this one," he said, bundled in a heavy overcoat and his trademark fedora, "and I don't care what happens after today." Then, alluding to his illness, Rockne asked, his voice rising, "Why do you think

I'm taking a chance like this? To lose? They'll be primed. They'll be tough. They think they have your number. Are you going to let it happen again?"

By now, Rockne was shouting, much to the chagrin of Doctor Keady, Wallace, Tom Lieb, and others in the room who knew how ill the coach was. As Wallace recalled, "Now he shot the works. He really let go."

Shouting as loud as he could, Rockne, in one of his most emotional pep talks, bellowed, "Go out there and crack 'em. Crack 'em hard. Fight to live and fight to win, win, win!"

After the last of the players had run out the locker room door, Rockne, sweating profusely, appeared to faint, where-upon Doctor Keady wiped the sweat from his face and his brow, took his pulse, and waved to a trainer to start pushing his wheelchair out onto the field before a crowd of about 60,000. On this day, as Wallace put it, Knute Rockne appeared to want to win more than he wanted to live. Fired up as they never had been before, Rockne's superb 1929 team battled ferociously in edging the powerful Tartans, 7–0, on a 1-yard plunge by Joe Savoldi on the last of four cracks at the Carnegie line starting at their 7-yard line. Two weeks later Rockne, again at the doctors' suggestion, remained home when Notre Dame played Drake in Chicago, but was back in front of the Irish bench in his wheelchair the following week for the Southern California game, where he received a huge ovation from most of those in the crowd of 113,000 when he was pushed out on the field at Soldier Field.

With the score tied at 6–6 at halftime, backup fullback Paul Castner got off his stool and, emotionally charged, told his teammates how much they owed Rockne, who had risked his life by travelling to Chicago by train to be with the team. It became even more emotional a short while later when Rockne was wheeled into the locker room, got up from his wheelchair, and implored his charges to "Go on out there and play them off their feet. Play 'em! Play 'em! Play 'em hard. Rock will be watching." Inspired to fever pitch, first by Castner, and then by Rockne, the players almost knocked the door down as they burst out onto the field.

Buoyed by their teammate and coach's words, Notre Dame drove for a go-ahead touchdown on its first possession of the second half, with Joe Savoldi crashing over from the 5-yard line. Carideo, the talented triple-threat quarterback from Mount Vernon in New York's Westchester County, had missed his first conversion attempt but made his second to give Notre Dame a 13–6 lead. But then USC responded dramatically as Russell Saunders ran back a kickoff 95 yards for a touchdown, something no other player had ever done against a Rockne-coached team. However, once again, USC missed the conversion attempt, and the Irish went on to win, 13–12. That night, what Doctor Keady had warned Rockne could happen because of his insistence on continuing to coach, did. While he was resting, the clot in Rockne's right leg became loose, passed through his heart, and finally settled in his left leg. It was a close call that could have been fatal.

Largely because of that scare, Rockne, at his doctors' insistence, remained in South Bend during Notre Dame's last two games. The Irish beat Northwestern 26–6 in Evanston, Illinois, then traveled to New York to face Army. With Tom Lieb at the helm for the fourth time, Notre Dame beat Army at Yankee Stadium, 7–0, on a 96-yard interception return by reserve half-back and track team sprinter Jack Elder, who picked off a pass from the Cadets' Chris Cagle in the second quarter and streaked down the right sideline untouched into the end zone. As he did, Rockne, surrounded by some old South Bend friends and listening to Graham McNamee's rousing radio call of Elder's run at his home, yelled, "That's it, he'll go all the way."

Highlighted by outstanding defensive play by both teams, the game was described, somewhat hyperbolically, by Robert Kelley of *The New York Times* as "one of the best football games of history." Primarily, it was a very good defensive struggle, but hardly "one of the best" ever. Mainly because of the cold and windy weather, neither team was able to complete a pass, with Army missing all seven of its throws, and the Irish failing to connect on any of Frank Carideo's passes. Despite the frigid conditions and the fierce hitting throughout by both sides, Army played the entire game without a substitute—not unusual at the time, but certainly hard on the eleven starters given the sub-freezing weather—while Notre Dame used seven substitutes. Notre Dame's All-American left guard Jack Cannon was particu-larly outstanding on defense, playing the entire sixty minutes, as he always did, without a helmet or even a cap to keep his head warm on that frigid afternoon.

Before the game, Rockne delivered a pep talk via telephone to his players from his home in South Bend, stressing once more how significant a victory over Army was to Notre Dame, its students, alumni, and its growing legion of fans. Whether it had a bearing on the outcome is difficult to judge, but it's more than possible that the coach's illness, and his long-distance pep talk, motivated the team. After the game, Rockne described the season as the toughest one his teams had ever endured and indicated that he might lighten Notre Dame's schedule somewhat in the future. "My boys were splendid," he said. "Not only today, but during the whole season."

Even though the Black Friday stock market crash was only a month old, a standing-room-only crowd of an estimated 85,000 packed Yankee Stadium for the game, played on a frozen field with the temperature about five degrees above zero. In all, West Point officials said, more than 200,000 people had applied for tickets to the game. Among those in the celebrity-studded, albeit frozen, crowd were Notre Dame's Four Horsemen (Jim Crowley, Elmer Layden, Harry Stuhldreher, and Don Miller); New York governor and 1928 Democratic presidential nominee Al Smith; New York City's flamboyant mayor, Jimmy Walker; Police Commissioner Grover Whalen; movie impresario Samuel Goldwyn; Yankee owner Jacob Ruppert and his star player, Babe Ruth; famed football coaches Pop Warner, Tad Jones, Bob Zuppke, Bill Roper, and Chick Meehan; congressman and eventual legendary New York City mayor Fiorello La Guardia; and a half dozen Army generals, including the Chief of Staff Charles Summerall.

In a complete turnaround from the disappointing 1928 season, the 1929 Irish team had gone undefeated—the fourth time a Rockne team had done so—and had turned a profit of almost $545,000, the largest ever, most of which went into the school's general fund. Still, not everyone at Notre Dame was happy with the success of the football team. Some administrators and faculty members still thought that the school's growth and recognition had been entirely predicated on its football accomplishments—which was true—and worried that many, if not most, people continued to perceive Notre Dame as a football factory, and not as the strong educational institution it had become, attracting outstanding students of diverse ethnic backgrounds from throughout the country.

That Rockne had skirted the normal entrance process and academic admission standards to acquire some players was undeniable. His predecessor and close friend, Jesse Harper, was to say years later, "I don't want to knock Rockne in any way, but he was a football man first and foremost, and he liked to win with the best possible squads." Harper was a highly literate coach who kept a close eye on the academic progress of his players, including George Gipp in 1917, his first varsity season. "At times, Rockne was a little too eager. He'd recruit from other schools' freshmen teams," Harper said, "or he would let a player slough off on his studies just to be a better football player."

Rockne never admitted he did so, though he kept George Gipp on the football team when he rarely went to class, but no doubt felt that he was justified in bending the rules since most of the greatest coaches of his era—Amos Alonzo Stagg, Fielding Yost, Pop Warner, and Bob Zuppke, among others—were doing the same, if not worse. Trying to rationalize his methods even further, Rockne felt he had to keep up with those coaching luminaries to achieve the success he had had over the last decade, not only in winning football games, but in focusing attention on Notre Dame to the point of making it a nationally known university.

One thing Rockne said that he never did, however, was visit a prospective player at his home while he was in high school. Rockne felt that if he recruited a player, the player would expect to play, even though he might not eventually cut it and be as good as Rockne thought he was and thus not play much, if at all. "I wouldn't ever want to find myself in that situation," he said, "so I primarily rely on my former players and other alumni to recommend good players, and the system has always worked." That was remarkable if indeed Rockne, once again, wasn't stretching the truth.

By the mid-1920s some coaches and sportswriters began to suggest that Rockne had lured some players to Notre Dame who either hadn't graduated from high school—which, of course, neither he nor George Gipp had—or had already played at other colleges before enrolling at Notre Dame. In some cases the latter charges turned out to be true, and the Notre Dame faculty board, which theoretically controlled the athletic department, if not Rockne, saw to it that a number of such players were forced to leave school. As to allegations of overemphasis of football by Notre Dame and some other schools, Rockne once said, "Has anyone ever defined overemphasis? They talk about football and its evils, yet they don't offer any clear-cut analysis of their charges. They do it to get publicity, and you can't blame them for that, but let's stop this scramble for the front page and hiding behind the skirts of fighting for football purity." It was a mantra Rockne would repeat often in his criticism of what he called misguided "reformers."

19

EVEN BETTER THAN THE HORSEMEN

AS GOOD AS 1929 had been, with nine victories, all on the road, 1930 portended to be even better for Knute Rockne and a team that returned virtually intact from the previous unbeaten season. Notre Dame would play its toughest schedule ever, and four of the ten games would be played on campus in the new 54,400-seat concrete stadium on whose every detail Rockne had been consulted. New opponents would include Southern Methodist and Pennsylvania, and for the first time the Irish would play Army outside of New York state—at Soldier Field in Chicago.

In the eyes of many students and players, past and present, the stadium, still standing today although expanded in 1997 to seat slightly over 80,000 spectators, would be a monument to Rockne. Largely because of his zealousness as a coach and fervent apostle of Notre Dame football, he had watched home game crowds grow from around 3,000 when he was a player from 1911 through 1913 to more than 25,000 at Cartier Field, and had lobbied steadfastly for a new stadium in recent years.

Both because Rockne had become the face of Notre Dame football and the endearment with which he was held by students and alumni, groups representing both of those factions had pushed to have the stadium named for the man whose teams had made a little-known, small, Catholic university in the Midwest famous throughout the land and even abroad. Rockne resisted those efforts, however, insisting that it be named Notre Dame Stadium, largely, it is believed, because he thought that naming the stadium for him would raise the specter of overemphasis on football and glorify, if indeed not sanctify, Rockne, to the chagrin of the school's administration. Remarkably, the stadium had been built in less than a year for $750,000, far less than the approximately $2 million that had been spent to build new stadiums at both Ohio State and Pittsburgh. By contrast, the addition of about 21,000 seats in 1997 cost $50 million. Making the stadium's construction all the more remarkable was that the stadium was built in just four months, with virtually all of the work done by a crew of 500 following the Wall Street collapse the previous October. Remarkable, too, was the fact that the stadium had been financed by selling premium seats in advance and also selling all of the leased boxes for ten-year periods, along with giving those buyers first shot at premium seats at Notre Dame road games over the next ten years.

Though still troubled by phlebitis, Rockne's condition was much improved by the time spring practice began in March 1930. Rockne and his wife had spent a quiescent six weeks in

Miami, most of it on the beach, but Rockne, rather than enjoy his time in the sun, became depressed over his phlebitis, which was painful at times and limited his mobility. A brief relapse while he was in Florida depressed him all the more and convinced his doctors to send him to the Mayo Clinic in Minnesota, where he stayed for two weeks. By then swelling had also developed in Rockne's left leg, and doctors told him that henceforth he would have to have both legs bound with rubber bandages. By summer his condition had improved considerably in time for his first football camp on the Notre Dame campus, from which the university, like Rockne, benefited financially.

Rockne had his entire starting backfield from the 1929 team returning, along with a solid line that included the remarkably talented 148-pound guard Bert Metzger, who would emerge as an All-American in 1930. Among those who had graduated was Jack Cannon, the bareheaded guard who had eschewed a helmet for three seasons without any serious consequences and who had been named an All-American (along with tackle Ted Twomey and quarterback Frank Carideo). Meanwhile, the shuttle involving former Notre Dame teammates Hunk Anderson and Tom Lieb continued. Anderson, who had left after the 1928 season to become head coach at St. Louis University, returned as an assistant coach after St. Louis decided to deemphasize football, while Lieb left again to become the head coach at Loyola of Los Angeles (now Loyola Marymount). Rockne also added three other assistants, including Jack Chevigny, one of the heroes of the 1928 "win one for the Gipper" Army game. That gave Rockne four assistant coaches, three more than he had when he became head coach in 1918, and the same number as that of most teams in the Big Ten. In addition, by 1930, the football team had a doctor accompany it on all road trips, and a full-time trainer in Eugene "Scrap Iron" Young. Young's route to becoming a trainer was serendipitous. As a 130-pound football prospect in 1924, Young had been badly hurt, and, as a reward for his enthusiasm and grit, Rockne offered to have him stick around as a part-time trainer. Until then, and even most of the time thereafter, Rockne also served as the team trainer, applying his own concoction of liniment, taping and bandaging players, and examining them for injuries, at which he was, according to his players, remarkably accurate in his diagnoses.

"Rock read a lot of medical books and really knew what he was doing," said Young. "He could feel a player's injured knee and tell right away whether he had torn or otherwise injured a ligament or cartilage. Even doctors were amazed at how much he knew. One doctor, after spending quite a bit of time with Rock, later asked me what medical school he had gone to. He couldn't believe it when I told him he hadn't gone to any medical school."

❧

By the fall of 1930, Rockne was the father of four children—the oldest fifteen and the youngest four—and had a salary of $10,000 a year, $6,500 more than when he became the head coach in 1918. He also was doing well financially as a motivational speaker, who, during the off season, when healthy, delivered as many as three talks a week, a few for as much as $500. He also received about $3,000 a year for his syndicated newspaper column, which he wrote, or, more correctly had ghost-written by Christy Walsh, during the football season. Additional income came from his summer football camps and for his work, mostly speaking engagements for Studebaker. It's unlikely that any other football coach was doing as well financially or, for that matter, as a coach.

During the last week of preseason practice, Rockne lost both his starting tackles—eventual Irish coach Elmer Layden and Dick Donoghue—for the season as a result of injuries, but because of his great depth was able to replace them with players capable of starting for almost any other college team. But then, by 1930, Notre Dame had a varsity squad of 110 players, most of whom would never play so much as a down. That was a testament to the allure of Notre Dame for high school football players.

Despite good weather, the opening game at Notre Dame Stadium on October 4 attracted just under 15,000 spectators, who could have all fit comfortably in the wooden grandstand at thirty-five-year-old Cartier Field, whose sod had been transported to the new stadium. On its opening drive, Southern Methodist needed only four plays, all passes, to score. But Joe Savoldi ran back the ensuing kickoff 98 yards to tie the score. Frank Carideo later returned a punt 48 yards for another Irish touchdown, only to have SMU respond with four straight completed passes, the last one good for a touchdown that drew the Mustangs even at halftime. Notre Dame finally pulled ahead for good in the third period on a touchdown pass from Carideo to end Ed Kosty. During that second half, Carideo, one of Notre Dame's greatest punters, repeatedly kept SMU bottled up deep in its own territory on "coffin-corner" punts, which invariably went out of bounds inside the Mustangs' 10-yard line. Carideo's finely angled punts became a lost art in later years when most punters—and their coaches—became satisfied to kick into the end zone, which gives an opponent the ball on the 20-yard line, or have a punter boot the ball high, but not into the end zone, in the hope that the receiver would call for a fair catch or that a defensive player would get downfield fast enough to tackle the kicker or down the punt somewhere inside the 20-yard-line.

The official dedication of the new stadium occurred the following Saturday when more than 40,000 spectators, including hundreds of former players, some of them Rockne's teammates, along with Rockne's predecessor, Jesse Harper, were on hand for Notre Dame's game against Navy. The night before, an estimated crowd of almost 20,000 people, including students, alumni, and South Benders, had turned out at the stadium for the dedication ceremony, which followed a torchlight parade from downtown South Bend. The ceremony included fireworks and the repeated playing by the university band of the "Notre Dame Victory March," which by the 1940s would rank with the "Star Spangled Banner," "God Bless America," and "White Christmas" as the country's best-known songs. Speakers included an emotional Rockne, who, in his talk, expressed his love for Notre Dame, his admiration and affection for his players over the years, and his gratitude to university administrators for agreeing to build the concrete oval. University President Charles O'Donnell, an accomplished poet and writer and perhaps the school's most intellectual administrator, devoted much of his talk to George Gipp, extolling the enigmatic Gipp by calling him Notre Dame's "spiritual guardian" and in effect the one mainly responsible for the stadium. That was a stretch, to say the least, and, much as he cared about Gipp, it must have bothered Rockne, who more than anyone else had pushed for a new stadium for years. Not surprisingly, Father O'Donnell also refrained from so much as alluding to Gipp's egregious academic performance, his poor class attendance, his expulsion when he was a junior, and his dubious off-campus lifestyle. The university president also read a panegyric poem by a Notre Dame student that referred to Gipp's putative deathbed conversion to Catholicism. Indeed, the tribute to "The Gipper" was so effusive that, at times, it seemed that the ghost of Gipp would emerge in a nimbus at midfield and proceed to drop kick several footballs over both goalposts.

Unlike the opening game against Southern Methodist, which ended 20–14, the contest against Navy was one-sided, with the Irish winning, 26–2, as Joe Savoldi scored three touchdowns. By now, after a successful season in 1929, Savoldi appeared on his way to an All-American berth. A bruising runner who had been born in Milan, Italy, the five-foot ten-inch Savoldi was hardly a quick study and had a tendency to forget signals and plays. Fortunately, in Carideo he had a quarterback who could speak Italian, in which Savoldi was fluent. In the game against Pittsburgh in 1930, Savoldi repeatedly was hit hard by a Panther tackle before he could get past the line of scrimmage, even after Carideo began to repeat signals to Savoldi in Italian. Finally, approaching the line of scrimmage, Carideo called out to the Pittsburgh linemen, "Any good Italianos here?" Whereupon the tackle who had been plaguing Savoldi raised his hand. "Thanks," replied Carideo who went back to calling signals to Savoldi in English. It hardly mattered. Pittsburgh had finished undefeated in 1929 and was expected to be in contention for the national championship again in 1930, but Notre Dame overwhelmed the Panthers by scoring 35 unanswered points in the first half, and then after Rockne had used reserves throughout the second half, gave up 19 points in winning, 35–19, before a capacity crowd of 70,000 in Pitt's new stadium The next three home games, easy victories over Carnegie Tech, Indiana, and Drake, drew disappointingly small crowds of 30,000, 11,000, and 10,000. A few Notre Dame economics professors and some sportswriters attributed the small Indiana crowd, in particular, to the first full year of what became the Great Depression, which had a severe impact on industrial South Bend. But three of the final four road games drew huge crowds. The first, after Pittsburgh, was played at Franklin Field in Philadelphia, where a capacity gathering of 73,000 turned out for Notre Dame's first ever game against Penn. For Marty Brill, the right halfback who had transferred to Notre Dame after his sophomore year because of a lack of playing time with the Quakers, it was a homecoming, and he made the most of it. Used primarily as a blocking backup until the Penn game, Brill, the son of a prominent Philadelphia industrialist (who was in attendance along with other family members), scored three touchdowns on runs of 66, 36, and 25 yards as the Irish romped, 60–20. As Grantland Rice put it in his account of the game, "Notre Dame's first team actually beat Penn 43–0 in 30 minutes of play." That was an allusion to Rockne pulling almost all of his starters after taking an insurmountable first-half lead. Rice, seeming to acknowledge the superiority of that Notre Dame backfield to the group that he had immortalized six years before, went on to write, "Rockne and Notre Dame passed on far beyond the Four Horsemen. With Carideo, Brill, Savoldi, and Schwartz, they put on a combination of four antelopes, four charging buffaloes, and four eels."

Savoldi, though he gained more than 100 yards rushing against Penn, blocked ferociously for Brill and Marchy Schwartz, who was on his way to becoming an All-American for the first of two consecutive seasons, as, apparently, was Savoldi. That is, until a story broke during the following week that the 22-year-old Savoldi had filed for divorce—in a South Bend court, no less. What made that news all the more stunning was that apparently no one connected with the team or the university in general knew that Savoldi had been married. That meant that Notre Dame had two reasons to expel him: for being married, which undergraduates were not allowed to be, and for getting a divorce, which was not permitted by the Catholic Church. Francis Wallace offered a third reason, writing that, "Joe hadn't learned not to sue for divorce in the middle of a football season, especially at Notre Dame." Unwilling to play favorites, even with a key member of perhaps Notre Dame's best team ever, Father O'Donnell informed Rockne that Savoldi had to go. For Rockne, it was perhaps the hardest thing he ever had to tell a player.

"Don't worry, Rock," Savoldi told the coach, sympathetic to Rockne's unpleasant chore, "I understand how it is."

In bidding good-bye to Savoldi, a personal favorite who he thought could become another Jim Thorpe, Rockne gave him a check for $1,500. Savoldi promptly signed with the Chicago Bears and appeared in three NFL games, scoring one touchdown. After that, "Jumping Joe," as he was billed, launched a successful wrestling career in an era when the sport included such legends as Jim Londos and Gus Sonnenberg, a former Dartmouth lineman, and was actually on the level. However, Savoldi never played football again.

For all of Savoldi's talents, replacing him was no problem for Rockne, since he had more than an adequate candidate in Larry "Moon" Mullins, who performed well during the next two games before being injured in the second one, against Army. In Army's first game in the Midwest, before a capacity crowd of 110,000 at Soldier Field on a cold, dank afternoon, Marchy Schwartz raced 56 yards for a touchdown and Frank Carideo kicked the extra point with four minutes remaining in the game to give Notre Dame a 7–0 lead. But then with less than a minute to play on Notre Dame's next possession, a Carideo punt was blocked and recovered in the end zone by Army to bring the Cadets to within one point, at 7–6. Fortunately for the Irish, three Notre Dame linemen burst through to block a drop-kick extra point attempt by backup Army quarterback Chuck Broshus, which enabled Notre Dame to prevail, 7–6. The following Saturday, in Notre Dame's last game of the season—and what would be Rockne's final game as the head coach—the Fighting Irish crushed Southern California, 27–0, before a crowd of 74,000 in Los Angeles. Moon Mullins's replacement at fullback, Paul "Bucky" O'Connor, a backup halfback from New Hampshire, was the star, running for three touchdowns while gaining more than a hundred yards. The decisive road victory secured Notre Dame's second consecutive unbeaten season and national championship. It was the fifth time a Rockne team had gone undefeated, and, as it turned out, a fitting coda to the Rockne legend. If the season marked the beginning of a new decade and a new stadium, it also was, undeniably, the end of an era in Notre Dame football.

Four players from the 1930 team were named consensus All-Americans—Carideo, Schwartz, the pint-sized Metzger, and end and captain Tom Conley—while Joe Savoldi, though he had missed Notre Dame's last four games, was named to the Associated Press first team, a tribute to his brilliance as a runner and blocker during the season's first six games.

Eight days later, Rockne would be on the sidelines again, this time at the Polo Grounds coaching the Notre Dame All Stars, a hastily arranged group of former Fighting Irish players, including the Four Horsemen and five of the Seven Mules who opened the holes for them to run through, along with playing defense. Others included Hunk Anderson, Jack Chevigny, and, from recent Notre Dame teams, Jack Elder and Jack Cannon, who, for this game, had the good sense to finally don a helmet. From the recently crowned national championship team came Frank Carideo, Tom Conley, and Bucky O'Connor, all who were in good shape yet worn out from the long ten-game season.

Their opponent was the New York Giants of the National Football League, still struggling to gain media and fan acceptance during their sixth year of existence. The game had come about when New York Mayor Jimmy Walker had asked Rockne, a longtime friend, if he could bring his Notre Dame team to New York to play the Giants at the end of the season to raise money for families made needy by the national depression that had just set in and which was taking a heavy toll on New Yorkers. Rockne agreed to come, but with a team of former players, feeling that his current squad had had enough football after ten hard-fought games. Save for the fact that the game did raise $100,000 for Walker's committee for unemployment relief, the game was a mistake from the point of view of Rockne and his players, most of whom hadn't touched a football in six years, as was the case with the Four Horsemen.

Nevertheless, the game attracted the second-biggest crowd the Giants had ever drawn, a capacity gathering of about 55,000 to the Polo Grounds, where Notre Dame had first played Army in New York City. (The larger-crowd was the 70,000 that jammed into Polo Grounds to see the Giants play and Chicago Bears team which included the great Red Orange in 1925, the Gianys first year in the NFL.) From the outset, it was a mismatch, with the Giants, who had finished second in the NFL that year, dominating throughout and winning, 22–0, a margin that would have been even wider had not the professional team used substitutes through most of the second half, and, at Rockne's request, taken it easy on his former players. The Notre Dame All Stars had spent four days practicing in South Bend before leaving for New York, but most of them were far from being in playing shape. In addition, their line was outweighed by more than twenty pounds a man, and they could not cope with the running and passing of the former Michigan star, and one of football's first great passers, Benny Friedman, who scored two touchdowns.

Before the first play of the game, John Law, a 165-pound starting guard on the 1928 and 1929 Notre Dame teams, who was from nearby Yonkers, took one look across the scrimmage line at 245-pound Giants tackle and eventual coach, Steve Owen, and said, mock seriously, to referee Tom Thorp, "Can you tell me how much time is left in the game?" Both Owen and Thorp couldn't help but laugh.

The first quarter was an omen as the All Stars gained only 5 yards rushing while losing 17. By game's end, the Notre Dame All Stars had managed only one first down, gained only 34 yards rushing—12 on a run by Rex Enright, the team's longest of the afternoon—and had failed to complete any of its seven passes.

In the locker room afterward, Rockne, who seemed to enjoy the game, said of the Giants, "That was the greatest football machine I ever saw. I'm glad none of you got hurt." The first sentence was probably Rockne hyperbole, intended to make the Notre Dame football alums feel better, while the second sentence was not only true but sincere. It was also the last time Rockne would ever speak to a team of Notre Damers—in this case a group that included some of the best players he had ever coached. At a banquet that night, he would raise a toast to the Four Horsemen and the rest of the Notre Dame All Stars, many of whom he hadn't seen in years and most of whom he would never see again.

20

THE END OF AN ERA

ROCKNE DID NOT dwell long on Notre Dame's second straight national championship. He was the toast of the college football world—the most famous coach with the best team—and an excellent salesman to boot, whether it was "selling" Notre Dame as an outstanding academic institution or selling Studebakers. But as usual he was anxious to get back to work.

Under contract with South Bend-based Studebaker since March 1929, Rockne made eighteen appearances on the company's behalf during the winter of 1930 and 1931. In late winter, the Studebaker hierarchy, so pleased with Rockne's performance on behalf of the company, made him its sales promotion manager. The work with Studebaker required considerable travel, but fortunately for Rockne his condition had improved, although his doctors cautioned him that if he overworked himself, his phlebitis, then in an arrested state, could flare up at any time. Several close friends said Rockne had told them that he liked the new challenge he faced in the business world, and that, at forty-three, perhaps it was time for him to leave coaching for another career. A full-time job with Studebaker would enable him to remain in South Bend and close to his beloved alma mater, which he had threatened to leave several times.

Meanwhile, John B. Kennedy, a veteran novelist and nonfiction writer and an associate editor for *Collier's* magazine, had finished Rockne's autobiography, which was based on a series of articles that had appeared under the coach's name in *Collier's* but had in fact been written by Kennedy. Kennedy stayed in close touch with Rockne while writing the book, which wound up including more than a few errors that Rockne, in skimming through the manuscript, apparently had overlooked. With all of his outside interests, it's not surprising that Rockne, though he was hardly averse to reading about himself, would merely skim through his own autobiography, which would be published later in 1931. However, he was hardly the first, or last, sports celebrity to thumb through his own autobiography, even when he was not entirely sure of its contents.

At his doctors' recommendation, Rockne spent a week at the Mayo Clinic before joining his wife, Bonnie, and their youngest child, Jackie, close by the Atlantic Ocean in Coral Gables, Florida, in early March. Encouraged by his progress in recovering from phlebitis, Rockne had also heeded his doctors' advice in taking a vacation, his first since the previous winter. Seemingly at ease on the Florida sand, Rockne knew he had a lot to be thankful for—a loving wife, four children (with whom he actually spent very little time, especially during the football season), a flourishing career that included two consecutive national championships, the satisfaction of knowing he had been instrumental in making Notre Dame nationally known, nationwide fame, and his work with Studebaker, which he enjoyed immensely. If he had one regret, it was not having devoted more time to his children: Billy, now 15; Knute Jr., 12; Mary Jean, 11; and Jackie, 5. Like many coaches, Rockne wound up being closer with his players than his own kids, who obviously adored their famous father. *From now on, though,* he would tell himself during the winter of 1931, *I'm going to spend more time with my kids.*

Visiting Rockne in late January, Francis Wallace found the coach playing with Jackie on the sand.

"You look great, Rock," Wallace told him.

"Good enough," Rockne replied. "They're letting me go swimming now. A year ago they only let me sit at the water's edge and wet my toes. My legs are a lot stronger, and I can play miniature golf. Best news the docs gave me was that I won't have to conduct spring practice from a chair." But late the following month, according to Wallace, Rockne had told one of his closest friends, Leo Ward, a Los Angeles attorney, that "coaching was a thing of the past, and he was looking for some means to capitalize on his reputation." Of course, Rockne had been doing just that for years: writing a syndicated column, doing radio commentaries, and ascending to a top executive post with Studebaker. But then his comment to Ward may have been a ploy to get Notre Dame administrators to stop trying to curtail his outside work in light of his phlebitis. And in March he did conduct spring practice at South Bend, indicating that he intended to be back on the sidelines that fall. By then Rockne had agreed to fly to California to discuss a proposal with Universal Studios to play a fictional football coach resembling him in a movie titled *Spirit of Notre Dame,* for which he would be paid $50,000. When President O'Donnell got wind of the offer, he asked Rockne to turn it down. Whereupon Rockne told O'Donnell that although he was going to meet with movie executives in Hollywood, he wasn't really interested in the proposal. That, of course, begged the question as to why he would bother to make the long flight. Before making the trip, he flew back to Coral Gables to spend a week with his wife and little Jackie, spending some of the time at the Hialeah racetrack with Bonnie, who enjoyed watching the horses as much as Knute did.

Rockne then flew to South Bend to see Father O'Donnell, but the university president was not available and Rockne left him a note telling him he was on his way to California. He then took a train to Chicago to see his mother, meet with Arch Ward, and have dinner with his business manager and agent, Christy Walsh, and another friend before taking a sleeper to Kansas City. There, on Tuesday, March 31, he had planned to meet his two older sons, Bill and Knute Jr., who were attending a boarding school, at the Kansas City station, but their train was late and Rockne had to hurry to the airport for his flight. Though commercial aviation was still in its infancy, Rockne felt it was not only safe but the most practical way to travel long distances, as he had already done a number of times. Five other passengers, a co-pilot, and a pilot who had already flown more than 4,000 miles were aboard when the ten-passenger Fokker monoplane owned by the fledging TransContinental & Western Air took off for Los Angeles with light rain falling. The combination passenger and mail plane was to make three stops along the way, the first one in Wichita, Kansas, where it was scheduled to pick up a few more passengers and more mail. About an hour and a half after the plane had left Kansas City, Ed Baker was feeding livestock on his family's farm in the small eastern Kansas town of Bazaar when he saw a red and silver plane, apparently flying at an altitude of under 1,000 feet. Suddenly he and some other nearby farmers saw a section of the right wing snap off, after which the red and silver plane plummeted to earth, landing in a wheat field. As it hit, five of the bodies were catapulted from the aircraft while the pilot, co-pilot, and the sixth passenger were pinned inside the front part of the wrecked plane, which was perpendicular to the ground with its tail facing straight up. With several members of his family, Baker ran to the scene, about a half mile away. He didn't know it, but one of the eight victims in the wreckage was one of the most famous people in the country.

Knute Kenneth Rockne had turned forty-three years old on March 4. A bulletin put out by United Press International about the crash said, "The first flash to Emporia (a nearby Kansas city) that Rockne was dead shocked the entire world, and business and industry halted while all sources of communications were placed into service." Speculation was that ice had accumulated on the plane's wings after it had taken off. Investigators subsequently announced that the propeller on one of the motors had broken off due to a structural defect, which caused the one wing to snap off.

Within minutes, the other two major news agencies, the Associated Press and the International News Service, also had put out bulletins on their wires about the crash, which had occurred about 100 miles from the cattle ranch of Rockne's former coach, mentor and friend, Jesse Harper. Harper immediately drove to the crash site, identified Rockne, and then accompanied his body to South Bend. In the hours after the crash, radio stations across the United States interrupted regular programming to announce that Rockne had been killed. Scores of newspapers put out extra editions that afternoon, whose headlines about the crash and Rockne's death stunned tens of thousands of people who had not heard the radio reports. Friends in Coral Gables hurried to the Rockne's rented house to break the tragic news to Bonnie Rockne. Knowing that five-year-old Jackie had heard what the friends had told her, she said softly, "Your daddy has gone away. He loved you so."

"Did my daddy get killed in an airplane?" little Jackie asked his mother.

"Yes, he did," Bonnie Rockne replied.

Within an hour, scores of telegrams addressed to Bonnie Rockne had arrived. One of the first was from Knute. It said, LEAVING RIGHT NOW. WILL BE AT BILTMORE. LOVE AND KISSES. The next wire was from Gus Dorais, the best man at Rockne's wedding, with whom Rockne had been immortalized for their performances in Notre Dame's upset of Army at West Point in 1913. Among those who wired condolences were President Herbert Hoover; King Haakon VII of Norway; Notre Dame President Charles O'Donnell; two fellow football coaches he had feuded with, Fielding Yost and Amos Alonzo Stagg; along with coaching counterparts Pop Warner, Bob Zuppke, and Tad Jones; comedian and friend Will Rogers; General Douglas MacArthur, who had wanted Rockne to coach at West Point; Babe Ruth; Jack Dempsey; Gene Tunney; former Notre Dame coaches including Jesse Harper; and scores of former players who had played under him.

A crowd estimated at 10,000 was on hand at the Dearborn Station in Chicago when the train carrying Rockne's body stopped there Thursday night before continuing on to South Bend, where thousands more had congregated at Union Station, the site where so many of Rockne's teams had been greeted by students and townspeople following especially significant victories, and even after surprising defeats. There would have been even more except that most of the Notre Dame student body of approximately 3,000 had already left for the Easter vacation. From the station, the hearse carrying Rockne's coffin traveled to the McGann Funeral Home, where George Gipp's casket had been on view following his death six years earlier. A guard of honor consisting mainly of Notre Dame football players was posted at the bier until the funeral and burial on Saturday, April 4.

Newspapers across the country ran front-page headlines about Rockne's death, along with obituaries longer than those of famed entertainers, political leaders, members of royalty, and other leading sports figures of the day. Inside, editorials lauded Rockne as a pioneering and innovative coach who had not only changed the way football was played, but through his coaching and dynamic personality had almost single-handedly made Notre Dame famous. Hailing Rockne as "a football genius," the *New York Herald Tribune* editorialized that, "He was not only a great coach, but a dynamic force that was able to turn mediocre material into extraordinarily fine teams." The paper declared that he was as great a promoter as he was a coach. "He might have been a P. T. Barnum or a Tex Rickard," the *Herald Tribune* stated, referring to the circus impresario and the legendary boxing promoter. "He molded fine teams, and he promoted them with a skill surpassed by no publicity agent. Scores of coaches adopted his football strategy and his promotion methods as well. He was everything to 'big-time' football."

In the *Chicago Tribune*, Arch Ward, Rockne's first press attaché, wrote, "Rockne was a driver, but he never became abusive. He was an insistent master, but an understanding one. He was an uncompromising demander of discipline and rules of training, eligibility, and method."

Except, Ward might have added, if your name was George Gipp.

❧

The plane crash that killed Rockne also was a blow to the burgeoning aircraft industry, given the worldwide publicity it received because of Rockne's celebrity. In all, there had been a dozen plane crashes in the world during the 1920s, which claimed a total of eighty-four lives. And in 1930 there had been only two crashes, one of which killed sixteen people in Oceanside, California, and the other, in Dresden, Germany, which took eight lives. But up until Rockne, no famous person had been killed in a plane crash, which made the story all the more significant and dramatic.

Of Rockne, President Hoover, himself a football fan, said, "Mr. Rockne so contributed to a cleanness and high purpose and sportsmanship in athletics that his passing is a national loss." Former Notre Dame president John W. Cavanaugh, whom Jesse Harper convinced to hire Rockne as head football coach in 1918, said of Rockne's death, "It is not too much to say that the world went pale, trembled, almost wept." Another longtime friend, the humorist, columnist, and actor Will Rogers, who once lassoed Rockne from the stage as the coach sat in a Manhattan theater, said, "We thought it would take a president or a great public man's death to make a whole nation, regardless of age, race, or creed, shake their heads in real sincere sorrow. Well, that's what this country did today, Knute, for you. You died a national hero."

Like Rockne, the nationally beloved Rogers championed flying and flew often in the late 1920s and early 30s. But, like Rockne, he, too, died in a crash when a plane piloted by the famous one-eyed pilot Wiley Post went down near Point Barrow, Alaska, in August 1935. Ironically, Rogers thus became only the second well-known person—and like Rockne an extremely popular one—to be killed in a plane crash, following his friend in death by a little more than four and a half years.

In South Bend, within hours of the crash most downtown stores and other businesses closed out of respect for the city's most famous, and beloved, resident. Everywhere one went—restaurants, speakeasies, pool halls, wherever—the talk was about Rockne's death. Over and over, the expression "I can't believe it" was heard, as if Rockne had been indestructible. Flags at Notre Dame and at all of the Big Ten campuses flew at half-staff for the next few days, an irony since Rockne had tried, unavailingly, to have Notre Dame accepted into the conference. Across the country, several state legislatures passed resolutions in the days that followed that expressed sadness and regret over Rockne's death.

On Good Friday, Rockne's coffin—blue and gold, the school's colors—was moved to the family home on East Wynne Street, where Rockne would lie all day in the living room in an old-fashioned wake as more than 1,000 mourners passed by, many after waiting for hours. On Holy Saturday, the pews in the awe-inspiring Sacred Heart Church were filled with 1,400 people, all of whom had been invited to the services, including Rockne's elderly mother and his two sisters; hundreds of former Notre Dame players, among them the Four Horsemen and scores of the more than 200 high school, college, and professional coaches who had played for Rockne; New York City Mayor Jimmy Walker, along with the mayors of Chicago, Philadelphia, and South Bend; Will Rogers; Notre Dame students who had delayed their Easter break in order to pay their respects to their beloved coach; and hundreds of friends. For those who weren't there, the service was broadcast live by the CBS Radio Network, which had also broadcast an hour-long tribute to Rockne by nationally known sportscaster Ted Husing the night before.

In his moving eulogy, Father O'Donnell, the university's poet-president, alluded to the national outpouring of grief and tribute by pointing out that President Hoover had sent a special tribute and the King of Norway had dispatched a delegation to the funeral. His death, O'Donnell said, had "struck the nation with dismay and has everywhere turned heads in grief." Behind Father O'Donnell as he celebrated the funeral Mass were three former Notre Dame presidents who served while Rockne was head football coach—Father John W. Cavanaugh, Father James Burns, and Father Matthew Walsh. By the end of the Mass, there were few, if any in the church, who had not shed tears.

Rockne's casket was later carried to a hearse by pallbearers Tom Conley, captain of Rockne's last team; Tommy Yarr, the captain-elect of the 1931 team; and the great backfield of Frank Carideo, Marchmont Schwartz, Marty Brill, and Moon Mullins. Thousands lined the route from the campus through downtown and to Highland Cemetery, where the final prayers were said as family members gathered around the grave.

Apart from presidents, no other American's death had ever drawn so much attention, attracted so many mourners, and evoked as much grief and sympathy as the onetime spindly legged and undersized end who had achieved immortality as a football coach. It would be fourteen years until America would again collectively grieve on such a grand scale following the death, in April 1945, of President Franklin Delano Roosevelt. And few people outside of the presidency have had as many places named in their honor. The largest tangible tribute was the Rockne Memorial, an intramural sports facility that was opened on the Notre Dame campus on June 3, 1939.

A statue of Rockne also was unveiled near one of Frank Leahy, one of his Four Horsemen and an eventual Notre Dame coach, outside of Notre Dame stadium in October 2009. Statues of two other former Fighting Irish coaches, Lou Holtz and Ara Parseghian, had previously been erected inside the stadium. For Rockne to be the fourth Notre Dame coach honored with a statue seems strange, since Rockne had largely been responsible for the construction of the stadium. John Heisler, the university's senior associate athletic director for media and broadcast relations, explained that Holtz and Parseghian's players had raised the money for their coaches' statues, while most of Rockne's players had died by the time sculptor Jerry McKenna, a Notre Dame alumnus, had created the statues of Leahy, Holtz, and Parseghian. Heisler also noted that Rockne had previously been honored on a much grander scale by the construction of the Rockne Memorial building. True, but until Rockne's statue was erected, most fans attending Notre Dame games got to see the statues of Leahy, Holtz, and Parseghian, but not the Rockne Memorial building, which is a considerable distance from the stadium. At the unveiling ceremony of Rockne's statue, Notre Dame Athletic Director Jack Swarbrick, perhaps trying to assuage the feelings of members of Rockne's family on hand, said, "We saved the best for last."

As it was, the Rockne statue was the idea of Joseph Mendelson, a lawyer and businessman from Santa Barbara, California, with close ties to Notre Dame. "I was running on a beach one day when I got to thinking how Rockne wasn't among the statues at the Notre Dame Stadium, and I said to myself, 'Hey, this is wrong,'" said Mendelson, who then put up the money for a statue of Rockne. Mendelson, who has two children who graduated from Notre Dame, previously had donated $2.5 million to endow the Mendelson Center for Sport, Character, and Culture at Notre Dame. "Not having a statue for Rockne at the stadium would be like having a Republican museum without Abraham Lincoln or a Democratic museum without Franklin Roosevelt," said Mendelson, who in the past has owned standardbred horses for harness racing named Rockne and The Gipper.

A similar statue of Rockne, also sculpted by McKenna, stands in downtown South Bend near the College Football Hall of Fame, which was scheduled to be moved to Atlanta in 2012. Other tributes have included streets named for the coach in South Bend, Taylorville, Illinois (a onetime hotbed of semi-pro football, where a number of Notre Dame players, and possibly Rockne, had played for money under assumed names before and after World War I), and Stevensville, Michigan, where the Rocknes had a summer home on Lake Michigan.

Shortly after Rockne's death, seventh-and-eighth grade students at the Sacred Heart School in the small, predominantly Catholic town of Hilbigville, Texas, inexplicably were entrusted with the task of renaming the town. The six boys voted for Rockne, while the six girls cast ballots for poet Joyce Kilmer, which posed a dilemma. The problem was solved the next day, though, when one of the girls, Edith Goertz, cast her vote for Rockne, breaking the tie and giving the farming community of about 200 residents a new name. Why Rockne? "Because almost everyone in town was Catholic and Notre Dame fans, and a lot of the residents listened to Notre Dame football games on the radio," Minnie Bartsch, the curator of the town's museum, said in the spring of 2010. And why did pre-teen Edith Goertz change her vote? "I think it was because her father was a very big Knute Rockne fan," Bartsch said. A memorial for Rockne in the form of a bust stands in front of the Rockne, Texas, museum; many of the town's approximately 200 residents are still Notre Dame fans eight decades after Rockne's death.

More than 2,000 miles Northeast of Rockne, Texas, the gymnasium at the Allentown Central Catholic High School in Pennsylvania is named Rockne Hall even though Rockne had no known connection with the city or state. Memorials also were established in Voss, Norway, the town of Rockne's birth, and in the wheat field in Bazaar, Kansas, where he was killed. Another tribute, in the form of a plaque, was hung in a bathhouse at the resort in Cedar Point, Ohio, where Rockne and Gus Dorais, while working during the summer of 1913, spent off-duty hours practicing passing routines that led to Notre Dame's historic upset of Army that fall and where Rockne met his wife, a waitress at the resort.

On April 9, 1943, during the heart of World War II, a cargo vessel known as a Liberty ship, the *SS Knute Rockne*, was launched in Richmond, California. A month later, another liberty ship, the *SS George Gipp*, named for Rockne's most famous player, was launched at the same shipyard. It was the only instance where two ships, named for a coach and one of his players, were launched during the war, if indeed ever. It also made Rockne the only football coach to have both a ship and a car named for him. Shortly after his death in 1931, the Studebaker Corp., for which Rockne had become its most magnetic sales executive and was on the verge of becoming a vice president, began manufacturing the "Rockne." A six-cylinder automobile that had been on the drawing board when the coach died, the Rockne sold for $575, slightly more than a comparable Ford or Chevrolet at the time, and was on the market for about two years.

Other honors would follow in the years to come, including the issuance of 160 million first-class postage stamps with Rockne's face on them on the hundredth anniversary of his birth, the first of which went on sale in Rockne, Texas. President Ronald Reagan, who had an unabashed affection for Notre Dame that stemmed from his memorable film portrayal of George Gipp, unveiled the stamp at a ceremony on the Notre Dame campus on March 9, 1988, after arriving in a Studebaker Rockne.

Reagan had won the role of Gipp forty-eight years earlier after campaigning vigorously for it while claiming that Gipp had been a hero of his when Reagan was a boy. Then in 1940, the year the movie came out, Reagan told an audience in Los Angeles that he had interviewed Gipp when he was a sports-caster in Des Moines, Iowa in the 1930s. That seemed highly unlikely since Reagan was only nine years old when Gipp died. Reagan, who was twenty-nine years old when the movie was made, also strongly urged the studio to cast Pat O'Brien as Rockne. However, Warner Brothers wanted Jimmy Cagney, a bigger star than O'Brien at the time, to play Rockne. But Notre Dame rejected Cagney because he had been a supporter of the Loyalist cause during the civil war in Spain in 1936. During the conflict, the Catholic Church opposed the Loyalists and backed the government of General Francisco Franco, which eventually was overthrown. As a pre-condition for their cooperation on the film, Notre Dame and Rockne's wife, Bonnie, had considerable say on the film, which accounted for the depiction of Rockne as a secular saint and Gipp as an unflawed hero. Portraying Rockne as a freshman at Notre Dame seemed like a difficult assignment for the forty-one-year-old O'Brien. But then Rockne came close to looking like a middle-aged man as a student, and O'Brien, after losing about twenty pounds in a month before the shooting started, managed to do a very creditable impression of Rockne, both as a college student and a young coach.

Part of the movie, including a depiction of Rockne's funeral at Sacred Heart Church, was shot on the Notre Dame campus. The movie made its worldwide debut on October 4, 1940, at the Palais Royale Theatre in downtown South Bend. Several thousand people massed outside the theater in the hope of seeing Reagan, Pat O'Brien, who portrayed Rockne, and Gale Page, who played the part of Bonnie Rockne. All three were introduced on stage before the movie was shown.

❧❦❧

Rockne established a record that has never been surpassed at Notre Dame. During his thirteen years as head coach, he produced five national championship teams, won 105 games, including his last 19, while losing only 12 and tying 5—a winning percentage of .881, better than any other football coach in history, college or pro. He also had five unbeaten and untied seasons, developed twenty first-team All Americans, starting with George Gipp in 1920, and coached an astonishing seventeen players now in the

College Football Hall of Fame—more than a third of the forty-three Notre Dame players who've been voted into that football shrine. Reflecting Rockne's influence on those seventeen players, fourteen became coaches, including two—Hunk Anderson and Buck Shaw—who coached on both the college level and in the National Football League. Further, Rockne, Gipp, and Layden were among the first group of inductees into the College Football Hall of Fame in 1951.

Far more significant than Rockne's record was the imprint he made on football and the recognition he brought to Notre Dame. Indeed, it is safe to say that Rockne, by his innovative skill as a coach and his engaging and outgoing personality, built the Notre Dame football team from a squad of about thirty in 1918 to one of about 125 by 1930 and made it America's team, even while an anti-Catholic bias, albeit a dwindling one, still existed in the United States. What was particularly remarkable was that he did so while warring with some elements at Notre Dame who felt that the school, and mainly Rockne, had over-emphasized football to the detriment of the school's growing academic reputation. As a football coach, he was neither as innovative as Walter Camp at Yale—regarded by many as "the father of American football"—nor Amos Alonzo Stagg nor Clark Shaughnessy (generally acknowledged to have been the first coach to use the T formation), but he was perceptive enough to have studied their methods and those of other outstanding coaches of the era, including his predecessor Jesse Harper, and develop his own distinctive coaching style, which, coupled with his knack for promoting himself, his football teams, and Notre Dame, made him the most-famous college football coach of all time.

Memorials to George Gipp are on a much smaller scale, which is understandable, since, dazzling as it was, his was a meteoric and much shorter career. In Gipp's hometown of Laurium, Michigan, there are two tributes. In August 1934, a small park and fifteen-foot tall pyramid-shaped stone monument that includes a plaque with Gipp's name and a football was dedicated. Not far away is the George Gipp Recreation Area, which includes the George Gipp Skating Arena, baseball and softball fields, tennis courts, and a basketball court. At Calumet High School, which Laurium teenagers still attend, a plaque with Gipp's name on it is awarded annually to a senior who has distinguished himself in sports and academics, then put back on display in the school's entrance lobby. That, of course, is somewhat ironic since Gipp was anything but a good scholar and played only one year of a varsity sport, basketball, for Calumet. At Notre Dame, Gipp is also memorialized by a plaque—in the football team's locker room—which includes Rockne's "Win one for the Gipper" oration.

If Gipp was the best Notre Dame football player of all time, Rockne, of course, was largely responsible, since he had both discovered and nurtured "The Gipper" while overlooking his off-campus transgressions at the beginning of a coaching career that would lead both of them to immortality and the university to both academic and sporting acclaim. The irony of their legacies, of course, is that neither Rockne, a Lutheran immigrant from Norway, nor Gipp, whose parents were Methodist and Baptist, had even graduated from high school when they came to Notre Dame six years apart with no intention of playing football, and yet they wound up as the school's greatest sports legends. It is highly unlikely that Notre Dame shall ever see such a disparate combination of football immortals again.

EPILOGUE

HE HAD BEEN one of Rockne's favorites, both as a player and an assistant coach, but as the new head coach at Notre Dame, Hunk Anderson, found Rockne a very hard act to follow, as most any coach would have. That Notre Dame had lost three-fourths of its best backfield ever—only All American Marchy Schwartz returned in 1931—and most of the outstanding line of the 1930 national championship team, made it even more difficult. Anderson also soon found out that he would not have the broad authority that Rockne had enjoyed in running the football team, but instead would be working under tightened institutional control.

First of all, President O'Donnell decided that Anderson would be the "senior" coach and Jack Chevigny the "junior" coach on the grounds that "Rockne cannot be displaced as head coach." That was a slight to Anderson, who had been an assistant to Rockne for five years, compared with Chevigny's one season as an assistant. That changed after the first season, when, after Notre Dame had gone unbeaten through its first seven games, the Irish lost to Southern California and Army. Following a 7–2 season in 1932, Anderson's 1933 squad lost five of eight games—at the time, Notre

Dame's worst season ever—and he became the first Notre Dame football coach to be fired after a barrage of alumni complaints. Abrasive and profane as he was, to the dismay of priests, both from Notre Dame and visiting prelates, along with some administrators, Anderson was not totally to blame. During his brief tenure, when, as he put it, he had to coach while wearing a straightjacket, Anderson had the number of scholarships cut from forty to twenty, something Rockne wouldn't have tolerated, although Anderson, using connections at Notre Dame, still managed to provide financial aid and jobs to more than 100 players each of his three seasons as head coach. But then Rockne's power and authority was probably equivalent, or even more powerful, than that of the university presidents when he was the head coach. As it was, Anderson went on to a successful coaching career in the NFL, both as an assistant and then as the head coach of the Chicago Bears for four years during World War II, winning a league title in 1943, when the team's founder and coach George Halas was in the service.

Two others who had played under Rockne, Elmer Layden, the 158-pound fullback for the Four Horsemen, and former tackle Frank Leahy, followed Anderson as Notre Dame's head coaches— Layden for seven years, during which he had squads of as many as 215 players (in 1938), and Leahy for eleven years. During Layden's tenure, tighter academic restrictions on football players were put in effect by President John O'Hara, and Pittsburgh was dropped from the schedule (after beating Notre Dame five times in six years) amid reports that the Panthers' coach, Jock Sutherland, was paying his starters weekly salaries. Mainly because of Layden's diplomatic efforts, the Irish also finally were able to book games with Big Ten schools Michigan, Wisconsin, Iowa, Illinois, Minnesota, and Ohio State, most of which had declined to play Notre Dame since Jesse Harper's days as coach before World War I.

Layden and Leahy were in turn succeeded by Terry Brennan and Joe Kuharich before Ara Parseghian in 1964 became the first

non-Notre Damer to coach the Irish since Jesse Harper. As a Pres-
byterian, Parseghian became the first Protestant head coach at
Notre Dame since Rockne, who, of course, eventually converted to
Catholicism in 1925, as, supposedly, had a dying George Gipp.

During most of that stretch, and then beyond, Notre Dame
remained "America's team," in the sense that the school had the
support of more non-alumni than any other, along with being
unique in that, for years, all of its games have been broadcast on a
national radio network encompassing about 150 stations and tele-
vised through an exclusive contract by NBC. That, of course, made
the "Notre Dame Victory March" the most listened-to college fight
song in the country. Academically, Notre Dame's undergraduate
enrollment, only 550 when Rockne arrived in 1910 and slightly
more than 3,000 when he died in 1931, was slightly over 8,000
by 2010.

While Rockne overshadowed his most famous player following
Gipp's death in 1920, the Gipp legend enjoyed a revival when the
movie *Knute Rockne: All American* was released in 1940 and Ronald
Reagan's portrayal of Gipp became the most memorable part of
the film. Forty years later, Reagan again revived Gipp's spirit by
frequently employing the "win one for The Gipper" rallying cry
while running for president, as did a number of his supporters,
including his eventual successor, George H. W. Bush. Then on May
17, 1981, Reagan made frequent references to his movie role as
Gipp, which he conceded he had campaigned for, when he invoked
the "win one for The Gipper" exhortation during a commencement
address at Notre Dame. As he always did, he pronounced Rockne's
first name as KUH-NUTE, the correct Norwegian pronunciation,
which had been anglicized by most people to Knute, with a silent
K. Three years later, Reagan urged the United States Olympic
Committee to "win one for The Gipper" before the start of the
1984 Summer Olympics in Los Angeles. Thereafter, the rallying
cry was heard more than ever, more often than not by people who

either had no idea who "The Gipper" was or who believed it was Reagan himself.

That was fine with Reagan, who reveled in being called the "Gipper." One of the most notable times he used the term in public was during the 1988 Republican National Convention when Reagan, addressing George H. W. Bush, who was the GOP candidate for president, said, "George, go out there and win one for the Gipper."

As was the case when Knute Rockne's football "Ramblers" were attracting far more attention to the football team than the university itself, to the chagrin of many of the school's administrators and alumni, many Americans still equate Notre Dame with football eight decades after Rockne's death. Even though the "Fighting Irish" were a perennial football power during most of those years, the university was by no means a "football factory," as some critics—mostly rival coaches—characterized it in the second and third decades of the twentieth century. No one was saying that in the twenty-first century when, for example, in 2009, Notre Dame, along with Duke, had the highest graduation rate for football players in the top tier of college football at 96 percent. Furthermore, by the beginning of the new century, Notre Dame ranked in the top twenty academically in most polls of American universities, as did several of its separate schools such as its law school, which George Gipp had attended, somewhat irregularly, during the 1919–20 academic year. Another irony: By 2010 the Big Ten, which had repeatedly rejected Notre Dame as a football member during the Rockne years, tried hard to lure the Fighting Irish, always an independent in football, to join the conference, but was unable to do so.

In truth, Notre Dame owes its development and subsequent academic acclaim to football. It is not the only university to have benefited, and even become nationally known, because of a football or basketball team. But Notre Dame was the first to do so, and in the process became the gold standard for attracting attention through athletics. Many others have tried to emulate the onetime small and virtually unknown Midwestern university by doing the same, but none have come even remotely close to succeeding. And in large measure it's been because only Notre Dame has had Knute Rockne, George Gipp, the Four Horsemen, and the affection and ardor of millions of loyal followers. It's the sui generis of American universities, and, with all due respect to Yale, Harvard, Stanford, and other outstanding schools, it no doubt will always remain so.

ACKNOWLEDGMENTS

FIRST AND FOREMOST, everyone I dealt with at Notre Dame was not only cooperative but in many instances went out of their way to help me in my research without ever asking what I might write about the university's most mythical, albeit flawed, sports figure, George Gipp. I am especially grateful to Charles Lamb, the head of the Archives department at Notre Dame and to his assistants Wendy Schlereth, Angela Kindig, and Sharon Sumpter for the time they spent with me during my research at Notre Dame and for the materials provided by the Archives department, both during my visit and in the months thereafter.

I am also indebted to John Heisler, the school's senior associate athletic director for media and broadcast relations, and his staff, particularly senior staff assistant Carol Copley, who was of immeasurable help, always quick to respond to a query in her joyful fashion. A tip of the hat also goes to Veronica Primrose in the university's Registrar's office for her help in obtaining academic information about Gipp and Knute Rockne. Certainly no one at Notre Dame ever tried to conceal the fact that Gipp, for all of his athletic brilliance, was hardly an academic standout. For assistance on Gipp's exploits as a baseball player at Notre Dame, I found

Cappy Gagnon, a historian on Fighting Irish baseball teams, to be a font of information.

Research on this book had a long life. It started with a story I did on Gipp more than 30 years ago for *Sports Illustrated.* During the course of that research, I interviewed a number of Gipp's former teammates, including Heartley "Hunk" Anderson, Fred "Ojay" Larson, Roger Kiley, and Chet Grant while all of them were in their eighties. With more notes and good quotes than I could fit into my *Sports Illustrated* story, I stored them in my files, determined that someday I would write what I hoped would be a definitive biography of Gipp. My timing for my interviews with Anderson, Larson, and Kiley, along with some of Gipp's boyhood friends, was propitious, since, sadly, they all died within the next few years. Looking back, it was a joy talking with Anderson, Larson, Kiley, and Grant about Gipp and Rockne and Notre Dame football in the years shortly before, during, and after World War II. As a boy who grew up hoping to play football at Notre Dame while the university band played the country's best-known fight song, the "Notre Dame Victory March," I was familiar with the Gipp legend and with the legendary Rockne, and so to talk to men who played with Gipp and for Rockne was both a labor of love and a pleasant trip down college football's Memory Lane.

As any writer of nonfiction knows, libraries and librarians are an immense resource and always willing to help. Once again, as in my two previous books, *Tunney* and *Giants Among Men,* Susan Madeo at the Westport, Connecticut, Library was invaluable in securing old and obscure books through the interlibrary loan and microfilm of old newspapers including the *South Bend Tribune,* the *Daily Mining Gazette*, which is published in Houghton, Michigan, and the long-defunct *South Bend News-Times.* Yvonne Robillard, an editor of the *Daily Mining Gazette,* which circulates in Gipp's hometown of Laurium, Michigan, and nearby Calumet, where Gipp, Hunk Anderson, and Ojay Larson went to high school, was also a great help.

Information on Gipp's irregular high school career and the plaque awarded in his honor at the end of every school year came from George Twardzik, principal of Calumet High, and Elsa Green, an administrative assistant at the school in Michigan's Upper Peninsula, close by Lake Superior. Extremely helpful about Gipp's pre-Notre Dame days in the Calumet area came from Bob Erkkila, a retired Calumet teacher, while Ed Vertin, the town administrator in Laurium, provided information about the George Gipp Recreation Area complex in his hometown and the memorial that was erected in honor of Laurium's most famous native son. Ron and Karl Gipp, cousins of George Gipp, also provided nuggets of information about the family, particularly George Gipp's early days, while Nils Rockne recalled what he had heard about his famous grandfather.

Writer Emil Klosinski, whose father, John, played on a semi-pro team with Gipp while Gipp was at Notre Dame and is also the author of a book about Gipp's days in South Bend, was an excellent source of information. So was Emil's son, Marc, who went out of his way to try to help me track down Victoria Adams Phair, the granddaughter of Iris Trippeer, the love of Gipp's life. Victoria Phair, in turn, was gracious and helpful in reminiscing about her beautiful grandmother, who for reasons still not known left Gipp heartbroken, but still professed her love for him in the years following his untimely death.

Others who contributed to this book included Joseph Mendelson of Santa Barbara, California, a longtime benefactor at Notre Dame, who put up the funds for a Knute Rockne statue outside Notre Dame Stadium; Joe Heintzelman, owner of Oscar's Billiards Club, a virtual landmark in South Bend, who recalled how his grandfather, for whom the billiards parlor is named, played billiards with Gipp while Gipp was at Notre Dame; Mike Stack, the public relations manager for the St. Joseph Regional Medical Center in South Bend, the hospital where Gipp died; Dr. Charles Higgs-Coulthard, a staff physician at St. Joseph; Patrick Furlong, professor emeritus of history at Indiana University, South Bend, who furnished information on what South Bend was like during the World War I era along with other historical information about both the city and the state of Indiana at that time; Kent Stephens, historian and curator at the College Football Hall of Fame in South Bend; Mady Salvani of the Athletics Communications Office at West Point for her assistance in producing materials on the long Army–Notre Dame rivalry; and Minnie Bartsch of the Rockne Historical Society in Rockne, Texas, who told me the delightful story of how and why a small Texas town is named after the most famous football coach of all time.

Once again, I must thank my agent, Andrew Blauner, for seeing to it that this book, like my two previous books, found its way into print and for his confidence in the project from the outset. Thanks, too, goes to my editor at Skyhorse Publishing, Mark Weinstein, for his editing skills after having left me to my own devices throughout the reporting and writing process. Last but most definitely not least, a ton of thanks to my computer guru, Paul McLaughlin of Norwalk, Connecticut, who was always quick to respond, by phone or in person, whenever I encountered technical problems and who, with his encyclopedic knowledge of computers, unfailingly resolved them, usually in a matter of minutes, often without having to make a house call.

ABOUT THE AUTHOR

JACK CAVANAUGH IS a veteran sportswriter whose work has appeared most notably on the sports pages of *The New York Times*, for which he has covered hundreds of assignments. He is the author of *Damn the Disabilities: Full Speed Ahead! (1995)*, *Giants Among Men* (2008), *Season of 42* (2012), and *Tunney* (2006), which was nominated for the Pulitzer Prize for biography. In addition, Cavanaugh has been a frequent contributor to *Sports Illustrated* and has written for *Reader's Digest, Sporting News, Tennis,* and *Golf* magazine, as well as other national publications. He is also a former reporter for ABC News and CBS News. Cavanaugh is currently an adjunct professor at the Columbia University Graduate School of Journalism and at Quinnipiac University in Connecticut. A native of Stamford, Connecticut, he is also a columnist for the *Stamford Advocate*.

BIBLIOGRAPHY

BOOKS

Army Football 2009 Media Guide

Beach, Jim. *Notre Dame Football.* New York: Macfadden-Bortell Corp., 1962

Brondfield, Jerry. *Rockne. The Coach, The Man, The Legend.* New York: Random House, 1976

Chelland, Patrick. *One For The Gipper.* Chicago: Henry Regnery Co., 1973

Klosinski, Emil. *Gipp at Notre Dame.* Baltimore: PublishAmerica, 2003

Maggio, Frank P. *Notre Dame and the Game That Changed Football.* New York: Carroll & Graf Publishers, 2007

Notre Dame 2009 Football

Perrin, Tom. *Football: A College History.* Jefferson, North Carolina: McFarland & Company, Inc., 1987

Quakenbush, Robert and Bynum, Mike. *Knute Rockne: His Life And Legend.* October Football Corp., 1988

Rice, Grantland. *The Tumult and the Shouting.* A.S. Barnes and Company, Inc., 1954

Robinson, Ray. *Rockne of Notre Dame.* New York: Oxford University Press, 1999

Sperber, Murray. *Shake Down the Thunder.* New York: Henry Holt and Company, 1993

Steele, Michael. *Knute Rockne: A Portrait of a Notre Dame Legend.* Champaign, Illinois: Sports Publishing, Inc., 1998

Total Football: The Official Encyclopedia of the National Football League. New York: HarperCollins Publishers, Inc., 1997

University of Notre Dame Football Media Guide Supplement

Wallace, Francis. *Knute Rockne.* Garden City, New York: Doubleday & Company, Inc., 1960

NEWSPAPERS

Chicago Tribune	*New York Herald Tribune*
Chicago Daily News	*New York Sun*
Detroit News	*New York Times*
Daily Mining Gazette	*Philadelphia Inquirer*
Indianapolis Star	*Notre Dame Scholastic*
Los Angeles Times	*South Bend News-Times*
Miami Daily News	*South Bend Tribune*
Milwaukee Journal	*The Sporting News*
New York Daily News	*Washington Post*

MAGAZINES

Collier's
Esquire
Notre Dame Alumnus
Smithsonian Magazine
Sport
Sports Illustrated

INTERNET

Wikipedia.com

INDEX